Transitions

Writing in Academic and Workplace Settings

WRITTEN LANGUAGE
Marcia Farr, senior editor

Perspectives on Written Argument
Deborah Berrill (ed.)

From Millwrights to Shipwrights to the Twenty-First Century
R. John Brockmann

Collaboration and Conflict: A Contextual Exploration of Group
Writing and Positive Emphasis
Geoffrey Cross

Forming the Collective Mind: A Contextual Exploration of
Large-Scale Collaborative Writing in Industry
Geoffrey A. Cross

Contexts, Intertexts, and Hypertexts
Scott DeWitt and Kip Strasma (eds.)

Subject to Change: New Composition Instructors'
Theory and Practice
Christine Farris

Assessing the Portfolio:
Principles for Practice, Theory, and Research
Liz Hamp-Lyons and William Condon

Writing on the Plaza: Mediated Literacy Practice Among Scribes and
Clients in Mexico City
Judy Kalman

Literacy Across Communities
Beverly Moss (ed.)

Englishes in Contact:
Anglophone Caribbean Students in an Urban College
Shondel J. Nero

Artwork of the Mind: An Interdisciplinary Description of Insight and
the Search for it in Student Writing
Mary Murray

Word Processing and the Non-Native Writer
Martha C. Pennington

Self-Assessment and Development in Writing:
A Collaborative Inquiry
Jane Bowman Smith and Kathleen Blake Yancey

Twelve Readers Reading: Responding to College Student Writing
Richard Straub and Ronald Lunsford

Transitions

Writing in Academic and Workplace Settings

edited by

Patrick Dias
Anthony Paré
McGill University

HAMPTON PRESS, INC.
CRESSKILL, NEW JERSEY

Printed in the United States of America

Library of Congress Cataloging-in-Publication Data

Transitions : writing in academic and workplace settings / edited by Anthony Paré.
     p. cm. -- (Written language)
  Includes bibliographical references and indexes.
  ISBN 1-57273-269-5 -- ISBN 1-57273-270-9 (pbk.)
    1. English language--Rhetoric--Study and teaching. 2. Academic writing--Study and teaching. 3. Business writing--Study and teaching. 4. Technical writing--Study and teaching. I. Dias, Patrick. II. Paré, Anthony. III. Written language series.

PE1404. T76 2000
808'.042'071--dc21

                          00-025935

Hampton Press, Inc.
23 Broadway
Cresskill, NJ 07626

Contents

Series Preface   vii

Introduction   1

1. Writing Classrooms as Activity Systems
   Patrick Dias   11

2. Write Where You Are:
   Situating Learning to Write in University
   and Workplace Settings
   Aviva Freedman and Christine Adam   31

3. Diplomats in the Basement:
   Graduate Engineering Students
   and Intercultural Communication
   Ann Beer   61

4. Writing and Design in Architectural Education
   Peter Medway   89

5. Bridging the Gap:
   University-Based Writing that is More than Simulation
   Aviva Freedman and Christine Adam   129

6. Writing as a Way into Social Work:
   Genre Sets, Genre Systems, and Distributed Cognition
   Anthony Paré   145

 7. What Do We Learn From the Reader?
    Factors in Determining Successful Transitions
    Between Academic and Workplace Writing
        Christine Adam   167

 8. Revising a Research Article: Dialogic Negotiation
        Natasha Artemeva   183

 9. Organizational Cultures as Contexts for Learning to Write
        Jane Ledwell-Brown   199

10. Reinventing Expertise:
    Experienced Writers in the Workplace Encounter
    a New Genre
        Graham Smart   223

Author Index   253
Subject Index   257

Series Preface

This series examines the characteristics of *writing* in the human world. Volumes in the series present scholarly work on written language in its various contexts. Across time and space, human beings use various forms of written language—or writing systems—to fulfill a range of social, cultural, and personal functions, and this diversity can be studied from a variety of perspectives within both the social sciences and the humanities, including those of linguistics, anthropology, psychology, education, rhetoric, literary criticism, philosophy, and history. Although writing is not often used apart from oral language, or without aspects of reading, and thus many volumes in this series include other facets of language and communication, writing itself receives primary emphasis.

This volume makes a timely contribution to our understandings of the connections (or lack of them) between two types of settings in which writing is learned: in school and at work. Although most people assume that writing is learned almost exclusively in school, the research presented in this volume indicates that much writing is learned in the context in which it must be used, that is, on the job. Thus the particular characteristics of various genres of workplace writing are learned as people are enculturated into and participate in their workplace "culture." But what of writing in school? The editors of this volume argue that "classrooms are inadequate settings for learning workplace writing," even though they are "ideal settings for learning academic writing." And while the learning of academic writing does not prepare students for all kinds of workplace writing, it does develop capacities that are often crucial beyond the academy.

While the study of writing is absorbing in its own right, it is an increasingly important social issue as well, as demographic movements occur around the world and as language and ethnicity accrue more intensely political meanings. Writing, and literacy more generally, is central to education, and education in turn is central to occupational and social mobility. Manuscripts that present either the results of empirical research, both qualitative and quantitative, or theoretical treatments of relevant issues are encouraged for submission.

Introduction

This book grows out of a long-term study of writing in certain academic disciplines and their related workplace settings. For six years, the authors whose research is reported here have moved back and forth between university and professional locations in architecture, engineering, management, public administration, and social work.[1] As we have worked with practitioners in these diverse fields, we have heard a persistent complaint that students are inadequately prepared for writing on the job. This criticism is supported by surveys of workplace writers that suggest that people often feel work experience, rather than university instruction, has taught them how to write at work (Anderson, 1985; Bataille, 1982; Ledwell-Brown, 1988). In Odell and Goswami's (1985) ground-breaking book on nonacademic writing, and in response to those findings, Anderson raised a pertinent question for those of us involved in the composition field: "It remains unanswered whether on-the-job experience is so important because of deficiencies in college writing courses or because the writing done at work simply cannot be taught adequately in the classrooms" (68). It was to answer that question, among others, that the research reported in this book was conducted (see also Dias, Freedman, Medway, & Paré, 1999).

---

[1]The editors and authors wish to thank the Social Sciences and Humanities Research Council of Canada for generous support of the research reported here.

That research focused on three key questions: What are the relationships between writing in academic settings and writing in the workplace? Given these relationships, how and to what extent is writing in university preparation for writing at work? What happens in the transition from academic to workplace writing? In other words, how might university graduates adjust to the writing demands of the workplace? These and related questions have directed our inquiries, which we have conducted primarily through interviews, observation of writing practices in both classrooms and workplaces, tracking and analyses of university and workplace documents, and responding-aloud protocols provided by readers in both workplace and school settings.

When we first began to interview practitioners and teachers in the disciplines we were investigating, we asked them how students learned to write for the workplace. Unanimously, practitioners replied that schools should teach them how (and, with a similar degree of consensus, felt schools were doing a woeful job of it). Teachers were equally but contrarily adamant: workplace writing can *only* be taught in the workplace. The following response from a teacher of social work was typical of the comments we heard from faculty members with whom we talked:

> I think the way they learn . . . is in their context of practice, because they learn what they need to write for whatever they need to write wherever they are. . . . the specific [skills of writing] around a case or a project or a community, you learn in practice. . . . You know, you look at your audience, and look at how one presents to that audience, and then you learn how to write for that audience. You learn that from experience. I think that's the way you learn it. I don't know how much of that can be taught.

In the years since, the research reported in this book has confirmed what that rhetorically astute social work teacher knew: writing proficiency is inextricably linked to setting and circumstance. Our answer to Anderson, then, is that people "learn what they need to write for whatever they need to write wherever they are," and therefore classrooms are inadequate settings for learning workplace writing (although they are ideal settings for learning academic writing). Moreover, our studies have indicated that workplace learning processes are rarely, if ever, guided by an explicit curriculum or training program to develop writing competencies. Teaching and learning occur uniquely in each setting—indeed, for each individual learner: the process is implicit, situated, spontaneous, improvised, and shaped by the learner's specific needs and knowledge and the workplace setting (cf. Freedman, Adam, & Smart, 1994). That is, the setting is not merely the inert backdrop or location within which learning takes place, but interacts with knowledge and learner in a dynamic though not always synergistic relationship. As a result, school-based simulations, no matter how detailed, cannot replace the workplace context, because what is learned in context *is* the context.

Most importantly for the topic of this book, our research suggests that the transition from academic to professional writing is an inextricable part of a larger, more comprehensive transition, one that involves the student in a process of gradual initiation or enculturation into the workplace community. (We use the term "community" guardedly, for a group of people linked together by location and/or common interests and goals; but we are also aware that although the term commonly implies collaboration and shared effort, there is what Herndl calls "the dark side of the force": "the ideologically coercive effects of institutional and professional discourse" [1996a, p.455]). Theories from various disciplines that attempt to understand more fully the individual as a social and socially constructed being point to a regular, barely perceptible process of immersion in the community's ways of seeing, saying, and doing. There is great resonance here with current rhetorical theory, particularly with recent redefinitions of genre as social action (e.g., Bazerman, 1988; Berkenkotter & Huckin, 1995; Devitt, 1993; Freedman & Medway, 1994; Miller, 1994). Studies of genre (e.g., Devitt, 1991; Giltrow & Valiquette, 1994; Paré & Smart, 1994; Schryer, 1993) indicate that participation in the regular discourse practices of a community shapes the individual's knowledge and ways of knowing.

Discourse practices—or, more broadly, symbolic action—is central in discussions of activity theory, a multidisciplinary perspective that underlies some of the chapters in this book. "An activity system integrates the subject, the object, and the instruments (material tools as well as signs and symbols) into a unified whole" (Engeström, 1993, p. 67). From that perspective, the process of enculturation into workplace values, attitudes, and beliefs begins when the student participates in the "activity system" of the workplace. Further, such participation begins to define one's identity as well. As Lave (1991) explains, "Developing an identity as a member of a community and becoming knowledgeably skillful are part of the same process, with the former motivating, shaping, and giving meaning to the latter, which it subsumes" (p. 65). It makes sense then to turn to activity theory, as Cole (1996) does, to broaden the psychological unit of analysis from the individual to the social collectives within which individuals think and act. The relevance of activity theory for writing research and pedagogy has been explored in recent work by Dias (Chapter 1, this volume; 1998) and Russell (1995, 1997).

The individual's enculturation has also been examined by anthropologist Mary Douglas (1986), who writes of the social group's "thought style" and the process by which individuals adopt that style. "Institutions," she writes, "systematically direct individual memory and channel our perceptions into forms compatible with the relations they authorize" (p. 92). Douglas draws on ethnographic research to argue that our ways of seeing and making sense of the world are shaped by context and culture. "Even the simple acts of classifying and remembering are institutionalized" (p. 67). The individual adopts the institution's forms: its classifications and categories.

From a sociological perspective, the transition into the workplace can be considered in terms of Bourdieu's (1972/1977) notion of *habitus,* which he defines as "systems of durable, transposable *dispositions,* structured structures predisposed to function as structuring structures, that is, as principles of the generation and structuring of practices" (p. 72). Herndl (1996b) explains *habitus* as "the way of thinking we inherit from past experience which then makes sense of our current experience and allows us to act. Furthermore, this habitus is itself continuously produced by our ongoing activity" (p. 29). According to Robbins (1991), "Bourdieu means by 'habitus' a process of socialization whereby the dominant modes of thought and experience inherent in the social and physical world (both of which are symbolically constructed) are internalized by social agents" (p. 84). In terms reminiscent of Bakhtin (1986), Bourdieu speaks of linguistic *habitus*: "The linguistic *habitus* . . . is the product of social conditions and is not a simple production of utterances but the production of utterances adapted to a 'situation' or, rather, adapted to a market or field" (1984/1993, p. 78).[2]

Central to these and other theories that seek to explain the social construction of individual consciousness is a process of transformation or transition. As the following chapters show, transition refers not only to the shift from university to workplace, but also to movements within the workplace. As the individual joins the activities, rituals, and practices of the collective, s/he adopts its ways of making sense of the world, its ways of acting on and in the world through language and other symbolic action. Of crucial importance in the transition from school to workplace, from newcomer to community member, is the individual's engagement in genres: the sociorhetorical actions that operate

---

[2]Bracewell and Witte (1997) link Bourdieu's notion of *habitus* to the construct of expertise in cognitive psychology: "In cognitive theory the construct of expertise has been the principal one used to account for the acquisition of regular and skilled . . . performance or, if you will, habits of mind that distinguish particular pursuits or knowledge domains" (p. 4).

as part of a community's activity system. Those genres have a central role in determining the nature and production of knowledge in the community, and thus the individual's participation in that knowledge-making. By engaging in the communal enactment of those genres, newcomers are drawn into the beliefs, attitudes, and values of the community, into its thought styles. Through the linguistic habitus of genre, they enter into the community habitus: ways of saying become ways of seeing. As anthropologist Clifford Geertz (1983) puts it, "thinking . . . is a matter of trafficking in the symbolic forms available in one or another community" (p. 153).

The chapters in this book attempt to capture various transitions from one rhetorical context to another and from one symbolic form to another: within the university, from one course to another; from university to workplace; and within the workplace, from one genre to another. In sequence, the chapters roughly follow a movement outward from the classroom to the working world: Chapter One offers an activity theory analysis of a university classroom, and Chapter Ten uses genre theory to consider the process of learning a new genre in the workplace. In between, chapters provide glimpses into moments and locations that mark the transition from writing at school to writing at work.

In Chapter One, Patrick Dias opens up the question of the relevance of writing courses as preparation for writing in the workplace by proposing a modest reexamination of the place, function, and conduct of university writing courses. He draws on activity theory, derived from the Vygotskian school of Russian psychology, to uncover contradictions as they emerge in classroom writing practices and as they circumscribe and delimit the role and function of these courses within universities. The analysis points up the need to acknowledge these contradictions and suggests how course practices and goals might be modified to reduce the effects of these contradictions and even to eliminate them.

In Chapter Two, Freedman and Adam draw on theories of situated learning to contrast two contexts for learning—one in school and the other in a workplace. Although aspects of each context are similar, and the processes of learning in both locales are alike in some respects, Freedman and Adam demonstrate that there are radical differences between school and work that can make the transition from one to the other a challenging experience. As they put it, "when students leave the university to enter the workplace, they not only need to learn new genres of discourse, they need to learn new ways to learn such genres." The chapter makes a strong case against the possibility of replicating in the classroom the complex and dynamic rhetorical settings of the workplace.

Ann Beer further complicates the problem of transition in Chapter Three, where she adds movement across national cultures and languages to the already difficult task of adapting to and learning in new settings. Beer uses intercultural communication theory to frame her analysis of the learning processes experienced by international graduate students in the engineering department of a Canadian university. As Beer points out, increasing globalization adds new dimensions to the problems and possibilities of communication: "Every group is embedded in a cultural setting which is being changed and changing itself both through contact with other cultures, and through the process of historical change." This shrinking but always more complicated world cannot help but have profound effects on the learning and teaching of writing.

In Chapter Four, Peter Medway examines the place of writing in architectural courses. In a discipline where writing is ancillary to design and drawing, this chapter reveals a role for writing that is different from most of the other university writing discussed in this book: writing as self-initiated rather than assigned, and valued as a means of recording one's thinking, of organizing and managing one's ideas, as revealing and making explicit the design process and "therefore open to reflection, analysis, and evaluation"—purposes far broader and more vital than those that apply to most university writing; that is, writing as largely and primarily a means of displaying knowledge and justifying it publicly. Students as writers, we might conclude, respond differently, and not inappropriately, to the exigences that arise in each course, and as they move between courses, they appropriate purposes and goals for writing that are called for by the specific expectations of each course. This chapter also points up a need for writing researchers to acknowledge writing that, unlike most academic writing, is both fragmentary and intrinsically incorporated into multimodal texts.

In the following chapter, Freedman and Adam discuss attempts to create university-based assignments that bridge the gap between the classroom and the workplace, and therefore help students make that transition. Their particular focus is a final-year practicum in a systems analysis course in a university business school. Exceptional circumstances allow the teacher of this course to offer students a writing and learning experience that positions them precisely between school and the workplace, where the epistemic goals of the former and the instrumental goals of the latter combine to create a rich and unique opportunity.

In Chapter Six, Paré uses genre theory and notions derived from theories of situated learning and distributed cognition to explore the enculturation process that social work students undergo during periods of internship in multidisciplinary settings. His description of the students' gradually increasing participation in professional discourse demonstrates the extent to which learning to write means, as well, learning to share in the complex cognitive and rhetorical work of contemporary institutions. That division of labor, however, is not necessarily equitable, and Paré's chapter reveals the link between professional discourse and power relations, as the social work students and texts he describes are located within the ideological struggles enacted through workplace rhetoric.

In the next chapter, Christine Adam employs responding-aloud protocols to capture the experienced reader's rhetorical stance. As she explains, "When oldtimers are asked to respond-aloud to community texts, their commentary provides a window onto the norms, processes, and evaluation of writing within the community, and gives us useful insights into the differences between writing at school and writing on the job." To make that comparison, Adam contrasts the readings produced by a college professor and a manager in a government institution. She then uses that analysis to suggest factors that should be considered in the design and evaluation of university programs that seek to prepare students for writing in the workplace.

In Chapter Eight, Natasha Artemeva takes us beyond the student's experience and into the world of work. The professional setting Artemeva brings us to is the university, and the writers under study are two professors of engineering engaged in the task of revising a research article. The chapter offers convincing proof that learning to write does not end with graduation; as Artemeva suggests, "even experienced writers of scientific papers need to go through a necessary and sometimes painful transition in order to reach a new audience." Her case study offers a useful insight, one that echoes Freedman and Adam's discussion in Chapter Two: students will not only need to learn new genres when they leave school, they will also need to learn new ways to learn.

In Chapter Nine, Jane Ledwell-Brown considers how "the overall values and attitudes of an organization translate into specific expectations of writers" and how the roles and place of certain divisions within an organization determine particular rhetorical strategies. Although these rhetorical practices and expectations are not explicitly stated, they are implicit in the ways managers respond to the writing of their employees in order to ensure that they conform to the organization's goals and values. She is concerned to find out what newcomers must learn in order to become members of their new discourse communities, and interviews the managers of one large organization to record their responses as they respond to the writing of employees in their divisions.

Most of the chapters in this book are concerned primarily with the induction of learners (students, interns, new employees) into the discourse of the discipline or community they plan to join or have just entered. In the closing chapter, Graham Smart is concerned with a different kind of transition; he asks how experienced and accomplished writers within the workplace contend with and respond to genres that are significantly different from ones they are used to working with. The question, echoing one asked by Natasha Artemeva in Chapter Eight about experienced writers in the university, is a reminder that even in firmly established traditional working environments such as a central bank, new genres emerge and writers must continue to learn to write. Smart's study, however, is in aid of a larger question, a version of which we first encountered in Chapter One. What aspects of writing expertise are transportable across different boundaries, for instance, as a writer moves into a new division or discipline, or changes jobs?

It is not accidental that we open and close with such questions. The several areas these chapters traverse explore how much of writing knowledge is local knowledge, knowledge of setting and circumstance, of a community or discipline's ways of doing things. It seems reasonable to assume that much, if not all, of such knowledge will be acquired by one's being as fully engaged in local activities as one's current knowledge and position allow. What remains then to teach? Or what aspects of knowledge about writing are amenable to instruction to aid the passage from one genre to another, or from one discourse community to another, or from school to workplace? Although these contributions proffer no explicit answers to that large question, we hope readers will find how and where they might look for answers in their own milieus.

REFERENCES

Anderson, P. (1985). What survey research tells us about writing at work. In L. Odell & D. Goswami (Eds.), *Writing in nonacademic settings* (pp. 3-83). New York: Guilford.

Bakhtin, M.M. (1986). The problem of speech genres. In C. Emerson & M. Holquist (Eds.) and V.W. McGee (Trans.), *Speech genres and other late essays* (pp. 60-102). Austin: University of Texas Press.

Bataille, R. (1982). Writing in the world of work: What our graduates report. *College Composition and Communication, 33,* 276-282.

Bazerman, C. (1988). *Shaping written knowledge: The genre and activity of the experimental article in science.* Madison: University of Wisconsin Press.

Berkenkotter, C., & Huckin, T. N. (1995). *Genre knowledge in disciplinary communication: Cognition/culture/power.* Hillsdale, NJ: Erlbaum.

Bourdieu, P. (1977). *Outline of a theory of practice* (R. Nice, Trans.). London: Cambridge University Press. (Original work published 1972)

Bourdieu, P. (1993). *Sociology in question* (R. Nice, Trans.). London: Sage Publications. (Original work published 1984)

Bracewell, R.J., & Witte, S.P. (1997, March). *The implications of activity, practice, and semiotic theory for cognitive constructs of writing.* Paper presented at the annual meeting of the American Educational Research Association, Chicago.

Cole, M. (1996). *Cultural psychology.* Cambridge, MA: Harvard University Press.

Devitt, A. (1993). Generalizing about genre: New conceptions of an old concept. *College Composition and Communication, 44,* 573-86.

Devitt, A. (1991). Intertextuality in tax accounting. In C. Bazerman & J. Paradis (Eds.), *Textual dynamics of the professions* (pp. 306-335). Madison: University of Wisconsin Press.

Dias, P. (1998, January). *Activity theory and its relevance for genre studies.* Paper presented at the 2nd International Symposium on Genre. Simon Fraser University, Vancouver.

Dias, P., Freedman, A., Medway, P., & Paré, A. (1999). *Worlds apart: Acting and writing in academic and workplace contexts.* Mahwah, NJ: Erlbaum.

Douglas, M. (1986). *How institutions think.* Syracuse, NY: Syracuse University Press.

Engeström, Y. (1993). Developmental studies of work as a testbench of Activity Theory: The case of primary care medical practice. In S. Chaiklin & J. Lave (Eds.), *Understanding practice: Perspectives on activity and context* (pp. 64-103). London: Cambridge University Press.

Freedman, A., & Medway, P. (1994). *Genre and the new rhetoric.* London: Taylor & Francis.

Freedman, A., Adam, C., & Smart, G. (1994). Wearing suits to class: Simulating genres and simulations as genres. *Written Communication, 11,* 193-226.

Geertz, C. (1983). *Local knowledge: Further essays in interpretive anthropology.* New York: Basic Books.

Giltrow, J., & Valiquette, M. (1994). Genres and knowledge: Students
    writing in the disciplines. In A. Freedman & P. Medway (Eds.),
    Learning and teaching genre (pp. 47-62). Portsmouth, NH:
    Boynton/Cook Heinemann.
Herndl, C. (1996a). Tactics and the quotidian: Resistance and profes-
    sional discourse. *Journal of Advanced Composition, 16*(3), 455-
    470.
Herndl, C. (1996b). The transformation of critical ethnography into
    pedagogy, or the vicissitudes of traveling theory. In A. Duin &
    C. Hansen (Eds.), *Nonacademic writing: Social theory and tech-
    nology* (pp. 17-34). Mahwah, NJ: Erlbaum.
Lave, J. (1991). Situated learning in communities of practice. In L.
    Resnick, J. Levine, & S. Teasley (Eds.), *Perspectives on socially
    shared cognition* (pp. 63-82). Washington, DC: American
    Psychological Association.
Ledwell-Brown, J. (1988). A survey of writing practices in manage-
    ment. *English Quarterly, 21,* 7-18.
Miller, C. (1994). Genre as social action. In A. Freedman & P.
    Medway (Eds.), *Genre and the new rhetoric* (pp. 23-42). London:
    Taylor & Francis.
Odell, L., & Goswami, D. (Eds.). (1985). *Writing in nonacademic set-
    tings.* New York: Guilford.
Paré, A., & Smart, G. (1994). Observing genres in action: Towards a
    research methodology. In A. Freedman & P. Medway (Eds.),
    Genre and the new rhetoric (pp. 146-154). London: Taylor &
    Francis.
Robbins, D. (1991). *The work of Pierre Bourdieu.* Milton Keynes:
    Open University Press.
Russell, D. R. (1995). Activity theory and its implications for writing
    instruction. In J. Petraglia (Ed.), *Reconceiving writing:
    Rethinking writing instruction* (pp. 51-77). Mahwah, NJ:
    Erlbaum.
Russell, D. R. (1997). Rethinking genre in school and society: An
    activity theory analysis. *Written Communication, 14,* 504-554.
Schryer, C. (1993). Records as genre. *Written Communication, 10,*
    200-234.

CHAPTER 1

Writing Classrooms as Activity Systems

Patrick Dias
McGill University

My argument in this chapter is that we ought to reconsider in fundamental ways the place, function, and conduct of writing courses within the university. In the following pages, I explore the grounds for such reconsideration and argue specifically that we need to redefine our understandings of what it is we mean by learning to write in university and of the kind of teaching that might promote such learning. I argue that such redefinition begins largely in considering a view of language and writing as social. The social perspective on writing, however, needs to be extended by taking on a perspective offered by activity theory. Defining activity theory (AT) and considering its implications for writing practices becomes the main burden of this chapter. Activity theory, I will show, helps uncover the contradictions at work within writing classrooms and brings into question what Joliffe (1994) has called the myth of transcendence, an assumption that justifies writing courses on the grounds that what is learned in such courses prepares students to meet the writing demands of other courses and of the workplace.

As teachers and researchers of writing, we are used to regarding writing courses as a normal, necessary, and well-established component of most university programs in North America.

And given the widespread belief that a large proportion of university entrants may be unable to meet university writing expectations, however defined, it is unlikely that in the near future writing courses will be under any serious pressure to justify their existence against the competitive demands of other courses. Moreover, the last two decades have yielded theory and research on writing of a quantity and quality that has provided disciplinary body and focus as well as generated perspectives and paradigms that seek to frame these developments (Berlin, 1987; Bizzell, 1986; Faigley, 1986; Knoblauch, 1988; Nystrand, Greene, & Wiemelt, 1993; North, 1987). The study and teaching of writing has created jobs, reduced redundancy and revived careers, generated conferences, and given birth to new journals and new university departments. As members of such a community, we have a vested interest in advocating and ensuring the continuity of such developments; unlike most areas of university study and inquiry, however, that continuity is linked essentially to pedagogical rather than disciplinary concerns.

And this, we might say, is as it should be; for writing classrooms exist primarily because, whether we agree or not, they are generally seen to develop a necessary skill rather than, as with most other university courses, to induct students into disciplinary knowledge and practices. We can safely say that in most universities teachers of writing must live with the expectation (and they are exceptional in this regard) that they will produce demonstrable results and do so almost immediately. In this sense, writing courses are "service" courses; and as such, they will come or go inasmuch as they are seen to succeed or fail in meeting such expectations. And there's the rub. Whereas those who are not within the field of composition studies tend to agree with the traditional justification for writing courses—they provide training in a core skill for university and the workplace—those within the field are increasingly questioning this notion. Whereas the continuing existence of writing courses relies on our sustaining the myth of transcendence and demonstrating its claims, the liberation of writing teachers as "service providers" accountable to the expectations of client departments requires that we question that myth and develop a tenable account of what it is we hope to do when we teach writing and what we might reasonably expect to accomplish and why.

It is these apparently polar positions ("Yes we can and do teach them to write" and "No, we cannot assure anyone that they will write more competently in their other courses or when they graduate into the workplace") that we need to explore and reconcile if the teaching of writing in the university is to shed the temporal and tentative accommodation that is its most prevalent condition. If we consider, for instance, an approach that has dominated the teaching of writing since the mid-seventies and into the eighties, the cognitive approach to researching and teaching writing, we can see why and how the myth of transcendence can be sustained. The concern in such an approach has been mainly with discovering and teaching the processes involved in writing. Research directed by such concerns has focused, for instance, on the writing processes of expert and novice writers and described effective writing strategies that can be modeled and taught, and help students recognize in their own approaches to writing what inhibits and what constrains (Britton et al., 1975; Emig, 1971; Flower & Hayes, 1977, 1981; Murray, 1980; Sommers, 1980). The pedagogical impulse is well served by such an approach: strategies focus on individuals and their developing skills as writers, and are seen to apply across the curriculum in a variety of contexts. Given this orientation, the teaching of writing retains its view of writing as a teachable, autonomous, and transportable skill. The research that matters here is a search for finer and fuller accounts of the writing process, with the promise of further elaborations into classroom practice.

TOWARD A SOCIAL PERSPECTIVE ON WRITING

Since the mid-eighties, cognitivist views of writing as occurring "in the head" have expanded and modified to accommodate a more social view of writing. In our studies of group work in university and school settings (1988), Anthony Paré and I were struck by the extent to which the very reading and writing strategies we would wish to teach our students were seemingly already a part of their repertoire, clearly apparent in the transcripts of their discussions as they engaged in reading or writing collaboratively. Although these students had not in any discernible way displayed individually the productive reading and writing strategies that emerged in the group effort, we were convinced that such group interactive settings somehow enabled the deployment of these strategies. Thus in retrospect, we realize that we may have witnessed instances of what Vygotsky had formulated as his "general genetic law of cultural development":

> Any function in the child's cultural development appears twice, or on two planes. First it appears on the social plane, and then on the psychological plane. First it appears between people as an interpsychological category, and then within the child as an intrapsychological category. (Vygotsky, 1981, p. 163)

Although Vygotsky is speaking of the development of higher cognitive functions in children, the principle can be extended to the adult
plane as well; for Vygotsky goes on to say that "all higher mental
functions are internalized social relationships" (p. 164). Those functions that appear and develop (interpsychologically) in group discussion ought in time to emerge (intrapsychologically) in individual
activity as well. Our students were realizing and revealing in collaborative discussion those strategies for reading and writing we had
planned to teach them. Collectively the group, in the language they
used and the strategies they employed, were realizing and deploying
the relevant cultural resources available to them. The chief of such
resources is of course language, embodying within it attitudes,
beliefs, and understandings that enable the group to agree on a common goal and work towards it. Such a view of language as embodying
cultural knowledge and skills, a view of language as social rather
than individual, is best caught by Bakhtin's brilliant formulation in
his seminal essay, "The Problem of Speech Genres":

> That is why the unique speech experience of each individual is
> shaped and developed in continuous and constant interaction
> with others' individual utterances. This experience can be charac-
> terized to some degree as the process of *assimilation*—more or
> less creative—of others' words (and not the words of a language).
> Our speech, that is, all our utterances (including creative work),
> is filled with others' words, varying degrees of otherness or vary-
> ing degrees of "our-own-ness," varying degrees of awareness and
> detachment. These words of others carry with them their own
> expression, their own evaluative tone, which we assimilate,
> rework, and reaccentuate. (1986, p. 89)

Bakhtin is distinguishing between language as an abstract system
(something out there) and language in use, as performed, language
bound in context, extended across speakers, situation, and cultural
artifacts such as scholarly articles, computer programs, the Internet,
calculators, or personal notebooks. It is this view of language as
social rather than as the possession of individual users that returns
us to the question that drives this chapter: given this orientation,
how might we in university settings redefine learning to write and
the kind of teaching that promotes the development of writers?

At the heart of a social perspective on writing is the notion
that writing is a situated activity: writing is integrally bound up with
the contexts within which it occurs—integrally bound up in the sense
that context is more than just the container or surround, the place or
situation or conditions within which writing occurs; context enters

into the act of writing in ways that define the goals and direction of writing, the very character, process, and constitution of writing. A view of writing as socially situated involves a radical change in focus, a shift of attention from the writer as autonomous individual to the writer as integrally and inevitably bound up within a social context, as participant in the activities of a group or community. Such a shift in its most overt form has led researchers to study the discourse practices of the various disciplines as well as the workplaces for which writing courses are expected to prepare students (Bazerman, 1988; Bazerman & Paradis, 1991; Dias et al., 1999; Freedman & Medway, 1994a, 1994b; Odell & Goswami, 1985; Spilka, 1993) and to discuss how such discourse practices relate to what we do in writing courses. Intrinsically, such a shift represents a concern with language practices, including writing, as social practices and is best represented in the emerging field of genre studies.

Genre studies provide the main theoretical base for much of what is reported in the following chapters. Genre studies regard genre knowledge as social knowledge, knowledge of social practices, including textual practices, that become regularized through the repeated exigences that call for those practices—the exigences themselves are social constructs (agreed on categories, culturally defined events). Genre knowledge is much more than the knowledge of textual forms and guidelines that allows us to generate typified responses to specific exigences; rather, it is best to regard genre as a form of social action, a response to our interpretation of a situation with regard to our own and other people's motives and the role we must adopt as part of that response. To the extent that such a response is regularized, it is a matter of first learning to identify or "see" an exigence as calling for one particular mode of response rather than another. And yet modes of response are not predetermined as such, being constantly constructed and reconstructed in terms of past experiences, particular needs and demands; thus genre knowledge is always in flux. I provide this brief account of genre studies only to suggest how difficult it is to define what is teachable in writing. If writing is a form of social action, and genres are potentially always in flux ("stabilized for now," as Schryer [1994] puts it), we need to ask how writing courses ought to be constituted to take account of forms that are essentially unstable.

A view of writing as social practice sets a perspective for examining what it is we do and might do as teachers of writing; however, it does not provide a convenient or practical way into that inquiry. We can see how a view of the writer as an autonomous individual suggests a very different account of writing courses and classroom practices than an account deriving from a view of writing as social practice. Thus if we develop an approach to teaching writing consistent with a view of writing as social practice (assuming an approach can be worked out), how will such an approach accord with institutional practices that generally assume the myth of the autonomous individual? By and large, our practice (for instance, as it registers in composition textbooks) assumes an institutional surround that is a neutral, if not invisible, agent in classroom events. We assume as well that at least for the time they are in our classrooms, our student are similarly cocooned from the social, political, and economic realities that shape their lives as students. These are not points of criticism; such a stance may be for all practical purposes the only one that allows us to teach groups of students in the limited hours allotted for such activity.

ACTIVITY THEORY

An analytical tool that may help us conduct the inquiry we need to undertake is provided by activity theory (AT), which derives from the Vygotskian school of psychology, specifically as it has been elaborated by Leont'ev (1981) and made accessible to North American readers through the work of Wertsch (1985, 1991), Engeström (1993), Cole and Engeström (1993), and more recently for composition studies, Russell (1995, 1997). AT offers us the conceptual tools to analyze human activity in context; it acknowledges that human activities are embedded in cultural/institutional histories as opposed to regarding individuals and their social/cultural contexts as separate entities. Thus Cole (1989) would define "person-acting-in-context" as a basic unit of analysis in activity theory. Context implies mediational means as well: language, other symbolic means, computers and other cultural and technological artifacts, not as separable entities, but as extensions (when in use) of the subjects in the activity. In other words, AT insists that we relate the specific situations we wish to study to their material surrounds, to their larger social, spatial, and temporal contexts. North American accounts are not entirely agreed on the finer points of AT; and this partial sketch provides just those core concepts that enable us to study writing classrooms as they are situated within the university and the workplace world they serve.

    Leont'ev proposes three distinct but interrelated levels of analysis, each level associated with a specific unit of analysis (Wertsch, 1985, p. 202). In other words, Leont'ev proposes three distinct ways of answering the question, what is an individual or group (the subject) doing in a particular setting. The first and most global level is the level of *activities*. The *activity* is defined by the *object* towards which the *activity* is oriented or the *motive* which drives the *activity*. Examples of a unit of *activity* are playing, working (for instance, farming, teaching, or cabinet-making), or going to school. The *object/motive* is not discrete or independent of the *activity*. The *object/motive* is conceived by the subject and, it follows, the *activity* is defined by the subject. Because ╱ *activity* is inevitably grounded in a social setting, a web of cultural and historical interrelationships, we need not see such definition as a conscious deliberate act; rather, we may think of work, play, or school-going as socioculturally defined, commonly agreed upon ways of acting and naming we grow into. Now whether the subject is involved in play, work, or school-going depends very much on the subject's perspective (and the collective's understanding of what constitutes play or work or school-going); thus I may be configuring a computer and be involved in the *activity* of work or play or school-going depending on the motive that drives the *activity*.[1]

The second level of analysis posited by Leont'ev is the level of *action*. *Actions* are the particular goal-driven tasks undertaken by participants to accomplish the *object* of the *activity*. A *goal* may be to write a memo for work, read a novel for recreation, or prepare a meal. *Goal*-driven *actions* must be considered separately from *activity; activity* is by definition ongoing; *actions* have definite beginnings and ends. According to Leont'ev,

> an activity and an action are genuinely different realities, which therefore do not coincide. One and the same action may be instrumental in realizing different activities. It can be transferred from one activity to another, thus revealing its relative independence. . . . The converse is also obvious: one and the same motive can give rise to different goals and, accordingly, can produce different actions. (1981, p. 61)

Thus the *action* of rock-climbing may be directed towards and realize different *activities*: work or recreation. Conversely, the recreational motive, for instance, may be realized through different *actions/goals*: I may work on a puzzle, read a book, take a walk, or watch TV. What is important to remember here is that a specific *action* is inevitably, and most often unconsciously, defined by the larger encompassing *activity* within which it occurs. Thus the *action* of preparing a dinner

---

[1]Activity, object, motive, action, goal, and operation are italicized in this explanatory section of the discussion only to distinguish their specialized sense from their everyday, common usage.

cannot but be influenced by whether the preparer regards it as a domestic, wage-earning, charitable, teaching, or recreational *activity*—and, of course, such driving *motives* may overlap.

The third level of analysis is at the level of *operations,* the *conditions* under which the action is carried out and the *means* by which it is carried out. Depending on the weather, traffic, and the time available, I may decide to walk, take a bus, or cycle to work, or even link up from home by computer. Each of these different *operations* is subordinated to the same *action/goal,* which is getting to work; unlike *actions, operations* are routine and automatic. In time and with practice, the various steps involved in getting to work may be reduced to washing, getting dressed, having breakfast, and taking a bus. Leont'ev's oft-cited example of shifting gears while driving illustrates how what was initially an *action* oriented consciously towards the *goal* of moving off and accelerating becomes with habituation an *operation* (no longer consciously directed toward a *goal*), a means (as with other *operations* such as braking and steering) of accomplishing the *action* of driving, getting from A to B.

If we apply this three-tiered system to the *action,* for instance, of writing with the goal of completing a report at work (work being the encompassing *activity*), we can think of several *goal-directed actions* that may be involved: collecting data, consulting colleagues, writing and circulating drafts, and composing on the word processor. Some of the data-gathering and word-processing *actions* may have become *operationalized,* that is, they are no longer attended to as deliberate *actions;* however, *operations* do move to the level of *actions* and become matter for conscious attention when, for instance, data entry involves the use of a new spreadsheet program. Many aspects of the writing we do (writing sentences and paragraphs, punctuation, and spelling) move back and forth between *operational* and *actional* levels, depending on familiarity with topic and genre. Spelling a word, or forming letters, or even holding a pencil properly is an *action* for beginning writers that with practice and some instruction soon becomes automatic and *operational.*

David Russell (1997) suggests that genres provide an excellent example of an aspect of writing that, depending on the genre, has become operational for most writers. If genres, as is argued by Carolyn Miller (1994), are typified rhetorical responses to situations that are socially interpreted or constructed as recurrent or similar, we can see how such typification has become operational for long-time participants in that activity system, whereas for newcomers, the writing of such genres is an effort of deliberate, goal-directed action, an effort which with growing familiarity with the reading and writing practices of that activity system, will eventually become operational. But that flow between actions and operations goes forward and backward, depending on the contingencies and participants; so that the operationalized response becomes outdated, inappropriate, or dysfunctional and is reconstituted as an action. To illustrate briefly, the form of internal memos hitherto routinely produced within a particular business unit, for instance, may require deliberate and constant attention and effort while the department is involved in expansion or merger and the memos are addressed to a changed and wider readership. The point is that the repeated exigences that generated a memo genre have altered, and a situation in flux necessitates more deliberate action.

Writing in school, however, and particularly within a writing course, is less likely to become operationalized, that is, flow from goal-directed action to a routine operation as a means of accomplishing an action, such as providing requested information or assembling an assigned report. Unlike in nonschool settings, where writing is integrated within the broader economic activity of work, which shapes the goals, forms, and processes of writing as a constituent action, writing within writing courses, because it is recognizably discrete, becomes the activity: writing in order to produce writing.

THE WRITING COURSE

The university writing program I propose as the subject of a test-case AT analysis—in order to tackle the unresolved status of university writing courses—is centered in a one-semester course that enrolls approximately 1,800 students in fall, winter, and summer day and evening courses. Students normally meet twice a week for fours hours (once a week for three hours in Continuing Education programs) in classes limited to a maximum of twenty-five. Students from several different disciplines take the course, usually in their first year. The writing program also operates a drop-in writing tutorial center as well as advanced writing courses for graduate students. Recently, the course was reorganized into specialized sections that take account of the discourse practices of the particular disciplines in which the students are enrolled. Course instructors include two tenure-track appointees, seven full-time junior lecturers, and fifteen part-time teachers, some of whom are either part- or full-time graduate students. Instructors meet regularly once every fortnight to discuss course planning, writing theory and research, and its implications for practice. They strive to achieve some degree of consistency across the sections in terms of goals, classroom practices, writing assignments, and grading procedures. With an annual writing research lecture series involving invited speakers and a number of ongoing research projects related to writing, most instructors are fairly well-informed on developments in composition theory and practice.

The three-tiered AT structure affords several immediate insights on what goes on generally in writing courses. In the first place, we have two activities rather than just the one activity we would expect to consider. From the perspective of students, we can regard the primary activity here as "school-going," motivated variously by a desire for learning (including learning to write), getting a qualifying degree (for employment or graduate study), and in some cases, acquiring or maintaining social status. None of these motives are inherently contradictory. On the other hand, from the perspective of the teacher, the primary activity here is teaching motivated variously by a desire to promote learning, cultivate a writing habit, help students develop positive attitudes towards writing, and, of course, earn a salary. The activities from perspectives on two different sides of the desk, so to speak, appear to complement one another. Drawing on the three-tiered scheme, we might frame course goals as ones mainly of making strategies for writing operational, strategies that are now deliberately taught and addressed as actions. We might also ask to what extent such development is hindered by the fact that many of these strategies, for example, ways of generating ideas or analyzing writing problems, remain essentially at the level of actions rather than become subsidiary operations. We will consider this question at some length below. By far the most important question is the matter of importing context into our discussion in order to take fuller account of our view of writing as social action. For when we have been speaking of goals and actions, we have been speaking as though the subjects in the activity, teachers and students, act in a social vacuum. In fact, AT by some accounts proposes a very strong version of the situatedness of human actions. As Engeström puts it,

> For activity theory, contexts are neither containers nor situationally created experiential spaces. Contexts are activity systems. An activity system integrates the subject, the object, and the instruments (material tools as well as signs and symbols) into a unified whole. (Engeström, 1993, p. 67)

When Engeström suggests that we focus on an activity system as the unit of analysis, he is reminding us that subjects in the activity are participating as members of a larger institutional system, and as individuals may not be aware of or even have access to the system's motives and objectives. He cites Mary Douglas:

> The whole approach to individual cognition can only benefit from recognizing the individual person's involvement with institutional building from the very start of the cognitive enterprise. (Douglas, 1986, p. 67)

An AT analysis includes and takes into account the varying perspectives of the subjects: they bring different roles and histories to the activity and therefore regard the activity very differently from how it is regarded by people who occupy different institutional roles. A study of the writing class as an Activity System posits a dynamic reality: shifting interests, changing participants, roles, relationships, contexts, and goals; a multilayered reality operating on multiple planes, and continuously constructed.

THE ACTIVITY OF TEACHING

The university calendar course description states that the writing course is designed

> to help students develop the quality and effectiveness of writing in various academic and professional situations. Emphasis is placed on the writing process itself, which includes the following: analyzing writing problems; appropriate problem-solving strategies; ways of generating, developing, and organizing ideas; designing communication for different audiences and purposes; and revising and editing texts.

As an advertisement for the course, the description announces practices that disclaim any notions of remediation on the one hand and essayist elitism on the other. Key words appear to be academic, professional, quality, effectiveness, strategies, process, audiences, and texts, suggesting both relevance and intellectual rigor. As intended, this description should appeal across the disciplines. At the same time, a reading of several individual course section outlines reveals that the prime aim of the course is to confirm students as writers, that is, to help them realize and develop their own resources as writers. In fact, the set of guidelines for course instructors reminds them that the general development of the course "follows the movement from writing for oneself to writing for others." Teachers are at some effort to induct students very quickly into practices that may seem quite foreign to some of the students: sharing writing in groups and reporting back regularly to the large group. The course text, authored by members of the course team (Dias et al., 1992), allows teachers to refer students to relevant sections so that lecturing is kept at an absolute minimum, and the teacher moves to the sidelines to provide feedback and respond to questions.

The goal then of the various teaching actions is not to instruct directly but rather to create contexts that enable learning. If writing is social practice, it must be cultivated as such within the context of the small group transactions. The course textbook is just one of several cultural resources available to the groups, and writing tasks are designed to draw on such knowledge. Assignments range from asking students to write from their areas of expertise for actual readers (in class or outside class) who need to know and are willing to respond with feedback, including their own judgments on the effectiveness of the writing, to engaging a class of electrical engineers in writing to a similar class in Paris via e-mail in order to exchange and comment reciprocally on investigative papers they have written in groups. The effort is to participate in an actual social process involving writing rather than in a simulation of real-world tasks within the classroom. On another plane, all students are required to "write for themselves," to maintain a weekly journal in order to cultivate a habit of writing informally and experimenting with modes and styles of writing on a regular basis. Teachers respond as interested and supportive readers.

A key aim of the course is to create a climate of regular self-assessment, so students can exercise judgment on their own development as writers and determine for themselves what they need to do to improve. They reflect in writer's notebooks or logs on their own processes as writers and their use of the strategies they have been experimenting with. They rely on feedback from peer readers as well, gaining some sense of what is valued as writing in the group from their own joint efforts. Throughout these and other practices the stress is on helping students develop a high degree of self-awareness and confidence as writers, to recognize their own resources as writers and know how they might participate in the discourse practices of the discipline or profession they have joined.

Even this brief selective account of the course reveals hidden divergent goals in the actions that contribute to the encompassing activity of teaching. The calendar account describes the content of the course, promoting the impression that it is much like other courses in having disciplinary content and activities; on the other hand, the teachers' outlines indicate a concern with process and involvement in writing as a social practice. Yet the latter agenda is derailed by certain course conditions, two of which, the one-semester length of the course and the heavy workload generated by the student writing produced in the course, are particularly subversive in their effects.

COMPETING FOR TIME

With a multisectioned course of this kind, it becomes expedient to standardize work requirements so that both students and teachers can feel assured of workload equity across the several sections. Given just thirteen weeks, teachers are agreed that they will require four formal written assignments, each of a specified kind and length. To ensure even further consistency, the course handbook specifies that the total number of pages of written work must not be less than 25 pages of double-spaced typewritten text. Such a minimum requirement seems meager, especially for a writing course. But one must remember that this is only the formal requirement. In keeping with the process-centeredness of the course, students do a considerable amount of writing that is not formally assessed but is just as much a requirement of the course: regular journal writing, writing exercises of a wide variety to try out the strategies taught in the course, process-writing logs, and multiple drafts of the writing to be formally submitted. All or at least most of the writing done in the course is assembled into a formal portfolio accompanied by a fairly demanding self-assessment of what has been accomplished. One might say those four writing tasks are merely the tip of the writing iceberg.

The account of the course I have drawn thus far is framed entirely as a view from within the scene, so to speak. What happens when we withdraw to some distance to take in the wider contexts within which the course functions? Maintaining the analogy, I would say the picture gains both perspective and depth.

Our view now takes in the four other courses students are normally enrolled in, most of these courses directly related to the students' prime disciplinary or professional interests. In this context, the writing course requirements seem considerably lighter gauged against the substantial demands of the other courses. Substantial, simply because in those invariably large first-year courses (large in terms of numbers enrolled, so that students generally remain anonymous for the first few weeks), students must expend considerable effort to settle what is expected of them in the way of creditable, if not merely passable, work; much more so than in the writing course where, in fact, course time is given over to planning for and monitoring progress on the four final products set as course requirements—and all this with considerable peer support and teacher feedback in a course that deliberately cultivates interdependence and sharing. In fact, the regular written exchanges between teacher and student allow for a continual monitoring of students' progress in the course and timely intervention where necessary. Most if not all students are grateful for such enlightened practices; however, the net effect is that they must allocate disproportionately more time to courses that do not provide the safety net allowed for in the writing course. Unlike in the writing course, topics for study and reading are not so clearly demarcated. Just the required readings alone seem unreasonably extensive given available time; and the recommended reading list remains no more than just that, something to remind students how much more remains to be done. It would seem reasonable therefore that students borrow whatever time they can from the less demanding writing course.

It is not that the writing course objectives and plan if conscientiously followed do not realize a respectably demanding course; rather, because so much of the course is actually what goes on in the classroom (regular classroom attendance and participation are bottom-line requirements for completing the course successfully, and reading if and when assigned is undemanding), much of the writing that is done outside class as part of the required but not formally finished work (preparatory drafts, journals, feedback on others' drafts) can be perfunctory and superficial and yet retain all the appearances of concerted effort. Paradoxically, the teacher's easy availability and regular feedback feeds the very process of enabling students to replicate what the teacher wants. This is particularly true of the kind of writing called for in the journal and logs. Moreover, the process logs and multiple copies of preparatory drafts are not in themselves irrefutable evidence of students' having followed processes advocated in the course. Such material is easily produced retroactively, and word processors make such tasks even less burdensome. Those students who are committed to the process are far too aware of its importance to compromise the integrity of their work and their relationship with the teacher. Those under pressure from other courses can only blame the system for their small, most likely unwitting, betrayals. Well schooled in the activity of "school-going," they may also have mastered the skill of writing writing. Unfortunately, because their shortcuts seemingly go unnoticed and unpenalized, they seriously undermine the credibility of the course and its sensible assessment practices.

Such compromising of course goals would be a matter of lesser concern if writing were seen to be valued in other courses as a regular practice. Or if at least some of the writing course practices were somehow validated by being incorporated into the design and carrying out of class assignments. As they are not, students are denied sufficient opportunity to extend their experiences from the writing course into the very areas of the curriculum they are preparing to write for. And one cannot argue that the major term papers and examinations that crowd students' end-of-term schedules provide a convenient testing ground for the strategies taught in the writing course. Writing in those courses is an entirely different action. In most such courses, papers may be returned with grades and comments, but hardly as an invitation to revise and resubmit in light of those comments. The latter practice is normal in the writing course, and ironically, a given in academic publication practices. What is most subversive of the supportive social practices that the writing course is grounded in is that such teaching approaches are hardly ever employed in other courses; the large lecture framework remains the norm for most programs. I do not intend with such comments to be critical of practices in the disciplinary courses; neither do I wish to argue that all courses ought to operate in more or less similar ways. Rather, my point is that we ought not to expect that students will display similar competencies as writers regardless of the situations they write in. On a related matter, Wertsch (1991, p. 94) has questioned the assumption that underlies the "metaphor of possession," the belief that ability displayed in one context will also be displayed in another.

What an AT analysis can uncover for us is that the activity called school-going involves several tasks or actions, with the goals of promoting learning or demonstrating such learning. I had said earlier that the perspective each subject (in our case, student) adopts determines the goal of that task and the operations that realize that goal. Given the overwhelmingly competitive demands of other courses, it is quite likely that the perspective a student adopts towards the several writing course tasks defines the goal as one of meeting course requirements. Thus it is more than likely that a student reading that one of the criteria for evaluation is "unmistakable evidence of effort to employ recommended strategies," may decide that given this criterion, her goal becomes one not so much of using those recommended strategies but of so staging her writing that evidence of their use is clearly apparent.

A similar disjunction plagues the writing teacher. Learning is the ostensible object of the activity called teaching; but as the course is conceived, that object is diverted by the need for consistency across the sections in terms of workload (both student's and instructor's) to that of describing a specific number of writing tasks to be completed in specified formats. Although it is not intended to, I wonder if such standardization does not work against the effort to somehow fashion a community of writers within the classroom, a community whose members define and develop writing commitments in response to exigences that require such responses. Such an agenda is one I believe most consistent with our notion of writing as social practice, and the one that resists the contradictions that an AT analysis reveals. If a view of writing as social practice is to prevail, then writing class-rooms must be open to writing tasks that emerge as outcomes of situ-ations within the classroom (not simulations, which I believe would produce simulated writing), and with a degree of spontaneity and urgency that cannot be anticipated in preset assignments. If the goal of the course is ostensibly the completion of four formal writing tasks, that goal will frame students' efforts despite teachers' efforts to have students take on their far broader agenda. (As an aside, we might wonder how we can expect that writing courses will obtain the degree of engagement and commitment more often available to disciplinary courses without imposing the kinds of sanctions such courses normal-ly use to ensure compliance.)

Working from a notion of writing as social practice does not preclude teaching certain strategies which, for instance, allow stu-dents to write more efficiently, assemble and organize their ideas, or revise and edit in the light of readers' needs and expectations. All such strategies bring to conscious attention actions that ought to become routinized operations (in the AT sense); unfortunately such transformations take time and practice, and it is quite likely that these strategies as they are promoted in this course remain at the level of actions, actions performed as course required tasks.

Early in this chapter, I had asked whether it is possible to claim that we can teach writing and that whatever learning occurs will carry over into other arenas outside the course and into the workplace as well. What AT reveals is the impossibility of regarding teaching and learning in a particular course as somehow apart from the larger institutional and societal framework in which that course is set. Students and course activities are constantly subject to demands and pressures that redefine and compromise what it is we intend within the seemingly closed confines of a course. Course goals and demands are continually redefined by students depending on the perspective they adopt. A way of dealing with such unintended dis-ruptiveness is to rely on students to define course goals and actions/tasks (which is what they do anyway) in ways we hope will match our own goals as teachers. Thus in small groups students can begin to define the goals and frame the tasks that will help them realize these goals. The teacher can help bring the groups together to negotiate common goals and tasks and inform them about the kinds of writing practices she hopes to induct them into: writing strategies, journal and log keeping, revision and editing strategies, among oth-ers. My point here is that students need to appropriate those goals and tasks for themselves in terms that make sense for how they themselves are located within the overall program. The other prac-tices that the teacher is committed to presenting and cultivating remain in the service of their ends. In their own groups students can refine their goals and tasks, both individual and joint, in the face of their developing understandings.

Viewed as social practice, writing is defined very differently in the disciplinary courses, primarily as a way of displaying learning. As a way of lessening the burden for writing teachers (that is, the onus of responsibility for teaching writing for all manners and seasons), students can now be in a position to decide for themselves how they manage writing in those courses (the myth of transcendence is no longer operative). They will realize they are now members of generally similar or dissimilar discourse communities and must learn what goes as writing in this community, where it comes from, and the particular social identity they must adopt. If they are fortunate, they will have frequent opportunities (or they will have to seek them) to develop such recognitions in small group discussion and in opportunities to write and receive feedback. In some educational programs and workplace settings, as the following chapters show, such participatory structures are already in place and working well.

REFERENCES

Bakhtin, M. M. (1986). *Speech genres and other late essays* (C. Emerson & M. Holquist, Eds.; V. W. McGee, Trans.). Austin: University of Texas Press.

Bazerman, C. (1988). *Shaping written knowledge: The genre and the activity of the experimental article in science.* Madison: University of Wisconsin Press.

Bazerman, C., & Paradis, J. (1991). *Textual dynamics of the professions.* Madison: University of Wisconsin Press.

Berlin, J. (1987). *Rhetoric and reality: Writing instruction in American colleges, 1900-1985.* Carbondale: Southern Illinois University Press.

Bizzell, P. (1986). Composing processes: An overview. In A.R. Petrosky & D. Bartholomae (Eds.), *The teaching of writing: The eighty-fifth yearbook of the National Society for the Study of Education* (pp. 49-70). Chicago: University of Chicago Press.

Britton, J., Burgess, T., Martin, N., McLeod, A., & Rosen, H. (1975). *The development of writing abilities.* London: Macmillan Education.

Cole, M. (1989). E-mail posting, November 21. XCHLC list, University of San Diego, CA.

Cole M., & Engeström, Y. (1993). A cultural-historical approach to distributed cognition. In G. Salomon (Ed.), *Distributed cognitions: Psychological and educational considerations* (pp. 1-46). Cambridge: Cambridge University Press.

Dias, P., & Paré, A. (1988). *Making meaning in reading and in writing.* Paper presented at the annual meeting of the Conference on College Composition and Communication, St. Louis, MO.

Dias, P., Beer, A., Ledwell-Brown, J., Paré, A., & Pittenger, C. (1992). *Writing for ourselves, writing for others.* Scarborough, ON: Nelson-Canada.

Dias, P., Freedman, A., Medway, P., & Paré, A. (1999). *Worlds apart: Acting and writing in academic and workplace contexts.* Mahwah, NJ: Erlbaum.

Douglas, M. (1986). *How institutions think.* Syracuse, NY: Syracuse University Press.

Emig, J. (1971). *The composing processes of twelfth graders.* Research Report 13. Urbana, IL: National Council of Teachers of English.

Engeström, Y. (1993). Developmental studies of work as a testbench of activity theory: The case of primary care medical practice. In S. Chaiklin & J. Lave (Eds.), *Understanding practice: Perspectives on activity and context* (pp. 64-103). Cambridge: Cambridge University Press.

Faigley, L. (1986). Competing theories of process. *College English, 48,* 527-542.

Flower, L., & Hayes, J.R. (1977). Problem-solving strategies and the writing process. *College English, 39,* 449–461.

Flower, L., & Hayes, J.R. (1981). A cognitive process theory of writing. *College Composition and Communication, 32,* 365–387.

Freedman, A., & Medway, P. (Eds.). (1994a). *Genre and the new rhetoric.* London and Bristol, PA: Taylor & Francis.

Freedman, A., & Medway, P. (Eds.). (1994b). *Learning and teaching genre.* Portsmouth, NH: Boynton/Cook Heinemann.

Joliffe, D.A. (1994). The myth of transcendence and the problem of the "ethics" essay in college writing instruction. In P.A. Sullivan & D.J. Qualley (Eds.), *Pedagogy in the age of politics: Writing and reading (in) the academy* (pp. 183-194). Urbana, IL: National Council of Teachers of English.

Knoblauch, C. H. (1988). Rhetorical considerations: Dialogue and commitment. *College English, 50,* 125-140.

Leont'ev, A. N. (1981). The problem of activity in psychology. In J.V. Wertsch (Ed.), *The concept of activity in Soviet psychology* (pp. 37-71). Armonk, NY: Sharpe.

Miller, C. (1994). Genre as social action. In A. Freedman & P. Medway (Eds.), *Genre and the new rhetoric* (pp. 23-42). London: Taylor & Francis.

Murray, D. (1980). Writing as process: How writing finds its own meaning. In T.R. Donovan & B.W. McClelland (Eds.), *Eight approaches to teaching composition* (pp. 3-20). Urbana, IL: National Council of Teachers of English.

North, S. (1987). *The making of knowledge in composition.* Portsmouth, NH: Boynton/Cook.

Nystrand, M., Greene, S., & Wiemelt, J. (1993). Where did composition studies come from? An intellectual history. *Written Communication, 10*, 267-333.

Odell, L., & Goswami, D. (1985). *Writing in nonacademic settings.* New York: Guilford Press.

Russell, D. R. (1995). Activity theory and its implications for writing instruction. In J. Petraglia (Ed.), *Reconceiving writing: Rethinking writing instruction* (pp. 51-77). Mahwah, NJ: Erlbaum.

Russell, D. R. (1997). Rethinking genre in school and society: An activity theory analysis. *Written Communication, 14,* 504-554.

Schryer, C. F. (1994). The lab vs. the clinic: Sites of competing genres. In A. Freedman & P. Medway (Eds.), *Genre and the new rhetoric* (pp. 105-124). London and Bristol, PA: Taylor & Francis.

Sommers, N. (1980). Revision strategies of student writers and experienced adult writers. *College Composition and Communication, 31,* 378-388.

Spilka, R. (Ed.). (1993). *Writing in the workplace: New research perspectives.* Carbondale and Edwardsville: Southern Illinois University Press.

Vygotsky, L. S. (1981). The genesis of higher mental functions. In J. V. Wertsch (Ed.), *The concept of activity in Soviet psychology* (pp. 144-188). Armonk, NY: Sharpe.

Wertsch, J. V. (1985). *Vygotsky and the social formation of mind.* Cambridge, MA: Harvard University Press.

Wertsch, J. V. (1991). *Voices of the mind: A sociocultural approach to mediated action.* Cambridge, MA: Harvard University Press.

CHAPTER 2

Write Where You Are: Situating Learning to Write in University and Workplace Settings[1]

Aviva Freedman & Christine Adam
Carleton University

Our research, and that of our colleagues, has revealed the degree to which university genres differ from those elicited in the workplace. Even in courses where the instructor is directly simulating a workplace task through a factually based case study, the nature of the writing is fundamentally different because of the radical differences between the two rhetorical contexts (cf. Dias, Freedman, Medway, & Paré, 1999; Freedman, Adam, & Smart, 1994). In this chapter, we wish to make a separate, though related, point: when students move from the university to the workplace, they not only need to learn new genres, they also need to learn new ways to learn these genres.

To illuminate the differences in the kinds of learning experienced, we draw on the growing literature on theories of situated learning, or practical cognition. We then present some of our research, focusing in detail on two settings: a fourth-year course in

---

[1]Portions of this chapter appear in Dias, P., Freedman, A., Medway, P. & Paré, A. (1999). *Worlds apart: Acting and writing in academic and workplace contexts*. Mahwah, NJ: Erlbaum.

financial analysis in which students were asked to simulate work-place-like reports in response to actual case histories; and an intern-ship program, where novices were called on to learn and perform the normal writing-related duties of that workplace. Our primary aim is to illustrate and clarify the nature of the differences—not so much between the genres elicited but rather between the kinds of learning experienced in, and necessitated by, the two settings.

SITUATING LEARNING

In the past decade, a new field in psychology has emerged, variously called situated learning, socially shared cognition, everyday cogni-tion, or situated experience. A primary focus of this new field has been on knowing and learning, but these terms have been redefined so that they carry very different meanings from those held within traditional studies of cognition. In fact, this new field is not so much cognitive science as a response to cognitive science as currently con-ceived. Fundamental to this work is the notion that knowing is social—not in the sense that one mind transmits knowledge to anoth-er, but rather in the Vygotskian (1978) sense that the source of intrapersonal cognitive functioning is the interpersonal.

The field of situated learning, however, is not unitary. Whereas the importance of both social and collaborative perfor-mances in learning is commonly recognized, scholars and researchers conceive many of the key notions differently. The commonalities underlying this field are these: learning and knowing are context-specific, learning is accomplished through processes of coparticipa-tion, and cognition is socially shared.

Given these commonalities, however, there are different streams within the literature. Jean Lave (1991; see also 1988) has specified three different theories of "situated experience." In the first, the "cognition plus view," researchers simply "extend the scope of their intraindividual theory to include everyday activity and social interaction. . . . Social factors become conditions whose effects on individual cognition are then explored" (1991, p. 66).

The second, the "interpretive view," "locates situatedness in the use of language and/or social interaction" (p. 63). Furthermore, "language use and, thus, meaning are situated in *interested,* inter-subjectively negotiated social interaction" (p. 67; emphasis added). Individuals work together hermeneutically, through (largely verbal) interactions, toward a shared understanding, within contexts where they are each or all actively engaged.

Both the first and second theories are limited, according to Lave, in that they "bracket off the social world" and thus "negate the possibility that subjects are fundamentally *constituted* in their relations with and activities in that world" (p. 67; emphasis added). The third theory, "situated social practice" or, where appropriate, "situated learning," includes the interpretive perspective along with an insistence that "learning, thinking, and knowing are relations among people engaged in activity *in, with, and arising from the socially and culturally structured world*" (p. 67; emphasis added). A qualified version of this latter perspective informs our analysis.

Fundamental to that perspective is the recognition of the degree to which human activity is mediated through tools—especially that most powerful semiotic tool, language. In his discussions, James Wertsch (1991a, 1991b) emphasizes the need to complement situated learning with Bakhtinian notions. Wertsch emphasizes in particular the way in which speakers "ventriloquate" portions or aspects of their ambient social languages in attempting to realize their own speech plans. All our words are filled with, and are echoes of and responses to, others' words. (To quote Bakhtin, "No-one breaks the eternal silence of the universe" [1986, p. 69; see also 1981].) Our utterances are dialogic responses to earlier utterances as well as anticipations of our listeners' responses. The relations are multiple, complex, shifting, and dynamic. They demand and reward engagement and attention, and involve notions of complex interplay between an individual's free speech plans and the speech genres available, between an individual's own utterances and the ambient social languages.

The literature on situated learning has produced (at least) two analytic perspectives from which such learning can be viewed: Barbara Rogoff's "guided participation" (1990, 1991) and Jean Lave and Etienne Wenger's "legitimate peripheral participation" (1991). Although these two perspectives have not been developed as alternatives to each other, they do in fact foreground different aspects of the learning process.

Rogoff (1990) uses the term *guided participation* to describe the learning process or cognitive apprenticeship that primarily middle-class children experience within their homes.

> Guided participation involves adults or children challenging, constraining, and supporting children in the process of posing and solving problems through material arrangements of children's activities and responsibilities as well as through interpersonal communication, with children observing and participating at a comfortable but slightly challenging level. The processes of communication and shared participation in activities inherently

> engage children and their caregivers and companions in stretch-
> ing children's understanding and skill . . . [and in the] structur-
> ing of children's participation so that they handle manageable
> but comfortably challenging subgoals of the activity that increase
> in complexity with children's developing understanding. (p. 18)

This perspective echoes notions like "scaffolding" and Lev Vygotsky's
"zone of proximal development" (1978, pp. 84-91): that space in which
a learner can perform an action (cognitive or rhetorical) *along with* a
skilled practitioner but not alone. The assumption is that, by so performing the act along with the practitioner, the child will later be
able to operate alone: the intersubjective will become intrasubjective.

Guided participation can be contrasted with the learning that
Lave and Wenger (1991) call *legitimate peripheral participation,* a
process that characterizes various forms of apprenticeship—from
that of Vai and Gola tailors to Yucatec midwives to butchers' apprentices to newcomers in Alcoholics Anonymous. Central to all these
forms of apprenticeship is their focus on something other than learning. Apprentices and masters, or rather newcomers and oldtimers,
are both involved in activities that have a purpose above and beyond
the initiation of newcomers. The tailors learn by becoming involved
in making real garments. In all the instances, the activity as a whole
has an end other than the learning of its participants.

In both processes, however, the newcomers do learn. The two
processes are similar in very important respects: (a) Both are based
on the notion of learning through performance or engagement—
"learning through doing," as one of the instructors in our research
kept repeating—as opposed to earlier cognitive notions of learning
through receiving bodies of knowledge. "The individual learner is not
gaining a discrete body of abstract knowledge (s)he will then trans-
port and reapply in later contexts. Instead, (s)he acquires the skill *to
perform by actually engaging in the process*" (Hanks, 1991, p. 15;
emphasis ours); (b) Both processes are social: instructors and learners collaborate, in a broad sense, and one result is that learners are
able to do something at the end that they were unable to do before;
(c) In both, learning is achieved through sociocultural mediation of
tools and especially linguistic and other semiotic signs. Also, in both
kinds of learning the learners do not fully participate. The conditions
for performing are attenuated; only some of the task is given over to
the learner, and this attenuation (generally a subtle and highly
nuanced attenuation) allows for the learning.

On the other hand, there is at least this radical difference
between the two processes: in guided participation the goal of the
activity itself is learning; in legitimate peripheral participation the ⟋

learning is incidental and occurs as part of participation in communities of practice, whose activities are oriented toward practical or material outcomes. This difference has important consequences, as we shall see.

We have chosen to use the terms "facilitated performance" and "attenuated authentic participation" to differentiate between the two kinds of situated learning we observed. The echo in the names is intended to acknowledge their sources; the difference in wording is intended to reflect the fact that we use these terms in more specialized and possibly narrower ways than those intended by the originators.

RESEARCH STUDIES

Our goal in this article is to differentiate the processes of novices learning to write in the workplace from the processes of students learning new genres in their university courses. The specific sets of novices and students that we selected are described below.

Novices or Interns

The novices we observed were graduate students involved in full-time internships. The internships were organized by a Canadian university's school of public administration specifically for students in the midst of their MA studies. The internships were neither compulsory nor graded as part of the curriculum: they were opportunities for students to spend one or more semesters working in paid, full-time public sector jobs—the kind that they might aspire to upon graduation. The school facilitated the hiring procedure by advertising potential placements, collecting resumés from students, and providing a locale for interviews. The potential employers interviewed and hired interns using their own criteria.

We followed seven interns, each assigned to different government agencies, over the course of at least one semester. They presented us with copies of all their written work (and with all drafts of that work, including notations and responses by supervisors and peers). We interviewed the interns regularly, visited some work sites, interviewed superiors, and observed and tape-recorded work in progress on-site.

University Students

The university course we used for this study was an upper-level undergraduate semester course in financial analysis, where students responded to case studies (Freedman, Adam, & Smart, 1994). We selected this course because the instructor intended the writing assignments to be more like workplace writing than like typical academic essays. In other words, we selected course writing that was as similar as possible to that of the workplace in order to highlight the contrasts. These findings have been corroborated and refined in the course of the larger project by more extensive observation of several different courses and classes in our business and public administration programs. The findings are also consonant with those of an earlier intensive case study focusing on an undergraduate course in law (Freedman, 1987, 1990, 1996).

Of the 25 students in the finance course, three students volunteered for close observation. These students provided us with the following: (a) the drafts of and notes for all written assignments; (b) papers written for other courses; (c) extensive retrospective interviews focusing on their composing—at the beginning, middle, and end of each of the three major assignments; (d) tape-recordings of segments of their joint composing sessions.

Before, during, and after the course, we interviewed the instructor, using open-ended questions to get at his goals, expectations, and ongoing reactions to the course and the writing assignments. He provided us with the course outline as well as the guidelines and task specifications for all assignments. The instructor also performed reading protocols in response to students' assignments. In classes we observed and recorded field notes on both the instructor's lectures and students' presentations. We collected written essays and case studies from all students in the class, and observed oral case presentations.

The case study writing involved simulations based on actual case histories, in which students were asked to write reports, as though they were managers or consultants to boards of directors of real companies, suggesting courses of action for the beleaguered companies at particular historical moments of crisis. Students were expected to write their reports using a workplace format, with an executive summary at the beginning and the format one might expect in a business setting; at the same time, they were required to deliver oral summaries of their written reports, dressed like consultants and using professional accoutrements, such as overheads and briefcases.

ANALYSIS

Our observational data consisted of field notes taken during class presentations and work site visits; notes based on the tape-recorded and transcribed interviews with the instructor, students, supervisors, and interns; notes based on the tape-recorded and transcribed composing sessions; and the actual audiotapes and transcriptions. We analyzed our notes and transcriptions for recurrent themes and then cross-referenced and triangulated these themes with findings from the textual data. Working alone and cross-checking our observations with each other, we sought informant corroboration whenever possible (see Goetz & LeCompte, 1984).

Our underlying orientation throughout has been naturalistic: that is, our goal has been to elicit and value the participants' own constructions of the meaning of the discursive practices and on that basis to point to patterns in the richly textured, socially constructed realities of each discursive context.

Findings

In keeping with the naturalistic orientation of this research, we organized the findings thematically, largely according to the theoretic models of situated learning described earlier—which themselves were constantly cross-checked and refined throughout the observations and analyses.

The first subsection focuses on how the students learned to write the genres elicited in the university classes observed. The second focuses on the differences in the two settings and, in the course of doing so, clarifies further the distinctive nature of the learning in the university as well as the workplace. The third subsection points to some of the problems that arise when university graduates accustomed to one mode of learning are placed in a context that requires another.

Learning to Write at School: Facilitated Performance

The theoretical frame that accounts for how students learned to write in the university classes we observed is best captured by the term *facilitated performance*. Our argument is that this frame, based on Rogoff's (1990) notion of guided participation, accounts for how university students learn discipline-specific writing in the classes that we observed in much the same way as guided participation accounts for early child language acquisition or cognitive apprenticeship in middle-class homes.

The most salient commonality is that the guide in both cases, caregiver and instructor, is oriented entirely to the learner and to the learner's learning. In fact, the activity is undertaken primarily for the sake of the learner. (Presumably, parents do not read *Mother Goose* to themselves any more than instructors deliver lectures to themselves.) The guide's concentration is focused on the learner and the activity, which is quite different from what we will see in the instances of workplace-based learning (and also quite different from what Rogoff [1993] and Heath [1983] reported in non-middle-class child rearing).

Not only is the guide's attention focused on the learner, but the whole social context has been shaped and organized by the guide for the sake of the learner (recognizing that each such context is itself located in some larger institution whose goals are also at play: family, university, capitalist society, etc.). The caregiver organizes the story-time experience, and the instructor orchestrates the course (within certain temporal, spatial, organizational constraints): readings are set, lectures delivered, seminars organized, working groups set up, assignments specified—all geared towards enabling the learners to master certain material.

In the courses we observed, students did not learn to write new genres on the basis of explicit direction by their guides (the instructors and teaching assistants), except in the crudest terms with respect to format, length, and subject matter (Freedman, 1993). Nevertheless, the writing was shaped, constrained, and orchestrated from the first meeting of the course—that is, from its specification on the course outline and, more significantly, from the first words uttered by the instructor.

Our observations of these classes, and the students composing for them, revealed that learning new genres in the classroom came about as a result of carefully orchestrated processes of collaborative performance between the course instructor and students: students learned through doing, specifically through performing with an attuned expert who structured the curriculum in such a way as to give the students increasingly difficult tasks. The instructor both specified the task and set that task within a rich discursive context. Both the collaborative performance and the orchestration of a richly evocative semiotic context enabled the acquisition and performance of the new genres—whether these were traditional academic essays about political theory, analyses of legal cases according to appropriate statutes of interpretation, simulations of workplace proposals, or feasibility studies.

Collaborative performance

At the beginning of the course in financial analysis, for example, the instructor assigned cases to be written up at home, and then in class he modeled appropriate approaches to the data, identifying key issues and specifying possible recommendations for action. As they attempted to write up the cases themselves at home, the students were "extremely frustrated" because "[they had] to do a case before [they had] the tools to know how to do it." As one student described it: "It's like banging your head against a wall." However, after the instructor modeled appropriate approaches in class—*especially in the context of the students' struggles to find meaning in the data themselves*—the students were gradually able to make such intellectual moves themselves. As one of the students said, at the beginning, "When he would tell us the real issue, we're like—'where did that come from?'" Then, "When you're done and he takes it up in class, you finally know how to do it!"

Modeling what the students would later do themselves, the instructor presented a number of cases at the beginning of the course. Like the mother with the storybook, the instructor showed the students first where to look and then what to say, picking out the relevant data from the information in the case, very often in the form of questions:

> What's the significance of 7 and 8 in the text? Did it add to your thinking about this case?
>
> At what market share restriction would that growth strategy not work?
>
> Assuming best case scenario, what will this company look like in five years?

He constructed arguments, using the warrants of and based on the values and ideology valorized in the discipline. Drawing on the simulated purposes for the case, he pointed to the importance of looking at and presenting information in particular ways:

> As a consultant to the bank, is this a critical value to know?
>
> In real life, you have to quantify this relationship between business risk and financial risk.

And as he moved from modeling the performance to having the students present the cases themselves orally in class, he provided corrective feedback:

Walk people through how you thought about the problem.

Let people know what the agenda is and your role.

Gradually students were inducted into the ways of thinking, that is, the ways of construing and interpreting phenomena, valued in that discipline.

We see here many of the elements that Wood, Bruner, and Ross (1976) specified as functions of the tutor in scaffolding (qtd. in Rogoff, 1990). The tutor defines the task, demonstrates an idealized version of the act to be performed, and indicates or dramatizes the crucial discrepancies between what the child has done and the ideal solution. The element of motivation in scaffolding is unnecessary in the university setting because the institution of schooling itself, with its accreditation process, provides sufficient motivation for learning.

Discursive context
These processes of collaborative performance offer part of the answer to how the students learned to write the genres expected of them. In addition, the instructor set up a rich discursive context with his lectures and the readings, and through the mediation of these discourses the students were able to engage appropriately in the tasks set.

Wertsch (1991a, 1991b), drawing on Bakhtin, talks of the power of "dialogism" and of echoing (or "ventriloquating") social languages and speech genres. The students that we observed responded "ventriloquistically" to the readings and the instructor's discourse, as they worked through the tasks set for them. Initially, they picked up (and transformed in the context of their preexistent conversational patterns) the social language or register they had heard. Here are oral samples culled from students' conversations as they worked on producing their case study:

Mike: I figured this is how we should structure it. . . . First, how did they get there is the first thing.

Judy: So that's . . .

Mike: . . . business versus financial risk or operations versus debt, whatever. . . . Then . . . like we will get it from the bankers' perspective.

Judy: Yeah, that's pretty much like what I was thinking too.

Mike: So, right now I have their thing before 78. How do you want it, pre-78 post-78? This is what I did. I went through all . . .

Judy: . . . internal comparison and stuff.

*****

Mike: I guess the biggest thing is the debt-to-equity ratio. Notice that? X has way more equity. If you look at Y, their equity compared to their debts is nowhere near, it's not even in the ballpark.

Joe: Which company is it that took a whole bunch of short-term debt?

Then, as the students wrote their papers, the conversational syntax, lexicon, and intonational contours of their earlier conversations disappeared, and they reproduced discipline-specific terms in the context of academic written English, achieving thus the written social register of a financial analyst designated by their instructor (see Freedman, Adam, & Smart, 1994). In the final draft of a case study, we find the following:

Short-term debt restructuring is a necessity. The 60% ratio must be reduced to be more in line with past trends and with the competition. This will be achieved by extension of debt maturities, conversion of debt to equity, reduction of interest rates, as well as deferral of interest payments.

In other words, through the mediation and appropriation of the social languages provided by the instructor's lectures and the readings, students created the new genres expected of them.

Findings from other undergraduate courses
We have focused on this course in financial analysis primarily because its writing was intended to be most like that of the workplace, hence making differences particularly salient. To buttress our argument, however, we should add that analyses of learning to write in other academic courses revealed a similar pattern with the following qualification: in the other academic courses, there was typically far less collaborative scaffolding or modeling of problems to be solved; rather, "facilitation" was realized primarily in the carefully orchestrated and highly cued discursive context, established by the instructor(s) through lectures and readings, to which the students were expected to respond.

To repeat: learning to write the appropriate genres, in the courses we observed, was not achieved through *explicit* direction from instructors. The writing, nevertheless, was powerfully shaped and constrained by the instructor from the first meeting of the course. From the instructor's first words, a rich discursive context was created in the course—through the lectures, seminars, and readings—a context that was clearly demarcated and differentiated from the wider ambient discourse environments of the students' lives by its time slots, spatial location, and specification in course outlines. Students responded "dialogically" and "ventriloquistically" (to use Bakhtin's and Wertsch's terms) to this discursive context, when responding to the questions posed in the assignments.

To be more specific, the discursive context of the course—created through intonation, repetition, and other forms of cueing in the instructor's words and the words in those readings the instructor deemed relevant—shaped and constrained the writing in the following ways: the lexicon was echoed through the specialized usage of both the terminology of each field and common words appropriate to that field; certain kinds of modalities were echoed; syntactic relations were modeled (e.g., clauses of condition or concession in law papers, clauses of qualification and causation in others); lines of reasoning were modeled, and thus students learned which warrants were appropriate, the kinds of evidence they might (and might not) draw on, the degree of certainty to assign to different kinds of evidence, and the kinds of backing that might be necessary and when to use them. The instructors thus collaborated with the students and facilitated the production of each paper by providing this thickly textured and highly cued discursive context and then defining the kinds of questions in the assignments that encouraged the students to draw on the lines of argument and use the lexicon and syntax modeled in the classes.

From the perspective of situated learning, the disciplinary classes provided something like the "guided participation" that Rogoff describes (1990). The guide or instructor shaped the context in such a way that the learner learned through performing activities elicited in the context. Our research revealed that, through being immersed in the rich discursive contexts provided in disciplinary classrooms—where instructors lectured to students for three hours a week, with these lectures often accompanied by a seminar of one or two hours and certainly accompanied by relevant readings—students began to be able to ventriloquate the social language and respond dialogically to the appropriate cues from this context. Their learning was mediated through extraordinarily elaborated semiotic signs—that shaped, constrained, and enabled their responses to the tasks that were set.

Learning to Write Again: Attenuated Authentic Participation

The interns that we observed learning the genres appropriate to the government agencies to which they were assigned went through processes that, in some ways, were fundamentally similar to those engendered by the university settings. In both instances, learning resulted from collaboration, in the widest sense, or shared social engagement, as well as through the mediation of sociocultural tools (primarily, but not solely, linguistic signs). There were important differences, however, that are all the more significant for being tacit and implicit, complicating the transition into the workplace. Both the commonalities and the differences are suggested in the following scene (from one of our internship observations), which captures many of the significant features of the learning we call attenuated authentic participation. Any extended analysis and commentary is in square brackets. Douglas is the learner and Richard is his mentor or supervisor.

> Douglas and Richard are observed as they respond to a sudden request to prepare a briefing note on the state of a particular set of negotiations for a new government minister. [Political events such as the appointments of new ministers often interrupt the anticipated flow of business in Canadian government offices. Mentors or supervisors must improvise, if they are to include the learners in the new tasks. Both must be agile.]

> Douglas and Richard are standing in front of a desk that has a pile of previous briefing notes and reports on these negotiations. Their task is to develop a new briefing document, summarizing succinctly what the new minister needs to know.

> The two discuss the potential content in global terms, brainstorming on a whiteboard, and then they sit down to write. Richard suggests that they work collaboratively. Douglas understands this to mean dividing up the task in two, with each taking responsibility for one half. [Presumably this reflects his notion of collaboration, based on what passed for collaboration as it was undertaken in university.]

> Richard corrects this misconception, explaining that he means that they will actually produce the whole text together: the two of them sitting together to generate and compose text, with one person assigned to do the actual inputting. There is some joking and jockeying about who will do the inputting, but Richard decides

that Douglas's superior expertise in word processing (he can use Windows) warrants his taking the seat in front of the computer. [It is not untypical in the workplace for novices to display superior expertise in relevant areas.]

The two proceed to formulate and reformulate text together, with Richard taking the lead and providing feedback to each of Douglas's suggestions, but at the same time constantly eliciting suggestions and listening carefully to Douglas's comments about his own suggestions. The two respond to each other conversationally in a series of half-sentences, which reveals the highly interactive nature of the interchange. Each half-sentence responds to and builds on the previous, so that the product becomes more and more jointly generated. [This kind of interactive generating and composing between a guide and learner is hard to imagine in a school context, even in a tutoring center. The coparticipation often reaches a flow at which it is difficult to determine who is suggesting which words.]

Complicating this interactiveness further is the interaction with already extant texts. Each suggestion for the new text is based in large part on the briefing notes and reports that are already available in the documents in front of them, with the words and phrases being modified, echoed, reaccentuated, qualified. [These earlier texts are cultural artifacts, which have been shaped by, and encode, the cultural practices and choices of the organization as it has evolved to that point. In Bakhtin's terms, the words in the new evolving documents are being echoed from the earlier ones, and reaccentuated in the light of the current "speech plan" (1986), so that the words become reinfused with slightly different meanings. This dialogism and mediation through cultural artifacts is true of university writing and hence learning as well, but without the complicating factor of the intersubjective activities of guide and learner.]

In other words, the scene shows persons in activity with the world as mediated through the technological tools (word processors and software) and the other cultural artifacts available. It depicts a hermeneutic grappling with notions making it sometimes difficult to discover where one thinker's processes end and the other's begin and where the new speech plan begins and the older cultural artifacts end.

To sum up, this typical scene reveals learning as taking place through active processes (in this case, writing), guided by mentors, and mediated through cultural tools. In that respect, the learning parallels that of the university setting. The differences are the nature of the interactive coparticipation and collaboration between mentor and learner, the improvisatory nature of the task, the task's authenticity and ecological validity within a larger context (the institution and indeed society as a whole), and the varied and shifting roles played by mentor and learner. Furthermore, no conscious attention is paid to the learner's learning; all attention is directed to the task at hand and its successful completion. Figure 2.1 summarizes these differences, which will be fleshed out in the discussions to follow.

Goals of the writing task
Probably the most critical difference between the learning that takes place in the university and the workplace, one with far reaching implications, is that the goal of the writing task in the school context

	Facilitated Performance	Attenuated Authentic Participation
Setting	University	Workplace
Goal of Writing	Writer's learning	Institutional action
	therefore	*therefore*
	Learning task sequenced by the guide Context and task simplified	Improvisatory quality of learning occasions
Guide-Learner Roles	Static and fixed	Shifting and multiple
Evaluation	Texts' quality determined by guide's grade Individualistic culture	Texts' quality determined by rhetorical success Collaborative culture
Learning Site	Most guidance takes place before text is completed	Much guidance takes place through extensive iterative collaboration after draft is completed

Figure 2.1. Differences Between Facilitated Performance and Attenuated Authentic Participation

is clearly and explicitly for students to learn (with learning to write as a route to, or specialized instance of, learning); in contrast, the workplace operates as a community of practice whose tasks are focused on material or discursive outcomes and in which participants are often unaware of the learning that occurs.

Freedman, Adam, and Smart (1994) illustrate the degree to which learning and the learner are the foci of the writing tasks assigned in a university class (even when these tasks were presented as simulations of workplace situations, and the reports elicited ended with recommendations for action). As that study shows, the real goal of the writing was neither action nor policy but rather the demonstration that students knew the appropriate arguments to make in order to ground appropriate claims in the relevant arenas (as circumscribed by the course content). Both students and instructors understood that this demonstration of learning was the writing goal. We contrasted the university's writing goals with the action or policy orientation of workplace writing produced in the research unit of a government institution.

Our own research in the workplace and that of others has repeatedly shown that one consequence of this difference in writing goals is that it is often unclear to newcomers *that* they must learn, let alone *what and how* they must learn, and *from whom* they can learn. In the government agencies we observed, newcomers often asserted that they did not think that they would need to learn to write differently (see also MacKinnon, 1993). And when the supervisors were asked whether they considered what they assigned them, their response was an unequivocal: "Hell, NO! They can learn on their own time." (As it turned out, these very supervisors were expert masters and mentors; they simply did not think of learning as implicated in the enterprise because it was not their explicit task goal.)

Role of authenticity
Another way of illuminating this difference in orientation is suggested by the following: a key criterion of success in an internship relates to the degree to which the learner sees the task as authentic—that is, one that has consequences in its context. One intern we observed expressed his frustration over being assigned a "make-work project," one that his coworkers did not see as relevant to the operations of the office and whose ultimate audience was as undefined for his supervisor as it was for him. This intern characterized the situation not as a loss in learning opportunities but rather as an obstacle to his ability to function legitimately as a member of that workplace community. In contrast, any task in the university context is seen as authentic insofar as the instructor assigns it. From the perspective of the class-

room, simulations are as authentic as academic essays, or lab reports, or book reviews.

Attenuation

Assigning appropriate attenuated authentic tasks to newcomers requires mentors' skill, subtlety, tact, and imagination, especially given the complex and multifaceted nature of the work environments we observed. Not every mentor met that challenge. Sometimes, newcomers were given routine tasks at the outset, much to their frustration. At other times, however, tasks considerably below the ability and professional orientation of novices were assigned as a way of allowing them enough time to observe the complex operations. More imaginative mentors provided interns with authentic and more challenging tasks from the start, tasks that were both within the competence of very green newcomers and that engaged them in processes that ultimately enabled fuller participation. For example, one intern was asked to take minutes at a round of negotiations; the task was authentic and necessary, was within her ken, and allowed her to observe the complex dynamics of the negotiating process as well as gave her an overview of the whole activity in which her work was to play a part. Observing the negotiations helped her understand how the different parts of the task she would be involved in related to the whole. It also opened her eyes to the dynamics of negotiating as well as to the competing value systems at play. (See Paré, this volume, for examples of this process in social work contexts.)

Reflecting on this initial task in her placement, the intern emphasized the value of the experience in that it was relatively easy, familiarized her with a "government format" (for example, "notes to file"), emphasized the importance of accuracy, "showed them . . . you know when to ask for help," and provided an opportunity to find out about the context of the meetings. A second intern was asked to compare in detail different sets of land claim agreements. The point-for-point, careful (and later collaboratively performed) comparisons introduced the newcomer to the whole activity, and engaged him in thinking through and reorganizing the relevant issues by operating on the discourse that was one material outcome of the activity.

The necessity to involve newcomers in attenuated authentic tasks, however, has certain consequences for the nature of the involvement, consequences that sharply distinguished such learning from school learning. These include (1) the improvisatory quality of the learning opportunities in the workplace in contrast to the carefully sequenced curriculum possible in the classroom, and (2) the relative messiness of the workplace context in comparison to the simplified and facilitated context of the classroom.

Improvisatory Quality of Learning Opportunities. One consequence of the necessity for authentic participation that Lave and Wenger have noted and that we observed frequently in our work is the highly improvisatory character of the interns' tasks (as opposed to those in the classroom, where a curriculum can be more or less planned in advance, allowing for some degree of improvisation and responsiveness to learners). For example, we saw the intern from the scene we described earlier being pulled away from one task in order to prepare a briefing note for a newly elected minister.

A negative consequence of the opportunistic quality of learning in the workplace is that, because the tasks are authentic and respond to external demands unrelated to a learner's needs, the delicate apportioning of parts of the task at times must be truncated, and—even in the best internships—the master must take over. Sometimes, deadlines need to be met; at other times, the supervisor suddenly finds herself short-staffed. And often, the supervisor cannot be certain that the intern can operate under the added pressure. As one intern reflected, "He [the supervisor] would always think about it first before he would ask for my involvement—to see if he thought that I could function under that pressure. And if he thought I couldn't, he would do it himself alone." And even the best workplace guides find themselves having to fulfill responsibilities other than the apportioning of newcomers' tasks. One of the interns we observed described how his otherwise very successful internship had a rough start in that, for the first week after he arrived at the workplace, his supervisor was out of town. No one knew what work to give him, and so he was given "joe-jobs" (photocopying and filing) until his supervisor returned.

To put it another way, unlike the course curriculum, workplace tasks cannot possibly be carefully sequenced and designed. The institution of schooling gives instructors a degree of control, allowing them to sequence activities and to simplify tasks. (For example, in an undergraduate law course, we were struck by the sophisticated sequencing of the tasks, such that—among other things—the textual analyses showed increasing degrees of syntactic complexity and genre realization over the course of the year [see Freedman, 1987, 1996]).

Messiness of Workplace Context. As suggested in other studies (Dias, Freedman, Medway, & Paré, 1999; Freedman, Adam, & Smart, 1994), the workplace context simulated in a university course, even when case studies are used and even when the case studies are not invented but based on actual histories, is enormously simplified and abstracted from the untidy realities experienced in the everyday work world. No matter how much irrelevance and ambiguity these case histories include, they are still abstractions from the experience of the workplace—abstracted in order to facilitate learning. In other words, the noise is removed and the task is simplified; something like Bereiter and Scardamalia's (1987) procedural facilitation is taking place.

The tasks cannot be so simplified in the workplace. It is true that mentors will often model their thinking about issues in such a way as to reveal to the apprentices how to limit and define the problems, and newcomers may be assigned only a part of the task. The task itself, however, cannot be simplified.

For example, social and political relations in the workplace context are considerably more complex. Tensions among employees must be discerned and then navigated. Some of the complexities of relations are evident in the following extract where a supervisor explains to an intern why they have been having such a difficult time obtaining feedback on a document from a superior: "She was not too concerned, because she was ticked off that she wasn't invited to the meeting. That's why she wasn't consistent. . . . So that was an obstacle to my getting out of [her] what I was looking for." In fact, novices not only have to determine whom to trust as a guide (as we will see), but they also must learn to make that choice without alienating other would-be guides.

Guide-learner roles
A further difference between the two kinds of learning derives from the differences in the roles of, and interactions between, guides and learners in the two settings. The roles are more clearly defined in the university setting. The instructor is designated as the authority for the duration of the interaction (which is recognized to be relatively short). In apprenticeship situations, roles are more fluid and indeterminate: there are new oldtimers and old oldtimers; fresh newcomers and more seasoned newcomers. Furthermore, newcomers are often expected to become oldtimers.

In the workplace, novices must learn to discern (a) what their role is to be and (b) from whom they can learn. We observed in a number of settings that novices or interns resisted their would-be or could-be guides. Because no clearly sanctioned institutional teaching authority was vested in their superiors and because their supervisors were often less than seasoned oldtimers, interns often resisted and consequently missed opportunities for learning. One intern, for example, refused to acknowledge the opportunities for learning offered by his supervisor because of her relative "greenness." That is, he incorporated her revisions to his draft of a document because he had to, but he refused to acknowledge the appropriateness of, and hence learn from, such editing changes as "land claims" to "land claim agreements"—which to us he insisted were really synonymous and merely a matter of idiosyncratic personal style.

Furthermore, as the different terms connote, the relations between oldtimers and newcomers are far more complex, subtle, shifting, and nuanced than the relatively stable and straightforward relations between instructors and students. To quote William Hanks (1991):

> Legitimate peripheral participation is not a simple participation structure in which an apprentice occupies a particular role at the edge of a larger process. It is rather an interactive process in which the apprentice engages by simultaneously performing in *several roles*—status subordinate, learning practitioner, sole responsible agent in minor parts of the performance, aspiring expert, and so forth—each implying a different sort of responsibility, a different set of role relations, and a different interactive involvement. (p. 23)

We observed one intern taking on a range of these roles, all within one morning: with respect to the use of technology, he was the expert; however, when time constraints forced his supervisor to take control of the whole task, the intern's status as a subordinate was clear. For most of the morning, he operated as a learning practitioner, working collaboratively, but in an attenuated role, with his supervisor; at other points, he was named sole responsible agent for specific tasks (e.g., finding and contracting work out to a map maker). Later, in an interview with us, his supervisor kept stressing the degree to which he, as mentor, learns from newcomers—not only the most current academic theory but also different approaches to complex internal social and political relations.

Evaluation
Earlier we emphasized the fact that university writing is learning- and learner-oriented. To be fair, one must acknowledge the equally pressing institutional reality: university writing is also oriented toward evaluating and hence ranking students. Although the instructor's basic goal is that her students learn, that goal is limited by the equally pressing need to grade and rank. Thus, in the end, the university instructor has a vested interest in a quality spread, which necessarily qualifies and limits the degree and the nature of the mentoring and collaborative performance. The guide-learner roles in the university are affected by the fact that, in the end and at every point, the guide evaluates the learner.

In the workplace, both newcomer and oldtimer share the goal of producing the best work possible. There is some evaluation in the workplace, of course, but it is far less frequent and pervasive; more significantly, for specific tasks, newcomer and oldtimer are often on the same side: they are working together on a task that will be evaluated by some outsider, usually in terms of its rhetorical or material success—in persuading others, in effecting action.

Consequently, there is no use of tests and grades in the workplace, and sparse use of praise and blame. Performance is evaluated by the overall success of the endeavor—the success of the writing, for example, as a rhetorical or social action. One of the interns recognized that his success in producing an initial document earned him his supervisor's trust and resulted in more significant tasks. "So," the intern claimed, "it was a big test." The reward for success was that the novices were entrusted with more responsibility and riskier tasks.

Learning Sites
Perhaps the most striking difference, however, is that the learning sites in the two settings are distinct. Consequently, when students move from university to workplace (or, in some cases, those experienced in the workplace move to the university), they do not necessarily recognize the opportunities for learning in the new setting because they are used to the way they learned in the old setting.

In the classrooms we observed, the performance was always guided by a great deal of careful stage managing of the prompt, task, and discursive context. The writing itself took place either alone or sometimes in collaboration with peers, with an occasional visit to the instructor or teaching assistant for advice. The students' final submission of their papers almost always meant the end of their involvement with the task.

In the workplace, the initial task itself was less controlled and shaped by the guide; typically it was initiated and constrained by external sources. There was some collaborative interpretation of the task and often collaborative performance of the task at some stages of the writing. But the most significant difference was that completion of the draft began a long process of iteration. The most important learning site in the workplace, as a result, comes during the kind of extensive feedback Paradis, Dobrin, and Miller (1985) described as "document cycling": "the editorial process by which [supervisors] helped staff members restructure, focus, and clarify their written work" (p. 285). Graham Smart (1993) describes the typical process in a government agency that we observed:

> In all genres, composing processes are structured by a similar cycle of writer/reviewer collaboration. Typically [after composing

a draft for review], the writer incorporates rounds of spoken and written feedback from the supervisor into successive revisions until the latter is satisfied. At this point, another round of collaboration usually occurs, involving the writer, the supervisor, and a more senior reviewer. As the collaborative cycle continues, unnecessary technical detail is filtered out, key concepts are defined, and the argument becomes increasingly issue-centered, coherent, and succinct. When the chief of the department decides the text has been refined sufficiently, it is sent to its executive readership. (p. 131)

The intensive and extensive nature of the feedback offered at each writing stage is described by a senior executive at a government financial institution we observed:

When you do things at [this agency], it's a process that someone writes a paper (and it's an important paper—other than a one-pager or two-pager). When they write you a paper, you read it first from a high level—find out if the ideas are there, are the arguments consistent. So, when someone does something for me, I say, "Well, yeah, you're kinda on the right track." And I say, "Go back and try this, try that." So, it doesn't get down to the nitty-gritty of the writing at this point. You're still at the, almost the methodological stage, trying to deal with the question that's being posed. And so you go through a *number of iterations*. The person will come back with the paper answering a different question or adding another question to the analysis, and it's not until the very end that we'll say, "Now I know all the ideas are there. Now I'm going to read it from the perspective of how it's written. Are the ideas now expressed clearly?"

Another way of looking at the differences between the two settings is this: in the university context, most of the contextual shaping and coparticipation takes place *before* the preparation of the first draft. In the workplaces we observed, although some collaboration took place during the generating and planning, a long and intense process of responding and revising—a process during which attuned learners could intuit the expectations of the genre within that context and institution—began *after* the draft was handed in to the supervisor. The important point is that all the comments provided on drafts are collaborative, not evaluative. The revising itself is an intense period of participation where learning can and should take place. But newcomers often do not recognize this as a potential occasion for learning.

Complicating the fact that the learning site is different, especially at the revision stage, is the interference from their previous learning patterns that suggests that anything written in response to a text by a grader is evaluative and final. Because novices in the workplace are typically not accustomed to *using* these comments for further revision, they hit a roadblock when a supervisor returns a draft to them with comments that the supervisor expects to be incorporated into a revised draft. For these novices, then, the comments written on their drafts mean negative evaluation and thus evoke resistance rather than recognition of opportunities for learning (and further collaborative performance).

Learning to Learn Again

We found considerable evidence in our research (Freedman, 1987, 1990; Freedman, Adam, & Smart, 1994) and that of others (Herrington, 1985; McCarthy, 1987; Walvoord & McCarthy, 1993) that university students are expected to learn new genres as they move from class to class. Such learning is both so inevitable and so naturalized that students hardly commented on it (Freedman, 1987). Consequently, as students move to the workplace, they seem to hold the same expectation: they need to learn new genres, but the modes of learning will be the same (see initial assurance expressed in Anson & Forsberg, 1990). However, after some time on the job, the novices commonly reported feelings of disjuncture and anxiety not experienced in their schooling (Anson & Forsberg, 1990; Freedman & Adam, 1995; MacKinnon, 1993). We claim that these feelings are not so much due to the need to learn new genres (such as memos, briefing notes, reports), something they have been doing regularly throughout their schooling, but rather to the need to learn new ways to learn such genres.

Ronald Popken (1992) writes about the particular problems associated with learning new written genres, or "discourse transfer." We observed a related problem: inappropriate transfer of learning patterns. Many novices did not think that they would have to learn at all, and certainly not in new ways.

For example, one intern, Julie, viewed each task as though it was set in a university context, with its clearly defined beginning and end and its clearly demarcated occasions for learning (in class and through assignments). Consequently, she consistently insisted on "getting on with her work" rather than availing herself of the learning opportunity offered her twice each day by the supervisor who invited her to take a short walk with him and another intern. Every day she refused the opportunity for shared reflection on and learning about what had been happening in the complex political and social rhetorical context of their workplace. During these walks the other intern learned how to read and interpret meetings and other interactions as an insider.

Julie consistently missed opportunities for learning, misconstruing them as new assignments, rather than as occasions for learning. "I didn't know I was expected to go to that meeting," she said resentfully, when she was called into a meeting that, though one she was not required to attend, would have given her a broader picture of the activity as a whole and thus clarified her specific task. "Was I *supposed* to come?" she asked under her breath in annoyance. In other words, Julie was still mentally situated within the school context, where specific tasks are set out in clearly defined ways, within the context of clearly defined discursive environments (i.e., the assigned readings and the three or four hours a week of lecture and/or seminar).

Other interns failed to learn from their supervisors' comments for revising drafts of their work, dismissing these comments as simply matters of personal stylistic preference. Rather than learning from these suggested revisions—changed wordings that often signified a great deal about how that particular culture viewed the world and the distinctions that were important there—the interns chose to see these changes as idiosyncratic personal preferences that they were being forced to accept but that they could resist learning from. When asked about what she had learned from her supervisor's comments, one intern reflected: "I don't feel so much that it's the government way versus my way. It's just my way and Gill's way and Sandra's way. And my way isn't wrong, and when I'm the Director, I'm gonna write the memo however I want to."

One fundamental difference in the two contexts studied is the value placed on individualism in the university culture as opposed to the more collaborative ethos of the government agencies. (A negative view substitutes the words anonymous or leveling for collaborative.) In the end, all university students are graded individually, even when they collaborate on specific assignments. Novices' transfer of this individualist ethos sometimes interferes with their ability to do the kind of collaboration necessary for performing and learning in the workplace. In our early interviews, interns displayed a kind of egotism: "It's my style. Why should I have to change it?" This egotism is exacerbated by the fact that students rarely revise their drafts in response to their instructor's written comments accompanying the grade. The comments serve to justify the grade, and although the instructor has the right to give a "B," the students have the right to maintain their ideas and language.

Furthermore, the nature of the ownership is different. At least in theory, students' ideas belong to them, and instructors are berated for plagiarizing from students in a way not conceivable within a workplace. As suggested in Freedman, Adam, and Smart (1994), employees in the government workplaces we have been observing rely heavily on intertextual references to each other's work (sometimes cited, sometimes not). Employee writing is kept on file, often for frequent consultation; student writing is filed, if at all, at home, and rarely consulted thereafter.

SUMMARY

To sum up, in both contexts the learners learn new genres. The two processes of learning are similar in very important respects: both are based on the notion of learning through performance or engagement, "learning through doing" (as one of the instructors kept repeating) as opposed to earlier cognitive notions of learning through receiving bodies of knowledge. What is entailed for the "teacher" in each setting is, in Hanks' (1991) words, "not giving a discrete body of abstract knowledge . . . [but] instead . . . the skill to perform by actually engaging in the process" (p. 14).

That is, students learn through activity and through social engagement: instructors and learners collaborate, in a broad sense, and as a result learners are able to do something at the end that they have not done or been able to do before. In addition, learning is also achieved through sociocultural mediation of tools, especially linguistic and other semiotic signs.

Common to both processes as well is the notion of less than full participation by the learners. In each case, the conditions for performing are attenuated: in the university the curriculum is sequenced in terms of order of difficulty; in the workplace only some of the task is given over to the learner, and it is this attenuation that allows for the learning or fuller participation.

On the other hand, the two processes do differ radically. In the university, through processes of facilitated performance, the goal of the activity itself is learning; in the workplace, through processes of attenuated authentic participation, the learning is incidental and occurs as an integral but tacit part of participation in communities of practice, whose activities are oriented toward practical or material outcomes.

As a result, the guide-learner relations are different. In the workplace, the terms used are oldtimers and newcomers (or masters and apprentices), and different people represent varying degrees of each (relative oldtimers and relative newcomers); there is the further expectation that the newcomers will become oldtimers. In the classroom, the instructor remains the instructor throughout, and the learner remains the learner. The roles are more static and fixed, and power is more clearly distributed, which is augmented by the fact that the instructor is also the evaluator and consequently has extra dimensions of authority and power, and hence alienation from the learner.

In the workplace, newcomers and oldtimers typically work together on the same side for specific tasks (although not always, and tensions of a different kind are possible there). Whereas in the classroom, the instructor has a vested interest in a quality spread of performance among students, causing a different kind of built-in tension between instructors and students, and among students.

In the classroom, the instructor has enormous latitude and authority in setting up the learning environment. Consequently, the curriculum is often sequenced and tasks are simplified, and most of the classroom activities are explicitly designed to enable learning. This sequencing and simplification is largely replicable from one course offering to the next. In the workplace, however, although a number of regular activities are built around institutional schedules, unforeseen events offer spontaneous opportunities for learning and are typically exploited as such.

Finally, the learning sites are different in the two environments. In the university context, most of the contextual shaping and participation takes place before the preparation of the first draft; in the workplace, learning takes place primarily through collaborative composing and revising, especially after a first draft is produced.

The upshot is that, on the whole, when students leave the university to enter the workplace, they not only need to learn new genres of discourse, they need to learn new ways to learn such genres. The two kinds of processes, although sharing certain fundamental features, are different enough that the transition from one setting to the other poses particular problems for students, eliciting feelings of disjuncture, anxiety, or displacement. These feelings, so commonly cited in the research literature and in anecdotal evidence, are inevitable, given the differing nature of the institutions, and not signs of student or school failure.

DISCUSSION

The distinction we have been making between facilitated performance and attenuated authentic participation can begin to blur. Thus, if we focus only on the relationship between, and the activities of, newcomers and oldtimers in the work setting, we may very well find a kind of collaborative guidance through performance that is at least broadly similar to that in the university setting. Alternatively, one can find examples of university interactions that attempt to approximate more closely those of related communities of practice, where the learning is intended to be like that found in instances of legitimate peripheral participation or attenuated authentic participation (see Gutierrez, 1994; Rogoff, 1994). These are classes in which tasks with real-world consequences are selected and where students work in collaborative groups of peers. Without denying the value of such experiments nor the possibility of seeing interactions that resemble facilitated performance in some mentor-novice relations in the workplace, our claim is that it is very useful to continue considering facilitated performance and attenuated authentic participation as distinct in important ways, in ways that privilege neither one nor the other but rather reflect the institutional constraints and societal needs expressed in each.

For example, we must acknowledge that the institutional realities of schooling militate against a total appropriation of the apprenticeship model. A pervasive goal of schooling (not the only goal, but an inevitable one) is to rank or slot students. Hubboch (1989) and Petraglia (1995) have each commented on our discipline's deep discomfort with that reality, but denial is a poor refuge. This requirement to grade and evaluate contaminates the relationship between students and instructors, at least to some degree. We may be locked in Peter Elbow's (1986) "embrace of contraries" but at least one pole of the contraries pushes against the kind of collaboration and shared intention possible in the workplace.

On the other hand, although we may chafe at these constraints and seek different kinds of interactions, we should acknowledge as well the advantages of schooling, which also have become normalized through their tacitness. Schools do offer the opportunity for an exclusive focus on learning and the learner, uncontaminated by concerns for results or material outcomes. This allows for a kind of teaching—involving sequencing of curriculum and close attunement to the learner's pace—perhaps not possible in the workplace.

In contrast, the workplace privileges a kind of coparticipation: collaborative engagement in tasks whose outcomes take center stage and where the learning is often tacit and implicit. A subtly different alignment and attunement is at play. Guides and learners play different roles, with differently nuanced strategies for the necessary attenuation of tasks.

Our task, as a profession and discipline, is not to jettison one in favor of the other by aiming to replicate the processes of attenuated authentic participation in the classroom—a tendency that has been heightened by the identification of the modes of language use and learning in schooling with those of the middle class (Heath, 1983; Rogoff, 1993). This is neither possible nor necessarily beneficial. Our task, as a discipline, is to consider and weigh carefully (after considerably more research has been amassed) the advantages and implications of each kind of learning and its match with each kind of setting.

Our first step must be a sensitive anthropological analysis—perhaps even archaeological excavation—of each learning site as it now stands, assuming a certain ecological wholeness. But ecology can be a limiting metaphor too in that it implies conservation, and hence conservatism (see Freedman & Medway, 1994). After the first stage of archaeological unearthing, critical analysis must be brought to bear and, with it, consideration of the alternatives.

REFERENCES

Anson, C. M., & Forsberg, L. L. (1990). Moving beyond the academic community: Transitional stages in professional writing. *Written Communication, 7*, 200-231.

Bakhtin, M. M. (1981). *The dialogic imagination.* (M. Holquist, Ed.; C. Emerson & M. Holquist, Trans.). Austin: University of Texas Press.

Bakhtin, M. M. (1986). The problem of speech genres. In C. Emerson & M. Holquist, Eds.; V.W. McGee, Trans.), *Speech genres and other late essays* (pp. 60-102). Austin: University of Texas Press.

Bereiter, C., & Scardamalia, M. (1987). *The psychology of writing.* Mahwah, NJ: Erlbaum.

Dias, P., Freedman, A., Medway, P., & Paré, A. (1999). *Worlds apart: Acting and writing in academic and workplace contexts.* Mahwah, NJ: Erlbaum.

Elbow, P. (1986). *Embracing contraries: Explorations in learning and teaching.* New York: Oxford University Press.

Freedman, A. (1987). Learning to write again. *Carleton Papers in Applied Language Studies, 4*, 95-116.

Freedman, A. (1990). Reconceiving genre. *Texte, 8/9*, 279-292.

Freedman, A. (1993). Show and tell? The role of explicit teaching in learning new genres. *Research in the Teaching of English, 27*, 222-251.

Freedman, A. (1996). Argument as genre and genres of argument. In D. Berrill (Ed.), *Perspectives on written argument* (pp. 91-120). Cresskill, NJ: Hampton Press.

Freedman, A., & Adam, C. (1995, March). *Learning and teaching new genres: New literacies, new responsibilities.* Paper delivered at

Conference of College Composition and Communication, Washington, DC.

Freedman, A., & Medway, P. (1994). New views of genre and their implications for education. In A. Freedman & P. Medway (Eds.), *Learning and teaching genre* (pp. 1-22). Portsmouth, NH: Boynton/Cook Heinnemann.

Freedman, A., Adam, C., & Smart, G. (1994). Wearing suits to class: Simulating genres and simulations as genre. *Written Communication, 11*, 193-226.

Goetz, J., & LeCompte, M. (1984). *Ethnography and qualitative design in educational research.* New York: Academic Press.

Gutierrez, K. (1994, April). *Laws of possibility: Reconstituting classroom activity for Latino children.* Paper presented at American Educational Research Association, New Orleans, LA.

Hanks, W. F. (1991). Foreword. In J. Lave & E. Wenger (Eds.), *Situated learning: Legitimate peripheral participation* (pp. 11-21). Cambridge: Cambridge University Press.

Heath, S. B. (1983). *Ways with words: Language, life, and work in communities and classrooms.* New York: Cambridge University Press.

Herrington, A. (1985). Writing in academic settings: A study of the contexts for writing in two college chemical engineering courses. *Research in the Teaching of English, 19*, 331-361.

Hubboch, S. (1989). Confronting the power in empowering students. *The Writing Instructor, Fall/Winter,* 35-44.

Lave, J. (1988). *Cognition in practice: Mind, mathematics and culture in everyday life.* Cambridge: Cambridge University Press.

Lave, J. (1991). Situating learning in communities of practice. In L. Resnick, J. Levine, & S. Teasley (Eds.), *Perspectives on socially shared cognition* (pp. 63-83). Washington, DC: American Psychological Association.

Lave, J., & Wenger, E. (1991). *Situated learning: Legitimate peripheral participation.* Cambridge: Cambridge University Press.

MacKinnon, J. (1993). Becoming a rhetor: The development of on-the-job writing ability. In R. Spilka (Ed.), *Writing in the workplace: New research perspectives* (pp. 41-55). Carbondale: Southern Illinois University Press.

McCarthy, L. P. (1987). A stranger in strange lands: A college student writing across the curriculum. *Research in the Teaching of English, 21*, 233-265.

Paradis, J., Dobrin, D., & Miller, R. (1985). Writing at Exxon: Notes on the writing environment of an R and D organization. In L. Odell & D. Goswami (Eds.), *Writing in nonacademic settings* (pp. 281-308). New York: Guilford.

Petraglia, J. (1995). Spinning like a kite: A closer look at the pseudo-transactional function of writing. *Journal of Advanced Composition, 15*(1), 19-33.

Popken, R. (1992). Genre transfer in developing adult writers. *Focuses, 5,* 3-17.

Rogoff, B. (1990). *Apprenticeship in thinking.* New York: Oxford University Press.

Rogoff, B. (1991). Social interaction as apprenticeship in thinking: Guided participation in spatial planning. In L. Resnick, J. Levine, & S. Teasley (Eds.), *Perspectives on socially shared cognition* (pp. 349-364). Washington, DC: American Psychological Association.

Rogoff, B. (1993, April). *Guided participation of children and their families.* Paper delivered at the American Educational Research Association Conference, Atlanta, GA.

Rogoff, B. (1994, April). *Models of teaching and learning: Development through participation.* Paper presented at American Educational Research Association, New Orleans.

Smart, G. (1993). Genre as community invention: A central bank's response to its executives' expectations as readers. In R. Spilka (Ed.), *Writing in the workplace: New research perspectives* (pp. 124-140). Carbondale: Southern Illinois University Press.

Vygotsky, L. (1996). *Thought and language* (E. Hanfmann & G. Vakar, Trans.). Cambridge, MA: MIT Press.

Vygotsky, L. (1978). *Mind in society.* Cambridge, MA: Harvard University Press.

Walvoord, B., & McCarthy, L. (1993). *Thinking and writing in college: A naturalistic study of students in four disciplines.* Urbana, IL: National Council of Teachers of English.

Wertsch, J. (1991a). A sociocultural approach to socially shared cognition. In L. Resnick, J. Levine, & S. Teasley (Eds.), *Perspectives on socially shared cognition.* Washington, DC: American Psychological Association.

Wertsch, J. (1991b). *Voices of the mind: A sociocultural approach to mediated action.* Cambridge, MA: Harvard University Press.

Wood, D., Bruner, J. S., & Ross, S. G. (1976). The role of tutoring in problem-solving. *Journal of Child Psychology and Psychiatry, 17,* 89-100.

CHAPTER 3

Diplomats in the Basement: Graduate Engineering Students and Intercultural Communication

Ann Beer
McGill University

Setting 1: Basement labs of engineering building. Old, cluttered, noisy—but working surfaces neat. The research "home" of graduate students in mining and metallurgical engineering in a large faculty of engineering. Many of these students come from continents other than North America, and speak languages other than English. They go about their regular research tasks: designing and building test equipment, creating and manipulating the computer software necessary for their projects, gathering data, analyzing results, drawing conclusions, discussing ideas, and reporting to their professor. They must work on seminars that they are required to present in their department, drafts of their academic text (master's or doctoral work), and progress reports for sponsors, many of whom are private sector companies.

Sawing, drills, bell each hour, big trolleys trundling by. Red hard hats on shelf, computers, white boards covered with equations and notes, drawings of columns, old metal pipes across ceiling, heating panel in floor. Some technical manuals—in a tiny office beside one lab. A few little personal touches at one desk (photographs), none at others. Metals, liquids, camcorder strapped sideways to a bar along-

side a column filled with clear liquid. Basement smell: dust, chalk, age. Hard surfaces, hard place, metals everywhere. Coffee going all the time. Mugs beside computer terminals.

 The students are under great pressure, work long hours every day, and see almost no one except their peers and their research professor or post-doctoral supervisor, who come down from time to time to check on progress. It is grueling work, and professors expect good results. The departmental seminars, in particular, are tough: the audience is highly critical, competitive, and apt to pounce aggressively on a moment of weakness. (Notes reconstructed from Log and interview material.)

Setting 2: A communications class for the same graduates (those who are international students), who have walked over from their own building. The course takes place in a typical arts/education-style classroom, peaceful, large, with bright windows and chalk boards, where papers, folders and pens are spread across large tables. The room is quiet, the view from the windows one of trees, sky, and other buildings. The students, who may or may not know each other, work with their writing instructor individually some of the time. She also walks around the room, encouraging their collaborative writing activities, responding to their drafts and edited texts, and helping them with strategies and rules for English communication. She is respectful, good humored, and supportive. She lectures briefly but with enthusiasm, discussing technical communication and stylistic features of English. She uses an overhead sheet and pen, writing sentences on the overhead transparency. Her skills as an editor are obvious; in fact, her background includes many years as a writing teacher in a large university. She has also done a lot of professional work outside the academic setting (human resources workshops on communications, writing workshops in private sector companies, tutoring, and professional editing). She has researched the background to this particular course well, having read many publications on the teaching and practice of technical writing, and investigating the written documentation and the views of professors in the students' field of study. However, she is not an engineer and her focus is the writing itself, not the engineering research for which that writing is a tool. (Notes reconstructed from Log and interview material.)[1]

---

[1]The context of the study: the graduate students work in mining and metallurgical processing in a large, research-oriented university in Canada. Although some are Canadian by birth, many are from elsewhere, and are funded by governments, employers, or other agencies in their country of origin. These international students—the focus of this study— need to gain new research expertise, build professional networks, and complete a master's or doctoral degree,

These contrasting settings situate the discussion that follows. My aim in this chapter is to use the framework of intercultural communication to explore the complexity and the challenge of the tasks the students face, as they negotiate different genres. Those who kindly volunteered their time for this project provide an insight into the intensely contextual and collaborative nature of genres (using as foundational Carolyn Miller's [1984] definition, in which genres are seen as social action). Their responses and observations show the difficulty of negotiating different discourse practices when the context is one of internationalism and varying levels of language use, contrasts between academic and workplace perspectives, and contrasts between their different courses in the university itself. As Freadman says (using the metaphor of tennis), genre-users must be "positioned in the right game"—they must be "readers" of the genre, and of the culture in which that genre works, in the "very strongest sense," in order to become successful writers—to return the ball appropriately (1994, p. 63).

For these particular engineering students, the time in a Canadian academic context has tight limits and is closely linked to the pressures of competition and finance. Coming from developing countries, required to finish their degrees rapidly, under great pressure financially and intellectually, and being asked to function in a second (or third, or fourth) language, they face enormous challenges as genre learners. Yet all recognize the value of "immersion" in an English-speaking culture for their future careers, whether they remain in North America or not. As John Swales (1990) has shown, the global dominance of English in scientific communication is clear, even if different researchers argue about its extent (pp. 96-109).

The students' experience raises questions about transitions into new levels of learning in settings where different cultures and/or

---

under considerable constraints of time. All have enough ability in English to function, at least technically, in the new environment and some have experience of international business in their own country. Their studies lie on the borderline between academia and the workplace, as their engineering research work, though carried out mainly in the university laboratories, is sponsored by and has direct usefulness for private sector companies. Some of the students regularly travel with their supervisors to plants, mines, and to other research sites, university or government-run, to advance the collaborative research in which they are engaged. Each has an individual project (the subject, usually, of the master's or doctoral work, once courses have been completed) but works as part of a larger group, collaborating with other students. Students who excel may be asked to present at conferences with or for professors, and all are required to give at least two formal seminars that may be attended by the rest of their department and other interested professionals.

languages meet. Much North American discussion of genre and activity theory (except, of course, work such as Swales' that comes out of the discipline of English Second Language) assumes, reasonably, a common basis in English and a shared familiarity with North American cultural norms. What happens when different linguistic and cultural backgrounds come into play? What is the relationship and the balance between the student's home cultures in another country and the learning and working cultures of the new country? The pages that follow will explore these questions in the context of intercultural communication theory, drawing on the concepts of "involvement" and "independence" (Scollon & Scollon, 1995) which I will discuss below.

My claim is that these students' path to acquiring the new genres they must learn depends fundamentally on positioning or stance—their own decisions about what, and whom, they will be involved with or remain independent from. I use the word "decisions" with some caution, as it is, of course, impossible to tell to what extent their positioning depends on conscious or unconscious levels of thought and feeling, and it would be inappropriate here to probe such questions. I will show at least how their own words suggest that this positioning (level of involvement and independence) works on at least three levels. These levels only begin to sketch the real complexity of such communicative demands:

1. Involvement with the new country and/or the former country;
2. Involvement with the academy and/or the workplace;
3. Involvement with the engineering ("hard skills") and/or the communications ("soft skills") part of their program.

I will revisit the two settings described above, but will do so in a larger context, looking at the "macro" levels of involvement and independence in relation to certain genres in the students' situation, as well as the "micro" levels in which their decisions about material, words, and documents can be seen in detail.[2]

It would be more usual in a single article to focus on only one of the three levels of involvement and independence mentioned above.

[2]This qualitative study involved the gathering and analysis of documents, observations, interviews, and discussions with the students themselves, professors, workplace engineers and managers, and liaison personnel. In this chapter, I draw mostly on interviews, those with students spanning a period of almost a year, and written documents, as well as my own logs and reflections, written over the same period. My own positioning was that of a Writing Center Director involved in WID (Writing in the Disciplines) initiatives across my own university campus and participating in a team research project.

However, as we learn more about genres and activity theory (see Chapter 1), we come to see that such focusing and limiting almost inevitably oversimplify the contextual influences and forms with which a student must work as a professional communicator in training. By looking at these three levels together, I hope to provide a basis for further study, including that of the students' genre acquisition itself, that will be less inclined to oversimplify and partition what in reality happens simultaneously and in constant interaction.

INVOLVEMENT AND INDEPENDENCE

> Language, like consciousness, is a product of men's activity, a product of the group; only therefore does it also exist for the individual person. . . . The origin of language can be understood only in relation to the need developing for people in the process of labor to say something to one another. (A.N. Leont'ev, 1981, pp. 218-219)

In this statement, Leont'ev assumes that the group shares a common history or at least some sense of temporary community, established long enough for "the group" to develop a "language" equal to its working goals. Implicit in the statement, also, is the idea of cultural or national linguistic commonality. People in the process of labor need to speak and be heard in order to get the job done; they presumably have a sufficient level of common understanding to make that possible.

In the modern world and the global economy, however, many working groups, among them the group of engineering students described above, do not share that commonality. In science and engineering, especially, there may be many different levels of natural and national language competence at work within the group. Intercultural communication theory recognizes this problem:

> Interactive intelligence is an essential aspect of human intelligence. As such it is brought to bear upon any communicative interpretation. This process seems to work very successfully . . . when conversationalists share common histories, cultures, and life experiences. The inferences they draw by assuming others think just as they do are generally safe. Problems are encountered, however, especially in the complex environment of international communication in English, when participants in a conversation hold different assumptions because of membership in different groups. (Scollon & Scollon, 1995, p. 73)

Problems arise, in other words, through the tendency of people in conversation to assume common ground where little or none may exist. Participants may have different loyalties, ideologies, or worldviews that they are unwilling or unable to give up, even if they consciously recognize their existence. (Often they do not, which is when many of the problems occur.) The participants' lack of knowledge of the way of thinking of the person opposite to them can lead to miscommunication in international business and professional activities. This is especially acute in English, which is now a world language for international exchange, though a second language for many of those who use it within and beyond their own cultural boundaries. As one engineering professor in this study said: "Something we have to remember is that English is probably the most versatile, most rapidly changing language on the face of the Earth simply because so many people use it as a working language rather than as a cultural language."

"Independence" and "involvement" are useful heuristic tools for the analysis of discourse at either the micro or the macro level. They represent the two poles between which the spectrum of interpersonal, or intercultural, communication can occur:

> On the one hand, in human interactions, we have a need to be involved with other participants and to show them our involvement. On the other hand, we need to maintain some degree of independence from other participants and to show them that we respect their independence. . . . One shows involvement by taking the point of view of other participants, by supporting them in the views they take, and by any other means that demonstrates that the speaker wishes to uphold a commonly created view of the world. . . . The independence aspect on the other hand, emphasizes the individuality of participants. It emphasizes their right not to be completely dominated by group or social values, and to be free from the impositions of others. . . . [It] is shown by such discourse strategies as making minimal assumptions about the needs or interests of others, by "not putting words into their mouths," by giving others the widest range of options, or by using more formal names and titles. (Scollon & Scollon, 1995, pp. 36-37)

The concepts of involvement and independence make it possible to "read" the graduate students' learning experience in the three areas of tension described above. How do these students (established adults with extensive academic and work experience, families, and responsibilities) cope with the challenge of moving countries and languages, of becoming students again—in many cases a sharp downturn in terms of status—and being asked to show communicative flexibility within the new settings (academic-workplace) and courses (engineering-educa-tion)? To what degree do they try to show involvement in each situation, and to what degree do they maintain independence? To what extent do intercultural tensions operate subliminally, blocking even a strong con-scious motivation towards the new setting? Can we see different indi-vidual students taking up different positions between involvement and independence? What do they gain or lose by doing so?

As such questions suggest, the apparent tension between these different self-locations is not necessarily negative; however, it does show that the students' learning is being shaped by complex forces that may be suitably investigated with an "intercultural" approach. In each case, the students face a need to reposition them-selves, and to do so with few elements of explicit support or instruc-tion. I will show how they begin to recognize and come to terms with the challenges they face in communication, drawing not only on their own oral and written material but also on the views of professors and colleagues, and on my own experience of meeting them.

The graduate students' survival in the program depends on not only the success of their academic work, but also on the impres-sion they make on professors and workplace sponsors. Their arrival (in most cases, quite recent) from another country and linguistic group means that confidence and motivation may be especially diffi-cult to maintain. Errors are inevitable, and some allowances may be made, but very rapidly the students will find themselves competing with others whose knowledge of the "grammar of context" (Scollon & Scollon, 1995) in the new country has been acquired over a lifetime. Yet each of them is at the same time negotiating a position in the new culture and defining boundaries. As one of the students says:

> If you are not able to give an impression of intelligence, an impression that you know the topic you are talking about, you lose everything. You cannot work, you can get nothing at all. And it's indeed very important in any language. I remember when I was a student and there was some opportunity to represent the university or the faculty or to get some important position or whatever you want to attain in your life, the way you speak is going to decide if you are going to get something or not. . . . It's very, very important.

For graduate students such as these, working in technical areas, to establish an "impression of intelligence" in a new language and cul-ture, represents a major challenge.

INVOLVEMENT AND INDEPENDENCE BETWEEN THE FORMER COUNTRY AND THE NEW COUNTRY

The students' willingness and ability to learn are inevitably influenced by their degree of involvement in the new culture—how much they can and will change—or their continuing sense of connection to the country from which they come. This can be seen through their level of English, their degree of loyalty to the home or new country, and their knowledge of cultural/national differences in genre, as described in the following pages.

Level of English

A critical issue is the level of English itself. If their English, usually learned in that home country, is still far from fluent, it will be more difficult for them to become fully involved. In response to an interview question about whether there were any formal structures for supporting the newly arrived students in ESL courses, professors had the following responses:

> Professor Graham:[3] As in everything, there's kind of a trade-off. There's a cost associated with that, particularly with respect to time. And there's a motivational thing. And you say, is this person going to be around indefinitely? What are they going to do on graduation? Are they going back to Russia? Are they going back to China?

> Professor Henderson: We require a TOEFL [Test of English as a Foreign Language] score of 550, and now we're much more rigorous about that, so they probably won't get here unless they've got it. But there were times when they were accepted on condition that they have it. They came without it and then we've told them they have to go to [an advanced English second language class], and we'd accept that in place of it. There are still some who have the TOEFL and they still have real problems. We advise them to go and take English courses.

Professor Fenton gave a detailed and illuminating reply, showing that the whole question of ESL and students' communicative competence had been carefully discussed in his department:

---

[3]All names have been changed.

Students, at their own expense, will take a six-months to one-year period to learn English, [during] which they don't do research and I don't pay them. We have a student from Chile on that program right now. We had a student from Mexico who effectively was on that program but we didn't coordinate or organize it that way. . . . And we have another student coming from Chile who will also be on that same program.

These plans [the language-learning preliminary periods] come up from my group, from my colleagues and associates, particularly Marcos who is South American. And he's quite concerned about the TOEFL restrictions. Because, for him, a lot of people that he knows in small communities, and there are a lot of small communities, don't get access to English training, so he feels the universities in Canada are excluding these people and that's not fair. So there ought to be some mechanism by which people who are technically competent can come, and get the training that they desire, and not be at a disadvantage compared to their colleagues that have been in a big city. People from Santiago and Mexico City, it's not a problem. Punta Arenas and Antofagasta, it's a problem. But it's not fair that they should be excluded. They've always been good students. They're keen, they raise the level. They create a motivation amongst the local students that sometimes even demoralizes local students. Generally they've been good. And increasingly, on our part, we like to see the students go back, and Latin American students, in particular, this is what they do. They come on scholarships, many of them. And they have a strong commitment to go back to Chile, Mexico, which I like. I want them to go back and develop what's going on.

As two of these professors say, a critically important issue is whether the students know for sure they are going back to the former country; if so, their desire to learn may be huge, but their desire to maintain independence, culturally and even socially, may also be strong. In other words, their level of involvement with the new culture may remain highly specific and limited. It is also true that they may decide to stay in North America, either initially or after a period of residence. Professor Marchenko points out:

Formerly, foreign students used to go back to their own countries, where their standard of writing in English was more than adequate, indeed often better than those around them. Now, however, more are staying in Canada. And as the economy has shrunk, their positions are more demanding. They have to be both researcher and deliverer of information; it is no longer possible to have the "backroom" types, who are excellent technically but weak in communications and human skills. They have to be able to adapt to companies' preferred reporting formats, use of key words, and so on. Having relied previously on their mathematical/computational skills, they find that they are now asked to perform as communicators. It can be very hard for them.

For those with still-developing skills in English, a vicious circle may develop: a limited, technical vocabulary in English may make them feel most comfortable or only comfortable in the lab, but "hiding" in the lab will limit their opportunities to learn the language more fully. Their writing instructor in Education confirms this: "Many of them, when they are writing their technical papers, the vocabulary is there. They seem quite strong. The minute you ask them to write about something else, immediately their deficiencies in English become apparent." And certainly, students spend long hours working in the laboratory setting. As one told me: "When my family is not here, [i.e., in Montreal] normally I work the whole week, from Monday to Sunday and probably more than sixteen hours daily, because I'm available for my work."

Ironically, in the group that was my particular focus, much of the discussion in the laboratories took place in Spanish or Portuguese as well as in English, as a large number of the students were from Latin American countries, where their engineering specialization is currently in a process of rapid development. The whole question of culturally appropriate communication skills in English takes on a new dimension in a situation where students may use their first language at work, and also at home with their families. Given their long hours in the lab, what opportunities do they have, other than meetings with professors, formal seminars, and brief workplace visits, to experience the new language in the depth needed to master it?

Moreover, the students may not be the only ones with ESL concerns; as one professor admitted, "some of our professors, English is not their mother tongue, so they have their own difficulties in this field." In other words, the command of English needed for full cultural participation, rather than a tightly confined technical role, may be something even some new professors in this field, who come from many countries, are also still developing.

Loyalty to Home Country/Desire to Stay in North America

In interviews, different cultural positions become clear, and show how even among students with similar histories, language competence, and national heritage, degrees of involvement and independence are unpredictable. One student, who grew up in an intellectual household in Mexico, recalled how strongly he wanted to write and publish in his own language:

> I was sort of romantic, because all of my work, I tried to publish it in Spanish and in Mexican magazines. In Mexico I'm a member of a society. . . . They publish a journal. I was submitting all of my work to that journal on different topics. So most of my work was published in Spanish in Mexico. I published also some work in the States in English. I also presented some results from my work in different congresses, mainly in the United States. But most of the work has been published in a Mexican journal. . . . I did that because I think that for a society, it is necessary to create, to become a science society.

Another, however, who was also planning to go back to his own country, described years of familiarity with international business English, which made his adaptation while he was a student in North America far easier:

> I learned a lot about writing in English. I mean . . . because, usually, each country has their own ways to write, you know. Each language has a different way. But I learned a lot from a lot of communication with England.

A third student, strongly impressed with both the demands and the scope of his new setting, criticizes his own language (Spanish) and country (Bolivia) in a way that shows, once again, a strong sense of the linguistic, cultural, and genre-related comparisons these students are constantly making.

> I find that in Spanish, which is my mother tongue, we have been using—at least myself—a lot of terms which are not precisely the appropriate ones for a given expression. I don't know exactly if it is because we have been . . . changing the sense of some words. . . . However, here I found that it means something completely different. I reflected back . . . these words come from the Latin. . . . Analyzing the meaning of the word, I surprisingly found that in English you use the term in a more appropriate way than I was using it in my country. I don't know if the Spanish is the same, but in Bolivia, in all South America, we don't care too much about using a given term. As long as it means more or less the same, we continue using that. . . . When I reflect about this, I say, no, really it's not only all my fault. . . . I have been enjoying reading some books in English here. Technically, books that I have also read

before in Spanish, and I have a lot of trouble sometimes in order
to find the [meaning] of a given paragraph. However, in English,
at least, I think it's the quality of the people who are writing the
books, maybe. They are more, much more accurate.

This student seems keen to move towards greater involvement in
English.

Cultural Genre Differences

As well as the question of loyalties, the students had many reactions
to cultural differences in genre. Here are some brief statements, as
students speak about letters of application or letters requesting information, written in normal North American business style, compared
with what they are used to:

Manuel: The first shock for us is the different personal relationships [in these letters].

Luis: When I was writing this one I was thinking in Spanish,
actually, and the structure there is different.

Bernardo: Here the structure is different. So, after that I just
wrote this one, thinking about (the fact) that I am applying here,
to Canada. So . . . the structure is now different. But now it's
realistic.

Juan: In Mexico . . . we are more polite with the people that we
are sending that [letter] to. . . . [I]f I am applying I need at least
two pages.

Q: One page is not considered polite?

Juan: No, it's not. It's considered that I am not really interested. .

Manuel: When I was writing some reports for some people from
the industry . . . for a manager from . . . not an industry, but a . . .
previous company, Professor Jones asked me to send some sort of
letter. I sent about, I don't know, maybe one page of the letter
and . . . and I showed Professor Jones and he avoided the whole
letter and he just included two lines. (Laughter.) Because I was
also thinking in . . .

Q: In Spanish? So he made it much much shorter?

Manuel: Yes. And also I think that here people are not accustomed to receive something polite, as we are. Here they cut maybe 90% of the "nice" and send just two lines. (Laughter.)

These comments reveal that the students are working with a constant inner model of cultural comparison. As they write for their professors, for workplace readers, or in their communications class, each of them is seeking to establish the ways in which the new country's genres resemble and differ from the old. Moreover, as very often it is the powerful mentors in their lives, their supervisory professors, who respond to their engineering writing, they are absolutely bound to take those supervisors' concepts of genre norms into account. Yet the professors' priorities and views may be different from those of either engineering workplace managers or communications teachers. And when it is a professor who edits the student's letter to a private company, insisting on only two lines, the student may not ask for clarification. The professor will assume the lesson is learned and will be followed; the student, working from the home country's norms of courtesy, will not ask about the difference but may continue to feel and be troubled by it.

Their communications teacher confirms the fact that success for these graduate students depends to a large extent on their language and genre competence in the new culture:

They are an interesting group, because they are technically very sophisticated people, down to the last man, they seem to have excellent word-processing capability, software at their fingertips. They can figure out . . . what the fog index [a technique for assessing the difficulty of reading level in a text] means. They learn English abroad, almost invariably, and they could probably tell me more about the active and the passive than I could tell them, sometimes. They know the rules. What they lack is experience in English. They lack experience listening to someone who speaks English as a native speaker does. . . . What determines the stronger or weaker writers seems to be their exposure to English and . . . how international the company was that they're working for. That seems to have created a great deal more difference in their writing than location or something like that.

INVOLVEMENT AND INDEPENDENCE BETWEEN THE
ACADEMY AND THE WORKPLACE

As well as the largely unspoken tension between the cultural norms of communication, the students are negotiating a constant transition between the academy, where they are registered for their graduate degree, and the workplace, which helps to fund their research through professors' research grants, and where the students' discoveries are often of real significance for improved efficiency and quality. Often the students' awareness of issues in the research is heightened by the interplay between the academic (epistemic) purpose and the hard reality of a company's needs. However, for some of these writers, the genre differences can once again pose problems. The experience of three international students, all from South and Central America, will help to illustrate this.

Carlos the Scholar

Carlos came from an academic family, one in which reading, intellectual debate, and the pursuit of learning were clearly central. He had earlier thought of a career in medicine but had decided against it because "to be a medical doctor I would have to share the pain of people and that's very hard." He had worked in government research units and in universities in his own country. Carlos, a highly verbal person, enjoyed exploring ideas both in casual conversation and in the specialized language required in the scientific work of his chosen field. He was well aware of the double nature of the research he had to do:

> There are two aspects in all of this work. One of them is the academic interest, in that there is a part of the work which is done on the fundamentals . . . to study the basic concepts and principles and phenomena. The second future of this is the application of those fundamentals in the development of engineering. . . . In that case it has some sort of commercial interest, all this work. Because all these pieces of work are supported mainly by industry, we have to work towards that direction.

In an early interview his attitude was one of intense loyalty to the epistemic, knowledge-creating goals of his past career as a professor and researcher; his involvement with the academy was high:

> Actually I was working for a university because, first of all, I liked to share what I'm learning and when we are sharing what we are learning, we also get back information. So this is the mechanism of knowledge. I mean, if I say: "I'm finding this" . . . and the other person would say: "Well, I don't agree, because . . . I think that it might be something like that," [then] in that sense, you know, there is some sort of development of knowledge.

His enthusiasm for education was also clear: "When we are working with young people, it's really very exciting, because young people are very open-minded. We can get excellent ideas from young people, and it makes me feel young." He understood that his present work was supported by, and answerable to, the private sector, but seemed to regret this—his level of independence from the workplace was obvious. Speaking of the way his professor edited his writing for the workplace, he said:

> For me it is difficult to write in that sense. So when I start writing something, and I go to see my professor and I hand it in, he corrects everything, and I have to take a lot of information from that and just keep it for another opportunity and leave only the ultimate results, the applications. But for me it is difficult because I don't like it. To write in that way, normally I would say that for me the less important thing would be something like that. The most important would be to present the original of what we are talking about.

> Q: So the deeper levels, fundamentals, and the theories and so on are what interest you?

> [Yes.] But we have to live with this and we have to deal with all of this and I have to learn, you know, how to manage all of this stuff, in order to make it interesting for people. For people who work in engineering; after all, I'm an engineer and I have to live with that.

In a second interview, held some months later, however, Carlos's attitude had changed. There was at least a resigned acceptance of the writing demands of the workplace context:

> People . . . who work in industry, no matter whether they have high levels of education or not, probably they—the highly educated people—change very slowly when they are working in industry and eventually they think that many things that for us, working at the university, are important—for them are irrelevant.

> Industry is a business; they are dealing with money, they are
> investing capital and they want to get profits. For them it is not
> important to know if the attachment of particles . . . to gas bub-
> bles follows certain patterns. What they are interested in is to
> increase productivity and that's it, no matter how. . . . If someone
> is working and increasing productivity, that is good for them and
> they don't care about the reasons.

He even showed some appreciation of the workplace visits, showing a
little more willingness to be involved:

> In my personal case it's a wonderful thing because otherwise I
> would not have the opportunity to know these plants, to know
> what they call or what we call the "know-how." So for me it is
> very very interesting to participate in these sorts of problems
> with industry and to see in real life how we can join what we are
> getting in academic life with the applications.

But he remained sensitive to the human dimension—evident in his
earlier comments about medicine and students. He showed some discomfort about communication problems at the work site:

> [We have to let them] know exactly what is the process of our
> experimental work. Because sometimes they are really very con-
> fused, especially the workers. . . . [I]n these times, there is a
> trend in industry . . . to reduce the number of people who are
> working. This is because of the economic situation in the whole
> world, I would say. So when they (the workers) see people coming
> from the university . . . and introducing some equipment and
> putting some sensors in their processes, they believe, and maybe
> they are right . . . that we are doing all of this in order to make
> the plant more efficient, first, and secondly, in order to automate
> everything. . . . They are afraid of us when we go to the plant,
> because they think that the ultimate effect of this work is going
> to be in their own work. I mean, probably, they would be thrown
> out of the company.

Clearly "the pain of people" was still a factor in his experience of his
profession. In a telling section of his second interview, he showed
sympathy with a particular workplace contact whose preferences
resembled Carlos's own:

> In this last experience I met in the plant a superintendent, a very
> well-educated person, and his name is Robert Victor, and he is
> very concerned with fundamentals and how to relate those funda-

mentals to production. This is very interesting but the people in
the plant—the technicians and workers—they make a little joke
about this superintendent; they call him "Professor Victor."

Even with his new insights into the workplace environment, his real
loyalty clearly rests with those for whom knowledge itself is the central
aim.

Bernardo: Comfortable in Both Worlds

Bernardo had similar insights into the differences between the academic and the workplace audience, but a very different attitude, one
best characterized by the notion of balance: he seemed able to feel
some level of involvement in both settings, and some independence
from each. An engineer from Central America, he had worked for
long periods in both academic and industrial settings. In the former,
he had taught undergraduates and done research; he had also written and published a considerable number of articles. In the latter, in
a plant where he had worked, he had become used to the demands of
production and the dominance of immediate applications. He spoke
confidently about his writing, and indeed did not seem to distinguish
between academia and the workplace in so clearcut a way as Carlos,
perhaps because his broad experience had enabled him to see how his
research could be used and adapted by a variety of people in both settings. Asked about the contexts for his current writing he said:

> Each year we have one of the seminars or congresses, a big con-
> gress involving the people working in [our field], around the
> world. So we [the research group] have a meeting and it also
> depends on the supervisor because the supervisor is pushing, in
> this case, me, to try to present something in this meeting. This is
> one [audience]. Another one is that also each year we have a
> meeting with people from the plant, the people bringing the
> money, I mean, the financial support for us. We have to present
> the progress of the work [so] that they [will be] supportive. We
> have to prepare different kinds of talks. We'd have . . . just the
> results, and also it's informal, because most people working at
> the plant, they were here before and they know a lot [about]
> things here.
>
> Q: I see, there's a close connection then?
>
> Bernardo: Yes, it's a close connection.

Q: That's something . . . how you present it to people in plants. You say they don't want the theory, they want the results. Any other differences that you see?

Bernardo: When they ask something, we have to answer very — we have to be very conscientious. I mean, I have to not extend my answer. I have to be very — have to reduce the . . .

Q: Economical?

Bernardo: Yes, in some cases, just to say yes or no. Because, if I try to answer by giving some explanation based on theory, they say, "okay, never mind, I am not interested in theory, I just wanted to know if you can solve that."

Many instances show Bernardo's intercultural sensitivity and his confidence in working with a variety of academic and workplace readers. For example, in his second interview, he mentions the different readers or listeners possible in the workplace setting, "the general manager, the president or [person] organizing the plant; the superintendent of the plant; the set of . . . process engineers; the operators."

Discussing managers, he says that they prefer not to see too many details about the research itself:

They are not interested in the [figures], they only want to see writing. Let me tell you something. We went two weeks ago to [a mining town] . . . the industry asked [Bernardo's supervisor] to run some experiments . . . and we went and we got some results and we wrote the report for these people, but the engineering people there, they asked for this kind of writing . . . and they said, "okay, okay, I don't understand what you mean with this one . . . you have to explain what you are trying to show me in this one."

Q: Why is that? Is their training very different?

Bernardo: [W]hen we have to talk to the people from industry, in the same room there are the people working directly with the devices and people working . . . just in administration. Their questions are very different. People from administration ask, for instance, "Is that working or not? Is it possible that it works or not?" And that's it.

He acknowledges with amusement the workplace resistance to operational changes led by university-based researchers, a resistance especially strong among some of the process engineers and operators in the plant:

> They don't believe in that. Actually, it happened to me, because before I came here I was working for five years in industry. And when somebody was out there just to ask me: "What would happen if I changed that? Do you agree if I change that in your system?" I said, "No, I cannot change that, I am working fine."

He learns from experience and adapts to changing genres and contexts constantly, but has strong preferences of his own. Discussing the literature review in a research paper, for example, he says:

> [F]or me the normal [approach] is that it [the literature review] has to be no more than 10% of the whole work. . . . I cannot spend half the work just in the literature review. I think that it's a general rule.

Here, his knowledge of academic convention and his workplace experience perhaps speak together; he is concerned for both adequate depth and maximum economy. But he readily accepted his professor's suggestion to slightly lengthen the literature review in this case, for strategic reasons: the research, which is innovative and challenges accepted thinking, must be especially well-defended for the audience at a congress of specialists. In other words, the culture of the formal congress demanded a strategic approach that could only be known and employed by his becoming sufficiently involved with that culture.

Bernardo seems comfortable with both audiences and the differences between them. His tone and comments express no frustration with either setting and its demands; because he knows both intuitively, he simply accepts them as they are.

Leon: Committed to the Marketplace; Resistant to Academe

Leon, like Carlos and Bernardo, came from a Latin American country. But he was different from Carlos because of his considerable experience in the private sector, and different from Bernardo because he had not spent time as a university-based researcher or teacher. Instead, he had gone straight out into the workplace from his undergraduate engineering degree. Leon's interests were certainly not those of the pure researcher. He came to Canada with the support of his company to get a Master's degree, but made quite clear that the epistemic goals of academia were not his primary object; his involvement with the managerial and business culture of his profession was profound. In his first interview he talked confidently about his earlier work in a small mining consulting company where he communicated internationally with staff and clients:

> Well . . . that's what I learned from the people from [Europe], that we try to put most of the information in the first page, because most people, they don't have time, and usually, when you send something the people will just look up: "Oh, I don't want to read that." So if you send a ten-page document, nobody will care about it. So we had to put the most important information right away. And that's the way we tried to put it.

Asked about the elements of letters sent to possible clients, he could describe them succinctly:

> The elements would be, first, thanking [them] for asking us for more information about the system, as usual; then, we would write the strengths, or a little bit of history of the product, world-wide and in our country, and then we would write the strengths. . . . But usually, if I knew beforehand, that that company, for instance, had a strong link with a Canadian company, with an American company, I'd try to see in the U.S. what . . . they used and what problems they had, so I put a little bit of a comment, oh, for instance, in Australia, where I know your company has a lot of connections you use D, because of this, this and this. And if we know a guy, we try to make . . . a personal link, if you know what I mean. It's really important in business.

He also had a remarkable, and practically acquired, sense of the multiple audiences in the companies with whom he had done business:

> Okay. Because, if you start from the top—well, we tried in the beginning to start from the top, it's not going to work. . . . Because nobody likes to receive orders. I mean: "Oh, you are going to use this . . . because the board of directors decided to buy (it)." The guys in the mine, they will just say: "Oh, come on, they don't know what we do here!" So, it's really important, in mining at least, to start to get the people, I would say—what's the word in English?—the people's sympathy.

He is very firm about the need for brevity in all writing:

> For engineering we try to be very brief in whatever we write so
> we usually wouldn't have an abstract, just an introduction and a
> very brief description of the procedure and the results and the
> conclusion. . . . Because usually when we get a paper when we are
> working we try to look first at the results; we don't really pay too
> much attention to the procedure involved, you know, with the
> pressure of working. . . . I am talking about day-to-day engineer-
> ing in the workplace, so usually we know already the guidelines
> or the procedures involved so we usually don't waste our time try-
> ing to put everything on paper.

By the time of his second interview, three months after the first, his
exasperation with academic culture had, if anything, grown. In other
words, he was increasingly stressing his independence from the academy and reasserting his workplace involvement. Talking of what was
to him the enormous length of Master's and Doctoral dissertations,
he commented:

> Well, I don't like to say this, but some people, I think, in any
> department, any university . . . they just compare the size—the
> production according to the size—rather than the content.

In other words, he could not even see why long sections (such as the
literature review or detailed theoretical explanations) were needed,
unlike Carlos who delighted in the detailed exploration of knowledge
they represent; or Bernardo who could see their strategic usefulness
in defending a new research discovery. To Leon, the length of the literature review was more like a contest or a way of showing production visually: the longer the better. He also said:

> A friend of mine is taking his Master's at [another major
> Canadian engineering school] and . . . he said, "It is incredible; I
> have to write a 100-page assignment. . . . How can you?" the guy
> said. . . . It's quite funny. He has ten years' working experience
> and he was very amazed. . . . He told me: "I could write it in ten—
> or eight—pages. So they expect you to stuff it with the literature
> review, and so on."

The literature review seems the *bête noire* of students with strong
workplace sympathies. To Leon's friend, and Leon himself, the literature review is apparently not justified; it is, rather, a way to annoy
students by asking them to "stuff" the document to make it larger.

    The communications teacher who worked with these students
explained her own sense of their different intercultural self-locations,
closer to the academy or closer to the workplace:

Workplace writing is a no-nonsense kind . . . you've got to get right down and do it. Academic writing . . . [is] almost like a dance, a show, and readers are not important. In the workplace, whether you're writing in Spanish or in English or writing down there [Central America] or up here, I think there's an emphasis on reader friendliness and utility. It has to be practical, efficient, and I think that goes along with the whole notion of science. Those with highly academic backgrounds have more trouble with this than those with workplace backgrounds.

Her own years of experience with these students seem to have given her a strong, intuitive sense of the levels of involvement and independence individual students feel in each environment.

INVOLVEMENT AND INDEPENDENCE BETWEEN THE ENGINEERING CLASSES AND THE WRITING COURSE

Just as the students interviewed showed a range of involvement and independence in the levels of loyalty to their own country or North America, and loyalty to the academy or the workplace, so too they showed varying degrees of affiliation to their own courses in engineering compared to their communications course in the education department. In the communications course they had an opportunity to learn and practice communication skills, technical and persuasive genres, and editing, while engaged on their other courses and/or research work. It is quite obvious, as the initial description of the two settings illustrates, that moving between these two university faculties involved a further cultural shift. Among other things, there was a striking gender difference, the education building being full of women professors and students as well as men, whereas in the students' own labs there were very few women students and no women professors. All of the students' own supervisors were male; their communications teacher was female. There was also a difference of tone or mood backed up by the different physical appearance of the two environments. The mood of the education class was gentler and slower, more collaborative and exploratory than the highly energetic, competitive, product-oriented pace of the students' own lab. The teacher, though demanding in her own way, did not seek to set the students against each other in a "pecking order" (something they were very aware of in their own departmental seminars) and it was clear to all concerned that in this course what each person learned to do—use new skills and practice their English—had far more significance than the final grade or a body of content knowledge.

The graduates met in class twice a week for a total of 39 hours in a semester, and produced a variety of examples of academic and workplace genres for their communications teacher. The teacher was realistic about both the scope and the constraints of the course:

> They need one-on-one work and I've been fortunate that most of the classes have been small, they've been around twelve or fourteen people, because what the [students] require is for you to sit down with them individually. . . . They need practice. They need old-fashioned workshopping. They need to sit around and freewrite every day for a little bit without panicking about correctness. Those are the things that seem to strengthen them and make them move. . . . Students go out stronger, they go out with more strategies. Is it enough, does it take them where they want to go? I doubt it. Especially if it comes early on.

In her own view, the students at least get a chance to use English together in a relatively nonthreatening setting, to examine their genre assumptions and talk about them, and to gain greater fluency. However, much of their lives, and hence much of their genre knowledge and skill, remain located in the other two dominant cultural domains described in the sections above, domains to which, because of constraints of time, numbers, and her own professional experience, she could have only limited access.

One example of the students' different kinds of involvement in the writing class was visible in the work of Leon, who was mentioned above. Leon's confident internationalism and his strongly managerial, workplace-oriented approach led him to react in a very different way from some of his peers in the writing class. His writing teacher had asked the students to work on a genuine technical paper that they were writing for their engineering professor, and to use the writing class to support its development and editing. Carlos and Bernardo took this literally, working on the research papers they had to do anyway. Leon took a somewhat different approach. Into a course paper supposedly intended for a mining professor, he inserted the following lines, just after the introduction, in the version given to his writing class teacher, whom, incidentally, he greatly admired for her skill as an editor:

> Day after day, the economic aspects of human activity become more important. Competition, lack of resources, and customer demands motivate businesses and industries to reduce their costs and improve their revenues. Mining companies are no exception.

Leon explained:

> That's much more academic because I had to, for this specific
> paper, I had to explain some points.
>
> Q: Was that put in specifically for [the writing instructor]?
>
> L: Oh yes, yes, it's very general.
>
> Q: Would you put that in the version for your [mining depart-
> ment] professor?
>
> L: No, I had to change a few things. . . . Well, for sure I changed
> this paragraph. . . . The obvious part for mining engineers or
> geologists I just took away.

Leon was well aware of what his writing teacher seemed to want—in
this case, that he should simulate exactly for her class a document
intended for a very different audience, and then revise and edit it. He
was only too willing to comply. However, the strength of his involvement with his own workplace training provided a different perspective, prompting him (paradoxically) to go against the explicit instruc-
tions of the class. For Leon, sensitivity to audience was everything,
so much so that he was willing to tamper with his technical paper
(giving it a very odd impact on the first page) in order to satisfy the
person who—in this version—was his actual audience, his writing
instructor. He wanted to show her the courtesy of a helpful overview,
and this took precedence over his awareness of what was genre-
appropriate for the task as originally formulated. What a contrast
with Carlos, for whom adjusting to new audiences seemed an uncomfortable process and for whom the research material itself was of
prime importance.

   As Aviva Freedman argues (1993), the rhetorical demands of
the academic context are inevitably different from those of the setting in which the students are deeply embedded in their own professional work. There are, equally, sharp contrasts in academia itself,
between discipline-based and decontextualized courses, as Patrick
Dias shows in this volume. Among the students who made up this
writing class, it is clear that there were huge differences both of
background and motive. Their "involvement with" or "independence
from" this class was shaped in complex ways by their previous cultural history (degree of international involvement, intent to return to
their own country) and their academic and/or workplace history.

CONCLUSION

As this chapter has illustrated, these international engineering students at Masters and Doctoral level were being challenged to become truly diplomatic writers in difficult circumstances. They had to negotiate, on a daily or weekly basis, at least three levels of involvement and independence between different "cultures"—cultures as large as nations and as small as the difference between two courses in a single university. The evidence shows how complex were the tacit demands of the writing tasks they had to complete, and how many kinds of confusion were possible. Certainly second language problems remained, but these came to seem much less important than the issues of understanding and response to cultural patterns, the exigencies of each writing context, and above all their own (sometimes ambivalent) feelings of loyalty or distance.

The students' writing reveals vast differences within that elusive concept we call "personality," which A.A. Leontyev (1981) sees as both socially and genetically constructed, and which is crucial to an understanding of how writing competence will develop. In a metaphor of curious relevance to this group of learners, he states: "Personality takes shape as the result of absorbed socio-historical experience, and on the basis of innate preconditions; but one does not end up with personality just by adding the two together, just as one does not end up with steel by simply mixing iron ore with carbon" (p. 12). And he asks: "What processes take place in the 'blast furnace' in which man's personality is smelted, and what should the steel worker—the . . . teacher—know about these processes?" (p. 12).

It seems on the basis of this study that the teacher at least needs to know each student as an individual, and needs to recognize that what has often been called "weak writing" is far more often, especially at this level of motivation and experience, "wrong genre writing."[4] The students' struggles and achievements at these three levels of involvement illustrate how much intelligence and effort go into the processes of translation and adjustment that they constantly engage in. They can indeed be seen as "diplomats in the basement"—developing intercultural skills with both conscious and unconscious analysis of the writing environments in which they work.

I would like to end by considering the relevance of Charles Bazerman's (1988) powerful statement about science in this rather different, but related, setting:

---

[4]This point was discussed by Alison Lee and Anne Freadman at the Second International Genre Symposium in Vancouver, January 1998, in the discussion period of a session called "Genre and Pedagogy."

> One peculiar aspect of the accomplishment of scientific discourse
> is that it appears to hide itself. . . . (T)o write science is commonly
> thought not to write at all, just simply to record the natural facts.
> Even widely published scientists, responsible for the production
> of many texts over many years, often do not see themselves as
> accomplished writers, nor do they recognize any self-conscious
> control of their texts. The popular belief of this past century that
> scientific language is a transparent transmitter of natural facts
> is, of course, wrong. . . . It is nonetheless fascinating that such a
> misconception could have thrived so well in the face of the mas-
> sive linguistic work that has gone into scientific communication.
> This attests to the success of scientific language as an accom-
> plished system. So much has already been done, and hides so far
> behind the scenes of current practices, that using the language
> seems hardly an effort at all. (p. 14)

Bazerman is, of course, discussing the apparently arhetorical nature
of scientific discourse, in a study that goes on to show just how profoundly rhetorical scientific persuasion actually is. However, his
statement also gives a valuable insight into the underlying reasons
for the difficulty these graduate students face as they seek to make
transitions and become adept in new cultures. The frustrations of
professors, workplace sponsors, and the graduates themselves, which
are felt far more often than they are explicitly explored, must be
linked to the "invisibility" of traditional communicative practices in
science. As Bazerman says, the cultures of science "play down" the
rhetorical processes at work in texts: "To write science is commonly
thought not to write at all, just simply to record the natural facts."
But scientists, like other professional groups, are being tested to the
limits by changes in the academy, in the relation between academia
and the private sector, and in the increasing globalization of the field:
where previously there was no sense of "effort," now there may be a
great deal—an especially visible effort when newcomers to a team
are expected to acquire the genre skills and the level of cultural
involvement necessary for action under great pressure.

Globalization and rapid change show that intercultural theory, when applied to the study of genres, requires both spatial and
temporal dimensions: we need to consider the students in this study
in terms of their transitions through cultures, space, and time. Every
group is embedded in a cultural setting that is being changed and is
changing itself both through contact with other cultures, and through
the process of historical development (Freedman & Medway, 1994;
Miller, 1984; Paré & Smart, 1994). Genre theorists talk about genres
"as stabilized for now" (Schryer, 1994, p. 107). In the context of
applied science and engineering, the stability of genres is being chal-

lenged in many ways. Making the transition into the tacit and confident use of these genres is a key concern for educators, as scientists and engineers of nontraditional (in Eurocentric terms) background become ever more numerous in industrialized countries. Those practitioners and professors who are part of the European tradition, and who have, until now, been able to use their engineering genres largely intuitively, are being faced with a need to explore further the many intercultural dimensions of their work. Their collaboration with the writing teachers and technical editors who are also now exploring intercultural realities will enhance all three groups' understanding of communication and the transitions their students or trainees must make. Increased understanding of intercultural communication, and especially stances of involvement and independence, can support more effective teaching and learning within the different cultures, workplace sites, and sections of the academy where groups such as these graduate student engineers must learn.

ACKNOWLEDGMENTS

I would like to thank all those who agreed to be interviewed for this study: professors, students, and other professionals. I would also like to thank the following people who were kind enough to comment on the manuscript: Janet Blatter, Guillaume Gentil, Jane Ledwell-Brown, Anthony Paré, and Carolyn Pittenger, and some of the engineering professors quoted in the study who must remain nameless, but whose insights have been enormously helpful. Thank you all.

REFERENCES

Bazerman, C. (1988). *Shaping written knowledge: The genre and activity of the experimental article in science.* Madison: University of Wisconsin Press.

Freadman, A. (1994). Anyone for tennis? In A. Freedman & P. Medway (Eds.), *Genre and the new rhetoric* (pp. 43-66). London: Taylor & Francis.

Freedman, A. (1993). Show and tell: The role of explicit teaching in the learning of new genres. *Research in the Teaching of English, 27*(3), 222-251.

Freedman, A., & Medway, P. (Eds.). (1994). *Genre and the new rhetoric.* London and Bristol, PA: Taylor & Francis.

Herrington, A. (1985). Writing in academic settings: A study of the contexts for writing in two college chemical engineering courses. *Research in the Teaching of English, 19*(4), 331-339.

Leontyev, A.A. (1981). *Psychology and the language learning process.* Oxford: Pergamon Press.

Leont'ev, A.N. (1981) *Problems of the development of the mind.* Moscow: Progress Publishers.

Miller, C. (1984). Genre as social action. *Quarterly Journal of Speech, 70*, 151-167.

Paré, A., & Smart, G. (1994). Observing genres in action: Towards a research methodology. In A. Freedman & P. Medway (Eds.), *Genre and the new rhetoric* (pp. 146-154). London: Taylor & Francis.

Schryer, C. (1994). The lab vs. the clinic: Sites of competing genres. In A. Freedman & P. Medway (Eds.), *Genre and the new rhetoric* (pp. 105-124). London: Taylor & Francis.

Scollon, R., & Scollon, S. W. (1995). *Intercultural communication: A discourse approach.* Cambridge, MA & Oxford: Blackwell.

Swales, J. (1990). *Genre analysis: English in academic and research setting.* Cambridge: Cambridge University Press.

CHAPTER 4

Writing and Design in Architectural Education

Peter Medway
Carleton University

WRITING IN ARCHITECTURAL EDUCATION: ITS SIGNIFICANCE FOR WRITING RESEARCH

Architecture's place in the university is somewhat uneasy: its pedagogical traditions are distinctive and do not sit comfortably within conventional university structures and schedules; it is geared toward practice rather than knowledge; the achievements of its faculty are as likely to be measured in competition successes, accomplished buildings and exhibits as in books and articles, and are problematic in terms of academic procedures for evaluating scholarly worth. It is to be expected, therefore, that the use made of writing in architectural education will be rather different from uses in other disciplines described in this volume.

The difference is more marked in some areas of architectural education than in others. Testimony from a sample of students in two Canadian schools of architecture (Schools A and B)[1] and anecdotal

[1]The data on which this chapter is based are drawn from two studies funded by the Social Sciences and Humanities Research Council of Canada: Grant Nos. 884-92-0009 and 884-93-0008, entitled "The Relationships between

evidence from elsewhere suggest that students believe they do not write much.

> How much writing have you done at school?

> Not much. Not much at all. This past term I don't think I did any, actually. Just a few paragraphs, perhaps, in my final project, but no essays, no creative writing at all. (School B student)

> Writing is still something which I find that I don't do enough of. (School B student)

> I didn't write an essay, maybe like one or two essays my whole time here. Then I was in fifth year and I had to write something . . . because I did a research thesis. This was like hitting a brick wall for me, because I didn't know how to write anymore. (School A graduate)

> [In architecture] writing really falls by the wayside. (School A graduate)

> Some people in school I know never use writing at all. (School A student)

A survey of course outlines in School A, however, suggests that writing requirements in some courses are both normally onerous and conventional in relation to demands in other disciplines. Particularly in courses in architectural and cultural history, full-length papers and paragraph-length test answers force students to read the set texts and serve as vehicles for organizing and displaying knowledge in familiar academic ways. In three of the five "core" courses, moreover, quality of writing is explicitly named as an evaluation criterion.

The main body of an architecture program, however, consists of two sorts of courses. The state of affairs just described refers to writing in the courses that are most like those in other disciplines, dealing mainly with history or theory and taught through lectures,

Writing in the University and Writing in the Workplace" and conducted by Aviva Freedman and myself in Carleton University, Ottawa, and by Patrick Dias and Anthony Paré in McGill University, Montreal; and Grant No. 884-94-0030, entitled "Comparative Case Study of Co-operative Education in High School, College and University," conducted by Ivor Goodson at the University of Western Ontario and Aviva Freedman and myself in Carleton University, Ottawa. For their contribution as field researchers on the two projects I owe a great debt to Danica Robertson and Tariq Sami.

seminars, readings, and texts. It does not apply to the design studio. "Studio" in a school of architecture is on the one hand a physical place. Thus, there is second-year studio, which is where second-year students essentially live while they are in the building, and which has its distinctive form of life. But studio is also, on the other hand, a curricular element, a workshop course in which students do design projects and the teacher circulates and gives individual tutorials; review and assessment are based on pinned-up work and are oral and public. The scheduled studio sessions tend to be long—half or full days—but in addition students spend most of their unscheduled time on studio work. As the work load is extremely heavy, this regularly involves weekends and "all-nighters." In the students' eyes, studio work is the priority; work for other courses tends to be fitted into whatever time can be spared from studio.

Students' perception that they do not do a great deal of writing may reflect the fact that there is little required writing in studio, where the main product is almost always drawings, models, and photographs. Some instructors will ask for writing: perhaps an initial statement of the design intention, perhaps a log, perhaps a self-evaluation. Some students will choose to write, either for their own purposes or as part of their final presentation. This may be the result of a local blurring of the boundary between the academic courses and studio, as when the same professor teaches both or when a cultural history professor imports pedagogical methods from studio:

> So as you find yourself writing for that [cultural history] course, you find yourself also writing for your own project. (School B student)

And some students simply write because they find it useful:

> My sketchbook had probably about as much writing in it as sketches in it. It's filled with just notes that I write down, you know. (School B student)

Those who do use writing tend to value it highly, as a means of keeping track but also, beyond that, as a means of thinking:

> To me writing is related to how you think, and in that sense writing is more of a tool organizing information and organizing ideas within the development of your idea, within the development of the project. And for me I think it's the most important tool in studio, as a tool to organize, as a tool to record things that you couldn't fit. Like . . . the project starts as a very small seed but at

the end of a term at your final crit you cannot fit it all in your
head, and you can't think about the building in its entirety at one
time. So you have to be very careful to record the original thesis
of the proposal, what's motivating it at the beginning, and keep a
record of how things are unfolding, and how I see them unfolding,
and how I see them projecting, and only then, at the final crit,
can I, in retrospect, work it together as a type of thesis. And without writing, you couldn't do it. You couldn't do it just in sketches
either. And so, as the development of an idea, I think writing
plays a critical role. (School B student)

But there is no general expectation that writing will feature significantly in studio. It is not, like other practices such as the oral review,
an enshrined element in the pedagogical tradition, and its occurrence
is irregular and unsystematic.

No, it's very minimal. I think it's up to the student. Like, this
past term there's a very minimal amount of writing that has to be
done. But if that is your strong point as a student, you are more
than welcome to incorporate it into a final presentation, or a final
hand-in. (School B student)

Such manifestations of writing as do occur, however, tend to be
regarded as important by the students and are of special interest
within the perspective of this volume.

It is on the writing that is associated with the practical work
of design, and not on the more academically familiar writing within
history and theory courses in architecture, that I will focus in this
chapter, as on the face of it it has more relevance to the practical
activity of professional architectural work. Perhaps surprisingly,
however, that relevance is not to the writing element in the work of
the architect. Architects do a great deal of writing, but it is related
mainly to contractual matters and to dealings with other parties over
materials, costs, technical advice, the control of construction, and so
on, rather than to design. For those major functions of writing, the
schools we know provide little or no training. The same seems to be
true of the many different schools where the practicing architects we
have talked to were educated; looking back from years of experience
in the profession, some of these practitioners regret that absence.[2]

Writing associated with design in the university does not
therefore constitute a rehearsal of workplace genres. This is not to

---

[2]The rather oblique relationship of architectural education to professional practice is an issue discussed in Dias, Freedman, Medway, and Paré (1999).

say, however, that it does not contribute, albeit less directly, to professional preparation. I will suggest in the final section that the professional need addressed is not for particular writing abilities but, less specifically, for an ability to combine linguistic and nonlinguistic forms of symbolic activity in easy combination. The main body of this study will address the nature of that combination by investigating the manner in which writing functions in association with the very different, nonverbal medium of drawing.

My first task, however, will be to identify a number of features that make design-related architectural writing distinctive within the university and a worthy object of study for students of writing. I will then examine the part that writing played in a major design project undertaken by a School A student for his final-year design thesis.

CHARACTERISTICS OF WRITING DURING DESIGN

In this section I will consider the writing that occurs in association with the production of a design. What follows is a schematic description of those aspects that differentiate this writing from most of the other university writing discussed in this book.

Future Orientation

Where writing is used at all in the design studio, it is deployed in the service of bringing a new object into existence. This object is not, of course, a building, because most studio projects will not get built. (The planning typically proceeds, however, at least in some respects, as if it were leading to construction.) The object of a studio exercise is a drawn and modelled design for a building, in other words, an elaborated concept. The reality that is the reference point of the writing will not fully exist until the end of the process. The situation is thus very different from that of most university writing, which takes actually existing (as in physical science) or hypothetically entertained (as in some business "cases") states of affairs and seeks not to give them fuller realization but to represent, analyze, and explain them. Even when the overall orientation is toward future action, as in the (usually fictitious) business plan or social worker's report of recommendation that are produced by students as exercises, the emphasis is often more on the correct representation and evaluation of the existing problematic situation and circumstances than on what will be done. The architecture student's design project, on the other hand, is largely about fresh invention and new cre-

ation. And whereas most academic writing displays and organizes existing knowledge, writing in design makes known a reality previously
available only to the designer, and sometimes serves to *make* a reality
that *can* be known. (That architectural education places such a premium on the articulation of *intention* is one reason why it is so potent a
means of forming student identity.)

Orientation to Material Production

The end of the design activity, including the writing, is a potential
material artifact—a concept that requires only a fabrication stage to
make it a thing in the world. The writing thus concerns the composition, configuration, and construction of this object. Such a task poses
representational demands that are very different from those of most
academic disciplines and of the other professional disciplines in this volume, which tend to be about human or natural physical phenomena,
whether concrete (a social work client) or abstract (economic projections).

Shaping Action

Writing in design shapes action rather than knowledge; the fruits of
writing are effective and consistent action. One of the functions of writing in design is to formulate and record clear purposes for design
action, and to record decisions and actions taken. The record can subsequently be consulted to ensure that the progress of the design
remains consistent with the espoused purpose, and so that routes can
be retraced to decision nodes and alternative possibilities reconsidered.

> One of the things that I've only just started to do was keep a real
> log of decisions and what was going on . . . . It helps to make it
> clear for yourself . . . in terms of, it's easier to take two steps back
> and then say, "What if I went left here, instead of right, in the
> middle of the project?" It's easier to do that, and spend a little
> less time whenever you're moving in a particular direction and
> you think you want to change direction or play around with what
> you're doing, stop for a minute and reconsider how you're going
> before you develop your idea a little further. You end up ... there's
> always a little bit of wheel spinning that happens there. It always
> takes you a day or so to figure out where you're at and where
> you're going, and that wheel spinning for you is greatly reduced
> by simply using the same kind of "Be clear," whatever, technique
> stuff. (School B student)

The "technique stuff" is keeping a written record. It is, in fact, for its record-keeping function that many students claim writing principally to be valuable in design.

Fragmentary and Multimodal Texts

Because of the representational requirement just mentioned, writing is often used in combination with sketches and diagrams, which are better adapted to show spatial relations, relative sizes and other aspects of material objects. The writing that is associated with graphical representations typically comprises very short texts, often less than sentences, sometimes in the form of labels attached to parts of a drawing. Design writing may be fragmentary for other reasons too, some of which it shares with students' private notes in other disciplines. Writing may be used to record (in a sketchbook/notebook) ideas as they occur in the course of work, without regard for any textual coherence among the various items on the page; it may be used to accumulate separate items of "raw material" for a planned longer text. Writing also occurs as lists and charts.

There is a growing recognition that fragmentary and multimodal texts need to be considered seriously by students of writing. As has been pointed out by Witte (1992) and Winsor (1994), "researchers slight such texts as lists and diagrams in favor of extended arrays of connected sentences and paragraphs" (Winsor, 1994, p. 228). And research needs to take account of what may distinctively be achieved within speech and writing and within the various nonlinguistic media (Medway, 1996a).

Relationship to Spoken Language

Because the predominant forms of instruction, presentation, review, and assessment in design exercises are oral, written text may function as draft for, notation after, or accompaniment to an oral event. What has been spoken (for instance by the instructor in a one-to-one "desk crit" or review of work in progress, or by the writer herself during a studio conversation with peers) may get written down in the notebook; written formulations of design ideas may get an oral reformulation in the student's explanations to the professor or the final review jury; or a written text accompanying the final drawings and models may be the basis of oral discussion at the review event. In general, the oral is seen as primary, the written as secondary, a reversal of the order that is usual in university education.

This feature, in combination with the preceding one, suggests a research perspective that, as Witte (1992) proposes, takes as its subject acts of symbolic communication and seeks to locate writing in relation to other linguistic and nonlinguistic media within that process. When the student is maintaining activity on three channels—written, spoken, and graphical—and switching freely between them, the initial questions that must be asked about instances of writing are "Why was language used rather than a graphical medium?" and "Why writing rather than speech?"

Relationship to Instructional Prescription and Grading

Although some writing in studio occurs because the instructor has required it, most does not, and writing typically plays a minor or nonexistent role in the assessment of the student's design work. This has implications for the nature of writing as *activity* (see the discussion of activity theory in Dias, this volume). Whereas most university writing is conducted under the aegis of evaluation, so that the activity that produces it may often be *getting a grade* by impressing the evaluator *through the writing*, writing in architectural design generally takes place at some distance from evaluation, which attends primarily to drawings, models, and the student's orally presented justifications. This frees writing to serve other ends (or participate in other activities) more directly, more in the way that it might in many workplace situations (and that advocates of "writing across the curriculum" approaches, such as Applebee, [1984], Department of Education and Science [1975], Emig [1977], and Smagorinsky [1995], would like to see in education generally). The activity that writing serves can be design itself. Thus a written text may answer short-term, ephemeral needs—such as the provisional noting of an idea that arose incidentally to the main activity of the moment—and lose all its value once its content has been retrieved and used. Writing can be used for thinking without any immediate regard to the opinions of teacher or evaluator.

INTRODUCING THE CASE STUDY: THE DESIGN THESIS IN ARCHITECTURE

In the final term of the final (fifth) year of the undergraduate architecture program in School A, students may opt to do a design thesis. Unlike a research thesis (which they may do in the penultimate term), a design thesis is an argument developed not through written discourse, except for a short statement, but by the design of an architectural entity such as a building, presented in two- and three-dimensional visual form in drawings, photographs, models, and so on. The short written text that accompanies the design is, however, quite significant; it is referred to in this school as the *precis*. (That of the case study student, Innes, is reproduced here as an appendix to the chapter.) At an earlier stage a written proposal has to be approved by the thesis committee.

The main part of this chapter will be an examination of the writing that went into Innes's design thesis, produced over three-and-a-half months from January to mid-April. Although his final written precis was short (just over two pages), a great deal of writing had gone on in the weeks leading up to that composition, including drafts of the statement itself and the earlier thesis proposal, but also many other texts. Innes's supervisor, Barry, proposed one piece of writing and generally supported the idea of copious writing, but most of the text generated was produced at Innes's own instigation.

Innes's intention in the thesis, as explained in his proposal, was to follow up an insight he had developed in his earlier *research* thesis, a mainly written text produced the previous term. In that work, a study of the ways in which the memory of heroes and glorious deeds was marked and preserved in the world of Homer's *Iliad*, Innes had argued that the building of funeral pyres and erection of battle trophies were expressions of a mnemonic impulse that was later to motivate architecture in the temples and monuments of classical Greece. His plan in the second, design thesis was to explore the validity and viability within contemporary society of an architecture that sought to preserve what the city or nation wished to remember. As he expressed it in his final written argument:

> Despite any intention to the contrary, architecture persistently preserves the memory of some value or desire and shows it to the city. Through this unique capacity, architecture's role may emerge as one of resistance to the corrosive effects of cultural amnesia upon both a memory of public life, and the desire for memory itself.

The project through which Innes chose to demonstrate his thesis was a proposed building in the center of the Canadian capital, Ottawa, to house the Special Collections of the National Library of Canada. The thesis was orally presented at the public final review to a jury that comprised the thesis committee and visiting critics; the documentation consisted of the written precis already referred to, copied and distributed, and a number of pinned up drawings—plans, elevations, sections, and perspectives. Innes worked on the thesis over some three months, with regular meetings with his supervisor, Barry, and a midterm review with the thesis committee.

The research data on which I base my account of the project include copies of Innes's notebooks, written drafts and final texts; and audio and video recordings by Danica Robertson of her interviews with Innes, two of Innes's meetings with Barry, the midterm review, and the final review.[3]

INNES'S USES OF WRITING

Compared with other architecture students, Innes does a great deal of his design thinking in words on paper. The explanation he gave in an interview the previous year explains, in ways highly relevant to his practice in the thesis, how he regards the place of writing.

PM   It's a bit like a lab notebook, like physicists keep.

I   Yes, yes, it's the same kind of thing, except in the sense that you're not, you're not, searching for some sort of objective truth, but maybe. . . . You know that there is something that you're looking for, [but] you can never say that "O.K., this proves that," or that you've actually provided an answer for whatever question you had, because you'll never really produce something that's definite or objective hard fact. Well, the interesting thing about architecture is the things you end up doing are often, I mean, they may be something that doesn't communicate anything explicitly—it never really does. But the way that you actually think about it, and go about doing it, is fairly clear and explicit.

"Making it explicit" through writing is "for architects . . . a really useful thing, a way of keeping yourself responsible."

The major function of the writing that Innes did for his design thesis related to intentions. At the most general level, an important part of his intention was defined by the research question. Whereas the verbal definition of the one-sentence question (see

---

[3]I owe the biggest debt of gratitude to Innes Yates and Barry Bell for allowing me unrestricted access to their proceedings and documents. I should point out that the finished thesis greatly impressed the jury and was awarded a Distinction.

below) was quickly achieved (by 20 January), the formulation of the broader rationale and logic for the research was still being worked on right up to the final precis. Arriving at a clear statement of overall purpose was a major use to which writing was being put even after the design was well under way and, indeed, almost complete. Writing also served to work out, clarify, and record more local and subsidiary intentions. As we shall see, a major part of the effort went into ensuring that *intention* and *artifact* were thought about together and remained connected. Much of the writing was about the attempt to secure and maintain that connection, so that the designer did not get carried away by the "logic" of his drawn design and forget that its point was to demonstrate a thesis.

REPRESENTATIONAL REQUIREMENTS: FOUR ELEMENTS OF DESIGN

Designing seemed to involve for Innes the verbal representation of certain elements, factors, or considerations of design. I will illustrate the main categories with examples both from Innes's spoken and his written discourse, partly to demonstrate that they are elements of the *discourse* of architecture and not just features of a written or spoken *genre* (a point I will briefly return to in the final section of the chapter). Consider the following extract. (Quotations in this section are from interviews unless indicated otherwise.) Innes is indicating features of his drawings as he talks to the researcher:

> Those are the Rare Book Room and Manuscript Collection. . . . And that room is contained behind this wall. So this wall would be one of the first things that you'd see after you enter in the building. There would be this kind of huge cut. Or, actually, the main floor of the building is almost entirely eliminated and just replaced with circulation, bridges which go across it. So everything is directed downwards, and the wall is the one thing that captures your attention.

We note first that architectural elements (room, wall, main floor, bridge) have to be named, as do generic and specific functions such as circulation and Rare Book Room. Such structural and functional realities, representing aspects of the building that are more or less unproblematically identifiable, are the first "factor or consideration of design" that the discourse recognizes and provides for; some of these are able to be designated by simple naming whereas others, such as complex and novel configurations, have to be described.

The aim of architectural design, however, is not just a structure that meets certain functional requirements; it is also a particular architectural *experience*. The other main entities that feature in the representations of the discourse—its other *ideational* constituents—thus reflect architects' wish to influence the viewer's or user's experience of the building. This experiential aspect, the most exacting for Innes and the most interesting and complex in terms of demands on written and other representation, has three levels, constituting design elements two, three, and four.

Number two, which appears in the first extract, is simply the viewer's perception—what can be seen (as against what is hidden), the order in which things are seen, how the parts of the building will enter the viewer's awareness: "This wall would be one of the first things that you'd see"; "The wall is the one thing that captures your attention." Elsewhere, Innes's formulation, "this curved circulation ramp and the light filtering in," brings together elements one and two (the objective character of the structure and the perceptual experience of light entering in a particular way). The context of that reference, however, is Innes's hope that the sectional drawings will not only specify the structure and make it possible to predict the perceptual experience (of light), but will give an idea of the "experiential quality" of the built state of affairs:

> So that's why these characters are so different than the other
> stuff, experientially as well as formally. I guess the formal quali-
> ties come through in the section. . . . You can imagine, I think,
> the experiential quality of being in there, this curved circulation
> ramp and light filtering in, this mysterious light filtering in.

"Mysterious" takes us into a third order of representation. It goes beyond perception and into the complex of feelings and associations aroused in the viewer by the experience of the architectural condition. In other words, it is a matter of *meaning*.

Consider the first extract again. One's perception of entering the main (ground) floor level of the building is that the floor does not extend across the building but gives way to a large space the bottom of which is at a lower level; putting it another way (out of many possible ways) there is an abrupt drop in floor level. In describing it the way he does, however, Innes brings out the *phenomenological* experience of this condition:

> There would be this kind of huge cut. Or, actually the main floor
> of the building is almost entirely eliminated and just replaced
> with a circulation, bridges which go across it.

"Cut" and "eliminated" are not given to perception but are the viewers' interpretations. The empty space may indeed have been created during construction by cutting away the ground (though not by eliminating a floor, as there was no floor), but it is an act of interpretation, of meaning, that mentally attaches that imagined prior process of construction to what is objectively a configuration of solid and void in space. "Contained" ("that room is contained behind this wall") is likewise a phenomenological, not a literal statement.

The phenomenological dimension is prominent in another passage:

> So that's the Rare Book Room and the wall, which are really about density, solidity, containment, grounding, foundation, things like that. And those are contrasted by these two things that I called the transient characters, and those have the mark of an ephemeral or less solid, less artifact-oriented form of memory. And those are seen as floating things, floating things that are like little worlds of their own.

"These two things" are the Reading Room and the Music Listening Room. The phenomenological experience of "floating" is achieved by reducing the obviousness of their attachment to the main structure:

> They are physically, they have to touch the ground, but it isn't the idea of the thing weighted down that is rhetorically explored. It's more suppressed, so it's kind of hidden. This thing is floating, it's not as in the case of the wall. It's not really displaying its function of staying firm in one place. It's more a something that moves around potentially, although obviously it doesn't.

Here we have the clearest possible distinction between the physical structure and the viewer's experience of it. The phenomenology of the two rooms is that they float, are unanchored, and could potentially move; that of the wall is "about density, solidity, containment, grounding, foundation." "About" always introduces a designation of some aspect of meaning. "See as" ("seen as kind of floating things") can introduce any of the three sorts of experience, and "the idea is that" announces intentions about experience:

> The idea is that the experience of the thing is much more fluid, much more translucent and the idea is that you're always looking through filters. So you're looking through a screen or something, through into another kind of reality, or another realm, whatever you want, something else. . . . But the idea is these different things are all perceived together.

Whereas phenomenological meaning is to do with, as it were, bodily associations, the sorts of almost physical responses awakened by the experience of a spatial condition (Bachelard, 1994), like the sense of "density" and "solidity" we may get even though all we can see are surfaces, or the sense of "containment" even though nothing is trying to get out, or of "grounding" even though nothing is trying to float free, *symbolic* meaning—our fourth element—is the evocation of ideas that are inherently nothing to do with structural forms, such as "mystery," "memory" ("an ephemeral or less solid, less artifact-oriented form of memory") or "little worlds" ("floating things that are like little worlds of their own").

To recapitulate, then, our four design elements that have their equivalent in the ideational elements of the discourse are *structure/function* and then three elements that relate to experience: perception, and two types of meaning: *phenomenological meaning* and *symbolic meaning*. In practice, as we shall see, the boundary between them is often indistinct.

What I am calling "symbolic meaning" Innes and Barry refer to with the term "thematic." For example, in Canadian iconography the North has symbolic potency ("The true North strong and free" and all that), so Barry remarks about Innes's handling of the northward orientation of the building that it "depends whether you want to give a thematic value to looking into the north." Examples in Innes's account of his concern for symbolic meaning are:

The wall you could see as a kind of wall of memory.

The first experience of the building is the thing as a filter in the city. So it's this wall that functions to become a filter between these two different memories of public life—the monumental public life and the everyday world of the market.

The second passage refers to the geographical positioning of the building between the zone of government buildings and that of the market. To see the building as a filtering wall is to ascribe to it a meaning that is somewhere between the phenomenological and the symbolic. Later Innes refers again to "the idea of this thing as a wall within the city"—the words "idea" and "as" acting as indicators that some aspect of *meaning* is being introduced.

"Idea" occurs again in the following passage, in which literal structural specification passes easily into the description of phenomenological experience:

> That's almost 20 metres from there all the way up to there, and you have this thing, this is the Music Listening Room, so it sort of hovers in here, and you get that idea of hovering above something. . . . And then you're actually coming into this, so it helps you understand the nature of the thing as a kind of hovering world. It's tethered by the world below. It's pretty big. I mean, it looks like it's over 100.

The way in which Innes's intention, which is all about symbolic meaning (the representation of the preservation of memory) is to be achieved through the manipulation of the first, phenomenological sort of meaning is made explicit in the following passage:

> The architecture is probably the only thing that can do that, so there's no other medium and no other mode of communication or experience that allows that kind of solidity just from the sheer physical fact of, you know, a building is a building, it's solid, it's standing there, and the more rooted it is, the more permanent. That's a kind of logic. So this world of the earth, the world of gravity and mass, is proposed as a valuable part of this idea of grounding or permanence.

WHAT INNES WROTE

Innes's writing and drawing proceed in three formats: a notebook, 5 1/2" x 8"; 8 1/2" x 11" loose sheets (mainly writing, handwritten and computer printouts); and large sheets of drafting paper (development of the design and final presentation drawings). The writing on the loose sheets includes versions of the thesis proposal and of the precis.

The issue I want to explore in examining this corpus is the nature of the contribution that writing makes to the design, by which I mean the prefigured (or "virtual"—Medway, 1996b) building. Because it constitutes a thesis, the work maintains a particularly conscious and rigorous relationship between verbally articulated rationales and principles and the graphically realized concrete design of the building. Maintaining that tight connection between the originating intention and the worked-out design was evidently not easy. It appears that design in drawing has its own logic, or at least its own seductions, so that a conscious effort was required to keep the purpose of the exercise in view. Writing was the means of achieving this, as was made explicit by Barry in his advice to Innes immediately before the final three weeks of intensive drawing work:

> B . . . it's a good time to return to the original thematics. You
> know, get the original thesis statement . . . because now that you
> have all the raw material it's quite possible that it's gone in slight-
> ly different directions, which is not to say you should pull it back,
> just to address what you have. Because, I mean, it's no longer
> explicitly clear to me what this is doing according to your thesis.
> It's not that it can't. . . . I don't know whether you want to actually
> try and write a three-page thesis statement again, but. . . . So I
> would think if you could describe explicitly what you think the
> building is doing, or trying to do in terms of the thesis question,
> and then that would help to elaborate or at least to identify the
> areas.

That statement becomes the two-and-a-bit-page precis (see appendix)
that is presented at the final review. In the terms of the design elements identified above, it deals mainly with issues of symbolic meaning. Specifically, it identifies a danger in the "amnesia" and loss of
desire for a public realm brought about by the obsession with the
ephemeral and instantaneous, as manifested in electronic communications. It then argues that architecture, with its inherent associations of solidity and permanence, is well placed to offer effective
resistance to this trend and to support the preservation of civic and
national memory and maintain a sense of the reality of the public
sphere. As it is specifically concerned with such preservation, a
library will be an appropriate subject for an architectural project to
explore the thesis question, which is:

> How can architecture resist death—as the diffusion of amnesia—
> and remember how to live?

("Death" recalls the earlier research thesis, explicitly referred to in
the proposal for the current thesis; Innes had argued that it was as a
defence against what they feared most, being forgotten in death, that
Homeric warriors engaged in the proto-architectural practice of erect-
ing trophies and elaborate funeral pyres.) The statement then
explains the program —a Special Collections Library for the National
Library of Canada and its four types of collection—and explains that
"the building *proposes* [emphasis added] that the public realm encompasses a greater presence than that which can be immediately
viewed, consumed, and then forgotten"; in other words, that the
building will make people believe that their existence as a people has
a reality that goes beyond ephemeral experience.

    Finally, very briefly, the statement says how this effect will be
achieved, by "link[ing] the experience of attainment [that is, of the

knowledge that the library contains] with the experience of grounding; of a deeply rooted, permanent foundation which prevails despite the shifting, chaotic world around it." The strategy will be that "[t]hemes such as lightness, expansion, clarity, and control will be explored in conjunction with themes of depth, weight, density, and containment," and also of "threshold, horizon, and ascension." These themes refer to *phenomenological* experiences of physical conditions, but by their metaphoric import they simultaneously activate symbolic meanings. What is true of the *names* of the experiences is felt to be true of the experiences themselves; to experience depth when looking down into the bottom of a building is at the same time to have intimations of, perhaps, something fundamental, of gravity or of lastingness.

Tracing the Sequence of Writing

If we go back to the earliest notes and work forward, from the first entry of 17 January to the final notes made the day before the review of 18 April, we can plot a gradual development in the use and nature of the writing. The part of the notebook dealing with this project comprises 57 pages. The first eight of these contain no drawings beyond a couple of small sketch plans on pages 5 and 6. The first page makes it clear that Innes really did start, as his final precis suggests, not with the wish to design a library but with his theme of the public desire for memory. The choice of project through which this might be addressed is a secondary move. He considers a number of alternative "program possibilities": "National Library / rare book center," "Media (technologies) center," and "National film board center." In an observation that is not explicitly taken up later he comments that "The act of reading in public is something unique to a library and is also something that a computer cannot give." Innes then writes a heading, "Public expectations," and, in the manner in which he typically develops his thinking on paper, sets out a series of bulleted points, some expressed as sentences, others as phrases, organized in a hierarchy signalled by up to four levels of indentation. This half-page section and the next section deal with a particularly problematic issue; Innes's ideal for architecture is that it should embody a "public desire," but how can we know, in the absence of any obvious expression of it, that that desire exists, and especially that there is a desire for memory? He proposes that newspapers might be examined "as a way of speculating on the public imagination"—do they express or manufacture public desire?—and proceeds to do that, concluding that they "give an indication (a very structured indication) of what is defined as the public realm" and show "how [the] city sees itself, defines itself: what is public."

Innes's reflective examination of newspapers evidently proved unproductive and his focus shifts unannounced to themes developed in his research thesis—memory, permanence, and death.

—Desire for memory

—Desire for permanence

DEATH = Absence of memory

*REAL DEATH—Thesis p. 27 *[Innes's asterisk]*

To the right of that block of text he has written in smaller script, "Death is a dominant theme in the Iliad ⇒ dealing with death."

Innes has put a large square bracket round the next block of points, and against it has written "in intro." These points are indeed incorporated in the first paragraphs of the proposal:

• Architecture as "heroic"—transcending mortality, an act of defiance or an image of resistance

—Thesis p. 28

—See also Koolhaas essay

—Idea of permanence in architecture supported by weight, mass. (image of)—perhaps contradicted by lightness.

⇒ permanence as desire for memory

Death, heroism and the desire for memory have come from the earlier thesis, but the association of permanence with weight is new and proves central to the design as it emerges.

Despite this final insight, the thinking has hardly yet begun to be architectural; the concepts mainly relate rather to cultural psychology and are of the type that is conventionally dealt with in academic written discourse. The search for a way into a project that will satisfyingly engage with this theme has thrown up a variety of lines of thought, none of which is compelling and some of which lead nowhere and are never heard of again. Getting started is hard.

A couple of days later Innes asks, "What could one fear for the city?" and considers:

fear of death—

—loss of memory of how to live—loss of the grounding for architecture

—What are the different "degrees" of death? (death in the city)

RESISTANCE

—Idea of <u>memory</u> inexorably linked to these ideas

• SPEED—postindustrial technology   —RESISTANCE

• FEAR   —SLOWNESS

• DEATH   —PARTICULARITIES of
                                    architecture

• MEMORY

• PUBLIC LIFE

We note that "grounding" was a term that carried critical weight in the final statement, and that to supplement the continuous propositional discourse of academic explanation the writing starts to build structures of oppositions that have an architectonic quality. Some of the symbolic meanings that will eventually be in play are now being identified, but not the constructional and phenomenological realities that might express them in a building.

The next entry gets to the heart of the societal problem that Innes wishes to address: no memory, no good life:

—If memory is less important, then how one lives is less important; "actions" or their importance diminishes.

(Iliad shows strong example of connection between "well-lived" life and memory.)

The mission of architecture in relation to this problem is "offering 'a fragment of utopia' to hold up for all to see," a formulation that reappears in the continuous prose of the proposal draft handwritten on loose sheets on the same day; one element of the aimed-at *rhetorical* construction has thus already achieved definition and is "in the bag"; others will follow, in an accumulative process that makes itself visible at various separated points throughout the writing.

The writing does not yet begin to reveal the architectural means by which a vision will be held up to the city. On the same page, however, a more specifically architectural mode of thinking enters from another direction and in another medium, in the form of a sketch plan (Figure 4.1) of the nineteenth-century Parliament buildings, graphically emphasizing the distinctive library, a circular building located at a key point of the site.

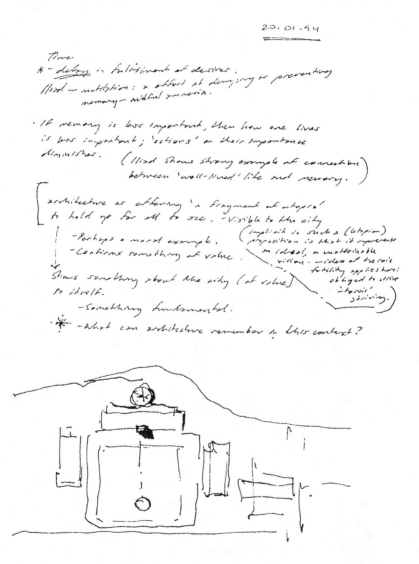

Figure 4.1. Notebook page, 20 January: Plan of Parliament buildings

There follows a verbal attempt to analyze the Parliament buildings in terms of their relation to the city, and to determine "What do the Parliament buildings remember?" No clear answer emerges to this question.

Next day, after a meeting with Barry at which the draft proposal is discussed, Innes is able to achieve a new level of clarity in defining the principles that will underlie his strategy for getting from the (nonarchitectural) civic aspiration to resist amnesia in public life to the determination of a specific built form. He notes that whereas he has been right to thematize a struggle that involves resistance to the prevailing forces of ephemerality and forgetfulness, these forces need to be given a more specific definition

> so that they can be speculated upon as actual spatial/tectonic conditions. (i.e. one must be able to draw them.) This can involve the more specific concerns existing as "sub-sets" of the more general themes.

One page later he begins to identify some of the subsets (Figure 4.2) and arrives at a lucid statement of the logic of his strategy:

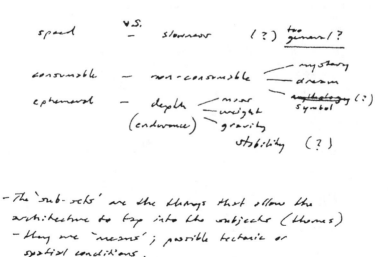

Figure 4.2. Initial schematic representation of the opposed themes, with "sub-sets" of the themes of resistance to the ephemeral

The "sub-sets" are the things that allow the architecture to tap
into the subjects (themes)

—they are "means"; possible tectonic or spatial conditions.

These insights are evidently liberating because two days later (27
January) Innes has shifted into a radically different, and specifically
architectural, mode of thinking, with drawing as the primary genera-
tor (Lawson, 1990) and writing occupying a secondary exegetical role
(Figures 4.3a, 4.3b).

The writing explicates the symbolic meaning that is to be
conveyed by the phenomenological experience of the built structure;
the drawing, on the other hand, begins to create that experience in
two-dimensional representation. On the next page, too, (Figure 4.4),
in considering how one of the "sub-sets," *dream,* might be drawn, the
drawing produces an idea of a different order than what has been
represented in the preceding text.

On 3 February Innes returns to the two pages of drawings
(Figures 4.3a, 4.3b), which he numbers 1-3 and analyzes in two pages
of writing organized under three headings. These headings are the
titles he has now retrospectively given to the drawings: in order of
treatment, "Depth drawing (#3)," "Weight drawing (#1)," and
"Symbol drawing (#2)." The analyses comprise further accounts of the
meaning to be created by the experience of the building. For example:

Weight drawing (#1)

—Speaks of value of "struggling" to resist gravity; the "glory" or
triumph of dealing w/ "weight".

—Idea of figure—Sectional ideas.

  ⇒ As opposed to relative "ease" of skimming the surface.

—Penetrates the layers of (?) mystery rather than skirting
across.

  —an attempt at permanence

  —difficult to "erase" or consume because of the "rhetorical"
  stance—the weight of the stance.

The impression is that in this case the "rationale" for the architectural
configuration is at least partly *post hoc*; Innes has discovered the con-

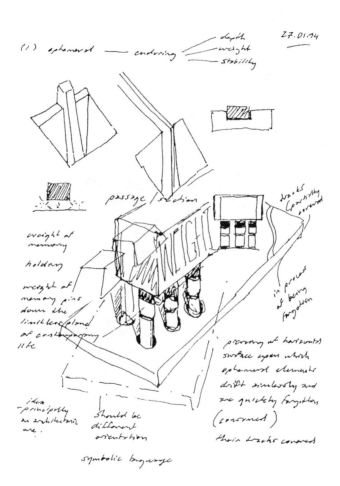

**Figure 4.3a. Facing notebook pages, 27 January:
Approaches to the design.***

---

*The numbers (1), (2), and (3) have been added, probably on 3 February in connection with
the written commentary on the drawings.

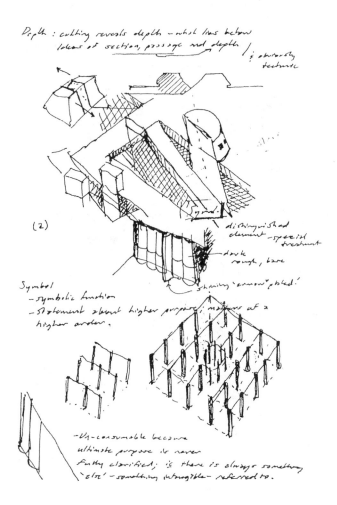

**Figure 4.3b. Facing notebook pages, 27 January:
Approaches to the design.**[*]

---

[*]The numbers (1), (2), and (3) have been added, probably on 3 February in connection with the written commentary on the drawings.

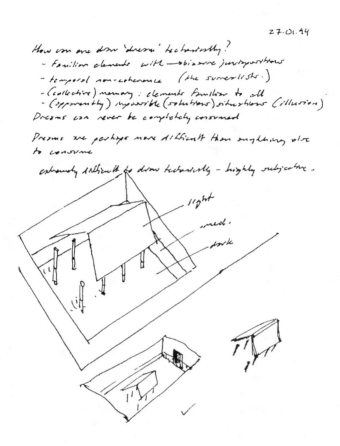

**Figure 4.4. Notebook page, 27 January:
"How can one draw 'dream' tectonically?"**

figuration in drawing and is now confirming that it does indeed fulfill his purposes. How else can one know that one's design meets one's verbally-formulated purposes except by rendering its character in words?

Meanwhile the proposal continues to be revised and developed. The sets of oppositions that had begun to take shape in the notebook take on a more schematic and developed form.

As an extension to the proposal, Barry had suggested that Innes write a description of the roles of the main elements of the building, and this text is appended to the proposal. As Innes explained,

Barry asked me to, actually, after the last meeting. So I describe the role of all these different parts and I gave them these goofy names. So this is the Wall of Eternal Memory.

Naming the things gives them an exactness or precision dramatically that you can then go on and try to achieve architecturally. So I named each thing and described what they did, without . . . it wasn't really a question of addressing the intention. It was more a descriptive account of how each of these things operated. So it's almost described from a point of view of, this is the experience of the building, this is what you encountered and this is how it related to what's come before it. So I do that with the Rare Book and Literary Manuscript Room and the wall. And then with the characters themselves, and then the vault which contains all the master copies of the magnetic and visually recorded information. . . . That clarified for me some of the things that are acting alone and clarified them architecturally. So that was pretty useful.

The first two sections of this new text are "The Wall of Eternal Memory" and "The Transient Characters" (which are small video-viewing spaces and the like):

The Wall of Eternal Memory is characterized by permanence—by the experience of depth, weight, and solidity. It is the very image of immutability—of the persistent desire for a grounding of memory that becomes the foundation for the entire building and by extension the nation, whose collections it carefully protects. The wall proclaims its sober task of holding all else in support. The depth and weight of its location within the earth is parallelled by the depth of the wall itself, revealed to the viewer during his or her descent as a filter which leads to a world of progressively increasing density: the rare book room. Behind the wall lie the deeper truths of posterity—a precious heritage of rare books and literary manuscripts, the core of which is a set of Pre-confederation imprints which tell stories of Canada's foundations: exploration, native culture and practices, voyages, travels, missions, and settlement. . . .

The Transient Characters tell their own stories as they float in the depths, hovering astride the wall of eternal memory. Juxtaposed against the solidity of the wall, they appear ungrounded and somehow adrift. In their fleeting, transitory nature they focus on an ephemeral memory; one which is less concrete and more independent from specific artifacts. The characters contain activities involving viewing: video, microfiche, computer software. They are explored via a system of walkways, bridges and stairs which descend from above. The world within the characters is independent and de-contextualized; relationships to the outside world are not important.

The language here effects verbally the same sort of unnoticed transition from the phenomenological to the symbolic that Innes hopes the building itself will accomplish in a viewer's experience. The literalness of the description of, for instance, the stored texts passes via the description of built features that have "depth" and similar qualities into the designation of meanings such as immutability, fleetingness, and transitoriness, with the aid of terms like "support" and "ungrounded" in which literal and metaphorical senses both operate. The ambiguity of the language is a sort of analogue for the dual experience of the building, as concrete object and as sign.

From this point in the project the forms that the writing takes, alongside those of bulleted sentences and points and of continuous prose, are increasingly diagrammatic—linguistic items organized according to a *visual* semiotic.

Innes is now mainly occupied in mapping in considerable specificity the way a symbolic idea will be rendered in the phenomenological experience of a structure (Figure 4.5).

He has to observe a tricky balance, maintaining a clear rationale for each designed element and avoiding the temptation to fall into less conscious, more intuitive processes of letting the design take him where it will, and at the same time not being seduced by the attractions of rational systems. Recording advice he has received from Barry, Innes notes

"Overall schematic idea of building ⇒ dangerous—get specific."

This relates to the earlier observation that "one must be able to draw them."

At the same time writing continues to be used for other purposes besides the control of meaning, as in an extended, continuous-prose description of the working of the CD-ROM, music, video, and microfiche area:

Master copies of all media kept in "control" safe. ⇒ "locus" of all information storage; the densest region of the zone. Access highly limited to certain members of staff. This locus is surrounded by second "copies" of the [?material] which are available for use—"dissemination" to visitors. The material is located through a cataloguing system and subsequently retrieved by the staff and given to the visitor for use on the appropriate technical system . . . etc.

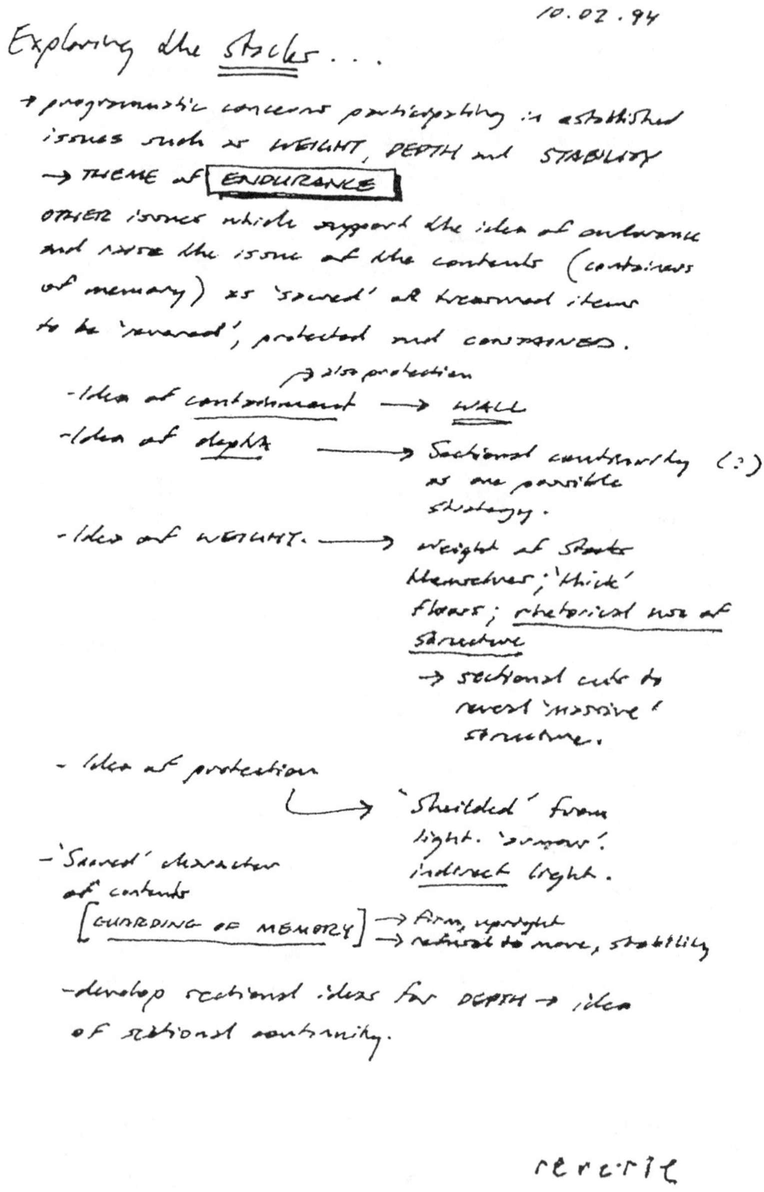

10.02.94

Exploring the stacks...

→ programmatic concerns participating in established issues such as WEIGHT, DEPTH and STABILITY

→ THEME of ENDURANCE

OTHER issues which support the idea of endurance and raise the issue of the contents (containers of memory) as 'sacred' or treasured items to be 'revered', protected and CONTAINED.

- Idea of containment (→ also protection) → WALL
- Idea of depth → Sectional continuity (?) as one possible strategy.
- Idea of WEIGHT. → weight of Stacks themselves; 'thick' floors; rhetorical use of structure
  → sectional cuts to reveal 'massive' structure.
- Idea of protection → 'Shielded' from light. 'sombre'? indirect light.
- 'Sacred' character of contents [GUARDING OF MEMORY] → firm, upright → refusal to move, stability
- develop sectional ideas for DEPTH → idea of sectional continuity.

reverie

Figure 4.5. Notebook page, 10 February: "Exploring the stacks"

This written detailing of the activity of the "zones" yet again prepares the way for another burst of drawing, in Figures 4.6a and 4.6b which develop visually the contrast between the zone just described (area "C") and Area "A," rare books and literary manuscripts.

This sort of written/drawn alternation continues, though the drawing takes place increasingly not in the notebook but on large sheets of drafting paper, which afford the possibility of larger scale and greater detail. Thus in Figures 4.7a and 4.7b (in the notebook) a short text of six words forming a caption to one sketch, and three individual words elsewhere, are enough to anchor the visually represented conditions to the overall thematic intentions.

This drastic reduction in the proportion of writing relative to drawing represents a successful breakthrough into essentially architectural thinking. Writing has for the moment served its purpose as a *design* tool; it continues to be produced but, as the conceptualizing and generative need falls away, its function becomes increasingly that of public justification.

CONCLUSION

Design can go on forever; every fresh drawing can be the basis of further discursive, sometimes written, reflection, which can in turn motivate further drawing. But Innes's project has a deadline, and for a thesis little may be gained by elaboration beyond a certain level. In this study, therefore, we see successive parts of the project achieve a provisionally settled state, a point marked by the almost complete displacement of writing by drawing.

Architecture in the end is working with physical realities like space, light, site, and materials, and the architect's distinctive attribute is a feel for form and material in two-dimensional and three-dimensional space. After a certain point, therefore, design has to proceed in a visual medium so that fertile architectural thinking may be stimulated by the "talkback" (Schön, 1983) from the drawn lines. So it is a switch from writing to drawing that is implied when Barry advises Innes to leave broad schematic conceptualization and "get specific." The result that we saw in the notebook is a change in the relative priority of writing and drawing on those pages where they occur in combination.

The inception of the graphical process is nevertheless informed by purposes developed in writing; the structure that is to be drawn must be such as to bring about a particular verbally defined phenomenological experience in order that a symbolic meaning, also

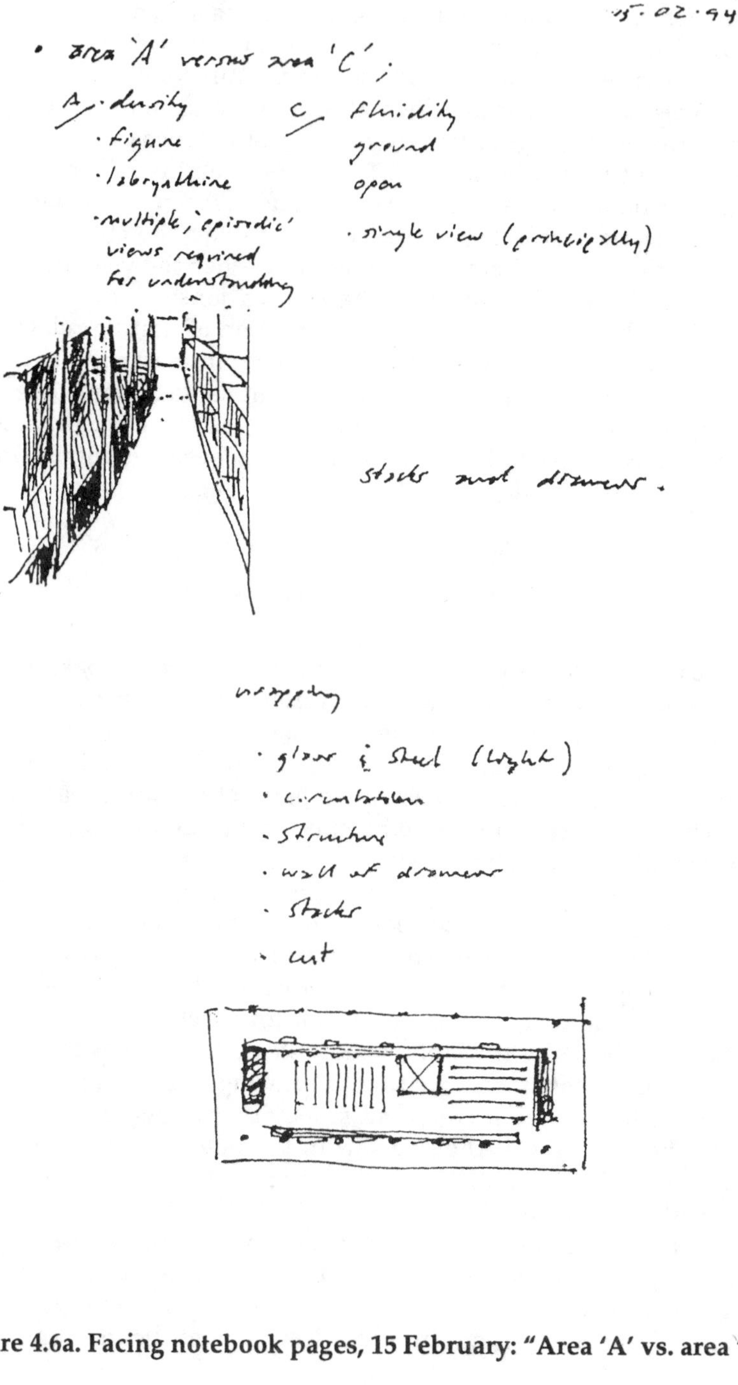

15.02.94

- area 'A' versus area 'C' ;

A, · density   C, fluidity
   · figure   ground
   · labyrinthine   open
   · multiple, 'episodic'   · single view (principally)
     views required
     for understanding

stacks and drawers.

mapping

· glass ¿ steel (light)
· circulation
· structure
· wall of drawers
· stacks
· cut

Figure 4.6a. Facing notebook pages, 15 February: "Area 'A' vs. area 'C'"

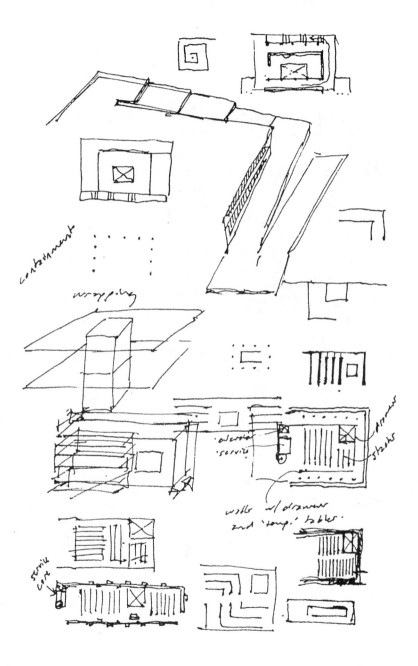

Figure 4.6b. Facing notebook pages, 15 February: "Area 'A' vs. area 'C'"

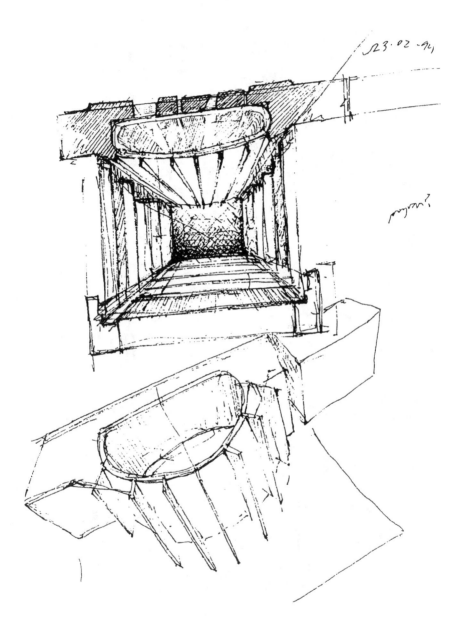

**Figure 4.7a. Facing notebook pages, 23 February:
Depth and containment**

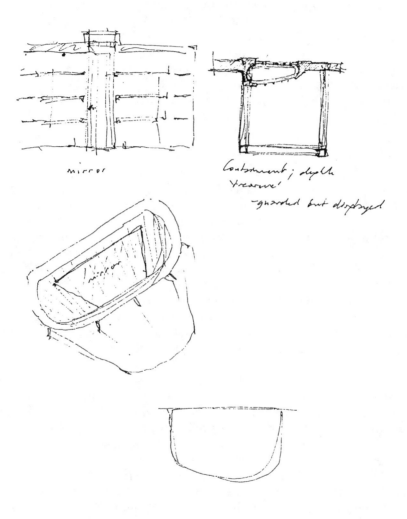

**Figure 4.7b. Facing notebook pages, 23 February:
Depth and containment**

verbally specified, may be conveyed or suggested. The verbal definitions, moreover, often go beyond the determination of symbolic and
phenomenological meanings and reach into the designation of the
physical structure itself. All the same, even the tightest verbal specification leaves options open for the designer who comes to draw the
building, the transition into that mode bringing in a new set of
ideational possibilities that give rise to new discoveries. Any writing
that then occurs in association with the drawing is likely to consist of
sparse labelling, whereas more extensive writing is for taking
account of what has been learned in the other medium; the articulated findings may then in turn inform another incursion into the
graphical, and so on in a dialectical process.

The Vocational Value of Writing

From the perspective of considering transitions from university to
work, Innes's activity appears paradoxical. Here is a learner designer
in the final stage of his academic preparation for the profession who
operates extensively in and relies, for central aspects of his work,
upon a process—writing—that rarely occupies such a role in professional practice. The relative unimportance of writing in office design
procedures may account for its lack of prominence in studio courses;
but in that case why does Innes exploit it so fully?

Part of the answer is that his supervisor, Barry, who has also
been his teacher for important parts of his undergraduate education,
is, somewhat unusually, convinced of the value in design of ways of
writing that are close to design thinking itself. Another part of the
answer is to do with the nature of the thesis, a form of activity that is
remote from workplace practice. The thesis, proceeding as it does from
a verbally framed question or proposition, invites verbal exploration,
even though its more important product will be a design. In addition,
the explicitly rhetorical perspective espoused by Barry encourages the
construction of a kind of verbal analogue to the spatial artifact.

Innes's writing cannot be seen as vocationally relevant practice in a genre closely related to one required at work, as much of it is
not a vehicle of communication, normally remaining unread even by
the teacher. In the thesis process the main sort of language that
appears in public and that matters is speech. It is possible, on the
other hand, to see the writing as in part a preparation for this speaking, and also as having educational value more generally, as learning
to see and speak within a discourse (Dias, Freedman, Medway, &
Paré, 1999). This is discourse in a Foucauldian sense (Fairclough,
1992; Foucault, 1977), a language practice that both represents and

constitutes the epistemic realities of a professional activity. The importance of the discourse that we may feel Innes is consciously exercising and mastering goes beyond communication; more fundamentally, it organizes the field of architecture's operations. Internalized as cognitive resource and deployed in oral discussion, it may well play an important part in professional design practice (though we do not yet have enough evidence on this). Within the school this discourse shows up in many instantiations, another reason that this is not a case of genre as that has recently come to be defined. It does not pertain specifically to either the spoken or the written mode; nor is it ecologically wedded to particular rhetorical situations, appearing indifferently in a student's design notebook or oral presentation, in a visiting critic's spoken remarks, or a professor's course prospectus. Learning the (or a) discourse of architecture involves coming to experience visual and spatial phenomena in particularly structured ways; the discourse enables one to conceptualize design possibilities in terms of a certain constellation of criteria, concerns, and options—such as the four design elements I identified above. "Architectural ways of seeing" depend on distinctions that are marked in language and are learned through a process that is in part one of language learning, although the language may be variously realized in speech, writing, or, presumably, inner speech, and not only in writing.

This may be the best light in which to ask about the audience aspect of the design writing that is seen by no one but the writer. Overtly, there is no audience but the writer's later self, but it is clearly unsatisfying to regard that observation as final. If the student is engaging in a discourse, his or her utterances are informed thereby with a particular addressivity. The answer to the audience question—the question of the latent or unacknowledged dialogic partner—is presumably to be gained by asking, Who gets talked to like this? Of what exchanges are these sorts of terms, discriminations, rhetorical moves, exemplifications, relationships of concrete to abstract, and so on, imagined by the student to be typical? In exchanges with whom are they thought to occur? Clearly, with other architects. Innes is speaking to himself but also, to an extent, to an idealized representative of Architecture—a representative who is also, perhaps, the double of the professional self he expects to become.

Writing for design seems in addition to serve a second educational function. It requires the student to make the design process explicit and therefore open to reflection, analysis, and evaluation. In particular, it is likely to induce awareness of the linguistic component of design. It brings into salience the distinction and the interrelationship between two modes of design, and makes it apparent that aspects of drawing and three-dimensional visualisation are under the control of ideas that are essentially nonvisual and that are capable of being, though in regular practice they may not usually be, expressed in language; and that there are ways of thinking that are specifically visual and that cannot be derived from or "read off" any discursive idea. One learns what pertains uniquely and inescapably to a particular medium, and what may or must be done across media; what normally looks like a straightforward graphical process of design visualization may actually be a joint production of visual thinking and an inner *speech* structured by a learned, verbally anchored discourse. Writing separates out and makes appear what really belongs to the verbal. At the same time, the experience of moving between writing and drawing makes student designers aware to what extent their ideas are shaped by the semiotic media in which they are framed.

Innes has learned, not necessarily explicitly, that there are areas where one may slide easily between verbal and graphical thinking and other areas where the differences are irreducible and the two modes are autonomous. So, as we saw, various sorts of *meanings* that the building is to have may be verbally designated, but no amount of such definition will give rise to a specific spatial configuration; devising the latter involves bringing in realities that do not feature in the discourse. Whereas the symbolic ("thematic") and phenomenological meanings that the building is to enact may be identified with verbal labels, it takes a visual representation to begin to make them happen experientially. (In regular architectural practice, of course, outside the school of architecture, there is a further experiential chasm between the drawn image and the actuality of a constructed building.) Barry is a believer in the value of writing in design; but he is also aware of its limits, and of the danger of seduction by one's own schematic constructions. In the end it is important to preserve the distinction:

> You can certainly develop an architectural idea in writing. . . .
> Thomas More's *Utopia* is an architectural project of sorts. Just
> like you can do architectural ideas in drawing. My only real argu-
> ment is with going from that ability to also equate them and say-
> ing that now they're the same because they're both architectural,
> because in the end the writing still has to follow the rules of writ-
> ing. In a work of architecture, it should follow the rules of archi-
> tecture. They're not necessarily the same. So, they might refer to
> an architectural essence, but as they become divergent . . . they're
> parallel activities, I think.

Writing and Architectural Work

The main conclusions of this study are that language, even though it might not be vocalized or written, is probably essential to design, and that writing is well capable of being the medium in which the linguistic aspect of design is carried out. Design questions and themes are expressible in words—if not directly then at least, according to Barry, "by analogy":

> I mean, they can never be replaced by those words. So I don't think the design question is ever one that can solve something in a way, say, a discourse can solve something. But you can perhaps lay out a thematic structure linguistically.

The "thematic" function, we recall, is what I referred to as symbolic. We saw that one of the essential uses of language in design is to allow the question of the experience and meaning of the building to be considered articulately and rationally. It may be true that buildings should "speak for themselves" without the aid of "program notes," but, as Barry says,

> the idea that it speaks for itself still implies that there is something being said.

It is useful, at least pedagogically, for the "something being said" to be articulated in words:

> In a school situation it's our job, at least I consider it my job to help students develop ways of doing what they want to do. And also to deal with the effect, if you're presenting something. Let's say it's a fifth-year thesis where a student's meant to have some competence. If the thing is not evoking anything then I think that's a reasonable discussion point, or if it's evoking a series of disparate or fragmentary allusions. So we can use language to try and decipher where the thing has gone wrong. Or we can do it in other ways, we can just redraw for the student, but that's considerably slower.

A final speculation: might it be that the transition from an industrial to a postindustrial economy, and perhaps from a goods-centered to a person-centered society, will lead to a shift in priorities away from the functional efficiency of the objects, environments, systems, and arrangements we live in, and toward their phenomenological character as entities to be lived *with* and even their symbolic value in reminding us of what is important about who we are? If that is correct, we may all need to learn that there is "something to be said" in those neglected realms of meaning; and the verbal representational challenges, currently so arcane-seeming, that are faced by architects like Innes and Barry, may become a central concern for the study and teaching of writing.

APPENDIX

Thesis Precis
The Memory Net
Design Thesis, 1994
Carleton University School of Architecture
Innes Yates
Tutor:Barry Bell
Committee member:***
Other:***

As with virtually every aspect of public and private life in the contemporary city, urban experience has been affected by technological developments which have come to be collectively termed the "digital revolution." These effects have exhibited both positive and negative aspects. The results of the digital revolution have in some cases dramatically enhanced traditional modes of thought and experience, and created entirely new ones. The efficiency, communicability, speed, and surreal quality of a digital world creates a strange attraction— even an intoxication—which seems to appeal to desires which run deeper than those for mere efficiency and productivity. This may be interpreted as a desire for effortless communication: as a dream of a global culture held together by an invisible network of electronic communication, unhindered by the weight, time, distance and physicality of the "real" world. While none of these desires are inherently negative, an increasing emphasis on or fascination with ephemera may be problematic in the context of public life. At a fundamental level, this problem has to do with the loss of memory.

Perhaps the most problematic aspect of this condition is the apparent lack of public fear surrounding the notion of a world which threatens anything solid with rapid dissolution. Through its neglect of the phenomenal nature of physical experience, such a world potentially negates the public realm, replacing the desire for collectivity with an electronically mediated reality, at the expense of the world of urban experience and human exchange. Unless consciously developed, the deeper mysteries, enigmas, and discoveries of urban life are threatened with replacement by a world of immediacy and artificial clarity. Memory is replaced by amnesia: the instantaneous consumption and gratification of an ephemeral, digital world. For public life, this vision represents a kind of death.

Within such a condition, architecture holds a unique status. Through sheer physical fact, architecture responds to a desire for permanence; it represents the values of order, grounding, and the establishment of place. Although it may frequently refer to conditions of movement, attempt to negate its fixity or dissolve its solidity, ultimately its physicality can never be successfully denied. Despite any intention to the contrary, architecture persistently preserves the memory of some value or desire and shows it to the city. Through this unique capacity, architecture's role may emerge as one of resistance to the corrosive effects of cultural amnesia upon both a memory of public life, and the desire for memory itself.

How can architecture resist death—as the diffusion of amnesia—and remember how to live? One possible focus is the struggle to remember itself; on the importance of establishing a memory that becomes a part of public life. The library is one public institution which clearly exhibits a desire for memory as a basis for fuelling multiple desires: information, knowledge, reflection, and dreaming.

The vehicle for exploring this question is the design of a Special Collections Library for the National Library of Canada. The program is comprised of four key areas, each of which involves a particular understanding of memory:

1. Rare Book Collection
   Literary Manuscript Collection
   Theses Collection

2. Newspaper Collection
   Software Collection
   Video Collection

3. Music Collection
   Audio Room

4. Reading Room

The building proposes that the public realm encompasses a greater presence than that which can be immediately viewed, consumed, and forgotten. As a strategy for resistance, it attempts to convince of the value of searching for this world.

The primary concern of the building is to link the experience of attainment with the experience of grounding; of a deeply rooted, permanent foundation which prevails despite the shifting, chaotic world around it. This is attempted by focusing on thematic concerns, chosen for their mnemonic value and potential capacity to support an idea of resistance. Themes such as lightness, expansion, clarity, and control are explored in conjunction with themes of depth, weight, density, and containment. These ideas are further elaborated and connected through encounters involving ideas of threshold, horizon, and ascension.

REFERENCES

Applebee, A. (1984). Writing and reasoning. *Review of Educational Research, 54*, 577-596.

Bachelard, G. (1994). *The poetics of space* (M. Jolas, Trans.). Boston: Beacon Press.

Department of Education and Science. (1975). *A language for life. Report of the Committee of Inquiry* (the Bullock Report). London: HMSO.

Dias, P., Freedman, A., Medway, P., & Paré, A. (1999). *Worlds apart: Acting and writing in academic and workplace contexts.* Mahwah, NJ: Erlbaum.

Emig, J. (1977). Writing as a mode of learning. *College Composition and Communication, 28*, 122-128

Fairclough, N. (1992). *Discourse and social change.* Cambridge: Polity Press.

Foucault, M. (1977). *Discipline and punish* (A. Sheridan, Trans.). New York: Vintage.

Lawson, B. (1990). *How designers think* (2nd ed.). London: Butterworth Architecture.

Medway, P. (1996a). Writing, speaking, drawing: The distribution of meaning in architects' communication. In M. Sharples & T. van der Geest (Eds.), *The new writing environment: Writers at work in a world of technology* (pp. 25-42). London: Springer Verlag.

Medway, P. (1996b) Virtual and material buildings: Construction and constructivism in architecture and writing. *Written Communication, 13*(4), 473-514.

Schön, D. (1983). *The reflective practitioner: How professionals think in action.* New York: Basic Books.

Smagorinsky, P. (1995). Constructing meaning in the disciplines: Reconceptualising writing across the curriculum as composing across the curriculum. *American Journal of Education, 103*, 160-184.

Winsor, D. (1994). Invention and writing in technical work. *Written Communication, 11*(2), 227-250.

Witte, S. P. (1992). Context, text, intertext: Toward a constructivist semiotic of writing. *Written Communication, 9*(2), 237-308.

CHAPTER 5

Bridging the Gap: University-Based Writing that is More than Simulation[1]

Aviva Freedman & Christine Adam
Carleton University

As repeated studies have shown (see, for example, Anson & Forsberg, 1990; Freedman & Adam, 1996; MacKinnon, 1993), the transition from university to workplace is often jarring. And it is typically with respect to acquiring workplace-specific discourse that the difficulties reveal themselves. Workplace writing, even when it appears to deal with the same content, is radically different in its social action (Miller, 1984) from university writing: the "rhetorical exigence" (Bitzer, 1968) and the sociopolitical context necessitate social motives, stances, and reader-writer relationships that are fundamentally different from those involved in the university classroom.

In an earlier essay (Freedman, Adam, & Smart, 1994), we attempted to highlight the nature of such differences by contrasting actual workplace discourse with university-based case-study writing, which attempted to simulate workplace discourse in the same field of endeavor through the use of actual case histories and role-playing.

[1]Portions of this chapter appear in Dias, P., Freedman, A., Medway, P., & Paré, A. (1999). *Worlds apart: Acting and writing in academic and workplace contexts*. Mahwah, NJ: Erlbaum.

Our analysis revealed that no matter how authentic the case histories seemed, the writing undertaken by the students was shaped primarily by the real rhetorical and institutional context in which the writing was staged—that is, the university classroom (see also Dias, Freedman, Medway, & Paré, 1999).

A potential conclusion from this analysis is that it is simply not possible at all to prepare students for the rhetorical demands of a workplace while operating within the institutional constraints of a university classroom. (Clearly internships and co-op programs do offer appropriate exposure, but the writing undertaken in such programs is almost always situated within the work world—as, for example, in the situation described by Paré [this volume]. The question we raise here is about writing assigned within the confines of a credit-bearing course offered on-site at the university.) The course that will be described in the pages that follow, however, provides a counterinstance. As we shall see, the instructor was able to create a facilitative context in which a useful bridge to workplace discourse was constructed. She was able to use her classroom as a site for practice in and real engagement with authentic workplace discourse.

Our goals in this chapter are to describe this course, to contrast the kind of writing elicited there with the kinds of "simulations" referred to in our earlier essay (Freedman, Adam, & Smart, 1994) and, finally, to specify why such successful instances of bridging the gap between university and workplace discourse are both possible and, necessarily, exceptional by their very nature.

THEORETIC BACKGROUND

The theoretic framework in which this study has been situated is the recently developed subfield of genre studies. In the past few years, the notion of genre has been reconceived: rather than referring simply to sets of textual regularities or text-types, genres have come to be seen, in the words of Miller's seminal 1984 piece, as social action or "typified rhetorical responses to recurring situations." It is not that textual regularities do not exist, but rather that these textual regularities have come to be seen as correlates or indications of larger contextual regularities—social, cultural, ideological, political.

To be more specific, the situations that elicit the rhetorical responses extend beyond the specific task set to the larger discursive context within which the task is set, to the sociopolitical context of the setter(s) of the tasks as well as of the rhetors or writers, to the larger institutional setting with its attendant values and political position and positionings, as well as to the larger cultural frames and ideological underpinnings. In all this, it is important to recognize that, again according to Miller (1984), the "recurrence" in the recurring situations and the "exigence" which elicit the rhetorical response are themselves socially constructed.

At the same time, Bakhtinian (1986) notions are powerfully represented in recent genre studies: genres are seen as essentially dialogic—anticipating readers' responses and responding to, as well as picking up on, earlier "conversations"; at the same time, genres are sites of struggle and contestation between centrifugal and centripetal ideologic and linguistic forces (see discussion by Schryer, 1994).

Using this theoretic context, we have been looking at genres of student writing produced at the university and genres of writing produced by professionals occupying the kinds of positions that our students are preparing for. What has become very clear, using this prism, is the degree to which writing at university differs, and *necessarily* differs, from workplace writing—even when the disciplinary focus is shared. In order to dramatize and provide sharper definition to the contrast, as part of our research we have focused on those kinds of academic writing that aimed at bridging the gap.

WRITING FOR THE PRACTICUM

Our primary focus in this chapter is on a fourth-year practicum course in a business school, a course in systems analysis. The course is organized as follows. Every year that she teaches the course, the instructor finds six client groups or organizations who need to have some aspect of their workplace computerized or some aspect that is already computerized redesigned. A total of 30 students is allowed to register, and students are selected according to their performance in a more technically oriented course taught by the same instructor the previous semester. Each client group agrees to meet with the students for a minimum of fifteen hours.

The instructor divides the students into groups of five. Criteria for the make-up of specific groups include the following: each group is assigned at least one student who is majoring in business, at least one who is majoring in computing, as well as at least one who has a car. A cardinal rule is that friends are to be separated, so that students gain experience working with people that they are not already familiar with. Student groups then draw the name of their client from a hat. The instructor then briefs each group on the specific problem that they will work on in that work environment. In order to do so, and in the course of doing so, the students produce the following three kinds of documents:

1. a problem definition document (on the basis of a feasibility study);
2. a systems specification document (on the basis of their systems analysis), to include several feasible alternatives as well as a recommended course of action;
3. a general design document (based on the client's selection of one of the alternatives from 2).

The course is a half-course, and the time-line is carefully spelled out at the beginning; NOTHING is handed in late.

In order to perform these tasks, students must go to the workplace to interview a range of participants there—the range determined by the needs and possibilities of that specific work environment. At the first interview, they are accompanied by the course instructor, who guides the interview when necessary and spends considerable time after the interview with the students involved going over what was learned.

In addition, each group reports back orally to the class as a whole three times, giving oral versions of their drafts of each of the three key documents. Almost all groups invite their clients to these class sessions as well. After their oral presentations, they receive feedback from the class, hand in their written document to the instructor, and then, at a separately scheduled interview, receive intensive feedback from her as to appropriate revisions. Sometimes further interviews with her are necessary; when she is satisfied, the written document is presented to the client, sometimes accompanied by an oral presentation in the workplace, if the client so desires.

The advantages of this process and these tasks are enormous. First, they are authentic tasks. As the professor said about this course (Duxbury & Chinneck, 1993), "the process involves coping systematically with the complexities of the real world, including both human and technological limitations." Students have to "limit the area of study, abstract essential features, subdivide a complex whole into parts of manageable size and model a real system to show the relationship among its components." As opposed to the preceding lecture course in systems analysis and design, which gives the students a tremendous amount of technical information, this course "conveys the real-world people skills needed to be a good systems analyst. The communication skills, diplomacy and other human issues are not easily transmitted in a book or in the classroom."

Second, according to the professor, this authenticity provided a taste of the complexity of workplace activity: "Students gain experience in handling ambiguous situations and in developing solutions subject to real-world constraints. Working with actual problems also develops analytical skills and problem-solving abilities, gives an understanding of the importance of organizational influences on systems design and the impact that a user-requested change has on the analysis and design process."

More specifically, the professor lists some of the strengths of the program as follows:

1. Students gain a "more global perspective on the systems analysis process";
2. Students "learn to work cooperatively in groups";
3. Students learn to "critique each other";
4. The tasks "enable students to integrate the knowledge gained from other business courses."

For us, however, the most striking feature was the degree to which the writing elicited indeed approximated workplace discourse from a range of perspectives. Perhaps the best way of clarifying the degree to which this was accomplished is by contrasting such writing with the case-study writing analyzed in Freedman, Adam, and Smart (1994). Like the course in financial analysis which elicited the case-study writing, the practicum course is situated within a university context: it has a course number, it counts as a half-credit towards a degree, and it is constrained by the time-limits of a single semester. There are, however, other important ways in which it is different, ways that reveal themselves especially when we think in terms of the rhetorical exigences.

CASE STUDY SIMULATIONS

The case-study writing involved simulations based on actual case histories, in which students were asked to write reports as though they were managers or consultants to boards of directors of real companies, suggesting courses of action for the beleaguered companies at particular historical moments of crisis. Students were expected to write their reports using a workplace format, with an executive summary at the beginning and the format one might expect in a business setting; at the same time, they were asked to deliver oral summaries of their written reports, while dressing like consultants and using professional accoutrements, such as overheads and briefcases.

Although there were important similarities to workplace writing (and consequently a rationale for the simulation), the discourse produced differed in fundamental ways from workplace writing, as Figure 5.1 indicates and as we explain below.

Real audience
For the case-study writing, despite the simulation, the real audience was not a board of directors (that the students in the class were sup-

	Case-Study Writing	Workplace Writing
Real Audience	Instructor	Supervisor
Social Motive	Epistemic	Praxis oriented
		Policy oriented
Reader's Primary Concern	Writer's knowing	Ultimate senior reader
	therefore	*therefore*
	Specification of shared knowledge	Omission of shared knowledge
	Concerns about plagiarism	Institutional intertextuality
	Originality	Collaboration
Goal of the Reader	To rank	To ensure the best text
Reader's Comments	Justify grade	Collaborative
		Revision oriented
Closure	Grade	Life beyond initial reading
		Indeterminate material consequences and readerships

Figure 5.1. Differences between case-study and workplace writing

posed to simulate) but the instructor—in his role as instructor, that is, as representative of a discipline and teaching a course within the university.

Social motive

Miller (1984) introduces the term "social motive" in her rhetorical analysis of genre as typified responses to socially constructed exigence. Broadly, the social motive of the case-study writing (like that of most academic writing and in contrast with the workplace writing) was identified as "epistemic" rather than action oriented, to use a distinction developed by Willard (1982). Willard differentiated between two kinds of arguments within the same disciplinary field: that kind of argument whose aim is knowledge oriented versus that kind whose aim is action oriented. An example is the distinction between the arguments of legal scholars, on the one hand, and those of practising lawyers, on the other.

That distinction proved very illuminating in our analysis. In the workplace we observed, all the writing—even in the research division—had a bottom-line value: its relevance to policy. By contrast, in the case-study writing, although the purported goal was to suggest a course of action, in fact the real goal was to show that the students knew the appropriate warrants and backing to ground appropriate courses of action, in the context of the discipline presented in this particular course (financial analysis). This became dramatically clear in one tape-recorded composing process, when students started working through one potential solution for a case, and stopped short suddenly: "Whoops, that would make it into a marketing case." And this was a course in finance. Wrong course. Find another solution.

Reader's primary concern

Related to the social motive, the focus of the case-study writing was on the writer: both the reader and the writer were concerned primarily with the writer's knowing, and the text existed to provide evidence of that knowing. For that reason, far more had to be spelled out (as corroboration of that knowing) than would be spelled out in an actual workplace report: even that which could be assumed to be shared knowledge between writer and reader. (See Giltrow & Valiquette, 1994, for a discussion of this phenomenon in student writing.) The instructor was also willing to forgive defects in the text, as long as there were indications of the student's knowing in the text and in the context of what the instructor knew about the student in classroom performance.

In the workplace, the focus of the writing was oriented towards some superior reader and towards producing a text that would take into account that reader's time limitations and knowledge base. Shared knowledge did not have to be spelled out. On the contrary, brevity was valued. For the same kinds of reasons, originality is not a requirement of the workplace, nor is proof that the writer has worked alone.

Goal of the assigner of the writing task

In the university, even case-study writing is evaluation oriented. To put it another way, instructors have a vested interest in a quality spread: it is important that there be some As (as confirmation that the appropriate teaching has taken place), but it is equally important that there be many Bs and Cs. Something that underlies everything that transpires at the university, and that so easily becomes invisible to us in its normalcy, is the institution's function as a gatekeeper. This function is not incidental, something that we must contend with from time to time and can ignore until, say, the actual time for reporting grades; it is pervasive and powerful, shaping the dynamics of the rhetorical exigence in powerful and ineluctable fashion. The goal is for the writing to be evaluated. This contrasts sharply with the workplace, where the employer's interest is in getting the best possible piece from all employees each time they write.

Reader's comments

The mode of reading is dictated by the reader's goals. The instructor reads with a view to evaluating (often reading a whole set of student assignments at the same time), and the comments written on the texts are focused on justifying the grades. In the workplace, the supervisor reads, often with pencil in hand, to improve the text, and the comments are made with the expectation that the writer will indeed incorporate those comments in future revisions.

Closure

Finally, for the case-study writing, as with most school writing, closure is achieved when the grade is given. Often the writing has no physical existence beyond that point. Typically, too, there is only a single one-time reader. In contrast, in the workplace, texts have a continued existence beyond any specific reader's response: there are many potential readers, and consequently a text has an extended and indeterminate function within the organization/workplace.

There are other differences, but we focus on these because they allow us to highlight ways in which the practicum writing becomes more like workplace writing, while still functioning within the institutional context of the university.

Writing for the Practicum

Figure 5.2 summarizes the contrasts among all three kinds of writing (case-study writing, writing for the practicum, and writing for the workplace), revealing the degree to which the practicum course functions as a way of bridging the gap.

	Case-Study Writing	Practicum Writing	Workplace Writing
Audience	Instructor	Instructor and client	Supervisor
Social Motive	Epistemic	Action oriented (+ epistemic)	Action oriented
Reader's Primary Concern	Writer's knowing *therefore:* •Specification of shared knowledge •Concerns about plagiarism •Originality	Value to client *therefore:* •Omission of shared knowledge •Institutional intertextuality •Collaboration	Value to senior reader *therefore:* •Omission of shared knowledge •Institutional intertextuality •Collaboration
Goals of the Reader	To grade	To ensure best text	To ensure best text
Reader's Comments	To justify grade	Collaborative Revision oriented	Collaborative Revision oriented
Closure	With grade	Life beyond initial reading Indeterminate material consequences and readerships	Life beyond initial reading Indeterminate material consequences and readerships

Figure 5.2. Differences between case-study, practicum, and workplace writing

Audience

Our analyses of student interactions, presentations, composing sessions, and drafts show how the practicum course offered an interesting hybrid of features from the university and the workplace—a kind of bridge across the gap between the two. The audience was both instructor and client. The instructor was always the first reader and her views, as evaluator and collaborator/expert, were always important. At the same time, the students always referred to their clients and to their clients' needs and goals in their composing sessions.

One indication of the hybrid nature of this transaction was that students kept having to adjust the amount of shared knowledge they provided. In the dialogue below, we witness a student group trying to determine whether they need to define "salary forecasting" for the other students in the class who will be watching their presentation.

Jill: I mean it [the definition] does not necessarily have to be in the written thing, but just in the presentation itself. I mean, I can see, you know, for three hours, people are just sitting in their chairs like bumps on logs. It just does not make sense.

Ivy: But if that's what she wants . . .

Jill: Well, you are having like thirty people sitting in the classroom . . .

Arthur: OK, what do we wanna do? Explain them or—what do we want?

Ivy: What is a "salary forecast," what is that, and why is it? Why do we have . . . ?

Marco: How much time do we have [for the presentation]?

Arthur: Oh, we have about twenty minutes.

Jill: Twenty minutes, ya. I mean we can say briefly, ya, taking three lines and say "salary forecasting is basically," you know, "knowing how much money you're gonna spend on the people you employ . . ."

Ivy: And how much is left . . .

Jill: Ya, and making sure you have enough left during the year to pay them off.

Ivy: That was a good definition.

Jill: Ya, I mean just something like that, so that people aren't like, well, what's "salary forecasting?"

******

Arthur: OK, it sounds good for the presentation, but I wonder whether we have to include it in the document?

Jill: No, I mean the document is basically for us and for the client, and for Susan [the instructor]. And, I mean, they know what they want from us. They know what it is, but I am just saying, for the presentation—I mean we could make some mention of it.

As they went from presenting their documents to the class and instructor to preparing the document for their clients, they needed to revise the amount and kind of shared information: a recurrent feature of their revision was the removal of information that they could assume to be shared with their clients.

Social motive

What distinguished the practicum writing from the case-study writing (and other university writing) was its underlying social motive. The social motive of the practicum writing, like that of the workplace, was to recommend real-world action. The student recommendations were taken seriously and, in all cases, were acted on in the workplace.

The success of the projects was measured by the degree to which they solved the workplace problem, as determined by the actors in the workplace. The instructor's own evaluation was always guided by what she perceived to be the workplace evaluation. The degree to which workplace criteria dominated was revealed when one group of students discovered that the solution to a particular problem could be found quite simply through applying a new piece of software that the clients were not familiar with. For the clients, the software solved the problem. For the students, this discovery truncated the entire process originally demarcated in the assignment. Significantly, the instructor simply congratulated the students on their fortuitous find, and awarded them the same grade as other students who ended up putting in countless hours to solve their clients' problem. We suspect that, if she were guided by considerations arising out of the context of a typical university assignment, this instructor would have asked this group of student to do some supplemental work—as a means of eliciting more learning (and as a means of ensuring equity within the classroom). In this course, however, she chose to establish as a social motive the motive of the workplace. This choice was to have the most far-reaching significance, as we shall see in the discussions below.

Readers' roles and goals

One consequence was the radically changed role of the instructor. She functioned more as supervisor than as evaluator: she collaborated with the students extensively; she accompanied them to the first interview, and discussed the interview with them afterwards, carefully pointing to key features and eliciting appropriate understanding; for each piece of writing, she both evaluated (gave a low grade at the beginning) and wrote extensive suggestions for revision, insisting that they revise until they produced the best possible text to be submitted to the client.

In the episode below, Susan, the instructor, meets with a student group to discuss the comments she has written on their initial draft of the problem definition report.

> Susan: Only two groups don't have to rehand it in [to me for evaluation], and you're one of them.
>
> Marco: Hey! (laughter)
>
> Susan: Very well written, um . . .
>
> Jill: Can we redo it if we want to?
>
> Susan: What?
>
> Jill: Can we rewrite it if we want to?
>
> Susan: Oh, I *want* you to rewrite it for your client. I mean, just 'cause it's the best [received the best grade among the student groups] doesn't mean that there are not changes. Okay? But they're minimal compared to the other groups'. . . . Here's all my comments and everything at the back.

The instructor then went through the report with the students, explaining each of the comments she had made. It is interesting to note here that all of the comments written on this report indicated changes that had to be made. Nowhere were there comments that justified the grade which had been assigned, and nowhere were there indications that the instructor was looking for evidence of student learning or mastery of particular disciplinary content.

This points to a larger kind of difference. This writing that the students were doing in the practicum was different from typical student writing in that the instructor regarded the writing as a reflection of her (and the university) in much the same way that a subordinate's writing is a reflection of the manager. This stands in sharp contrast to instructors' typical attitudes towards their students' writing, as Southam, an executive officer in a government agency who also taught an evening course in the public administration program, explained:

> [In the workplace] I feel it's more a reflection of me if someone's writing for me and then it has to be straightened out. I'm perhaps more critical, whereas in the case of a student's paper, I don't really have that much attachment to it other than did they learn what I wanted them to learn. . . . If someone's doing something for me [at work] I view it as part of my work, so I take it a little more seriously. It reflects me and other things as well.

Closure
Finally, to return to our comparisons, the case-study writers felt closure when the grade was given, and the texts ceased to have importance (and often physical existence) at that point. For the practicum, the writing was graded, but its existence was not delimited or circumscribed by that grade: the documents led a continued and indeterminate existence in the clients' workplace; like written documents we had observed in other agencies, their completion indicated their entry into a larger arena where their continued physical existence as documents along with their potential for material consequences could only be guessed at.

The instructor also encouraged the students to keep final drafts of these reports to use in the future at job interviews as evidence of their ability not only to conduct systems analysis but also to produce appropriate documentation. All of the students we interviewed in the class did keep copies; in one case we know of, a student took his group's written reports with him on all of his job interviews, and was offered a summer job doing systems analysis in a large local software firm.

The Exception That Proves the Rule

To conclude, although this course is a dramatic example of a wonderfully scaffolded introduction to workplace writing, at the same time, it also reveals the degree to which it is and must remain an exceptional course for the following reasons, among others.

1. This course was extremely time intensive to the instructor. Each year, new clients had to be found, with new problems, and the instructor invested a lot of time in working with students (who are free to call her at all hours). It is noteworthy that when this particular instructor could not teach the course, it was taught in a traditional university-course format.

2. The course had to be limited in terms of numbers—because there were a limited number of clients, and because the instructor had limited time. So only a few students—and only the best—were allowed to register.

3. Perhaps most significantly, all the students had to be able to receive As. No grade spread was required—as opposed to the expectations placed on every other course. The instructor had to make a special arrangement with the university to allow this to occur.

This kind of arrangement is only possible because it is rare, indeed exceptional, and the case must be made each time the course is given. In other words, there must be some kind of assurance that this course will not interfere with the overall gate-keeping function of the institution. The course is countenanced because it is an exception, and in that sense, it is the exception that verifies the rule concerning the fundamental and necessary radical differences between the rhetorical contexts of university and workplace.

This course, because it is an exception, provides a useful perspective on workplace-university differences. At the same time, it points as well to other kinds of programs (not so directly university based) that might allow for easier and more easily scaffolded transitions to authentic workplace writing contexts—sheltered co-ops, internships, apprenticeships.

SUMMARY

To sum up then, in our analysis of case-study writing (Freedman, Adam, & Smart, 1994), we pointed to the degree to which this writing was shaped by the rhetorical exigence of the university context despite the simulation attempted. The case-study writing thus revealed the degree to which the university context differs in profound and far-reaching ways from that of the workplace—ways that elicit very different genres.

The writing we observed in the practicum also points to the radical gulf between the two settings but in a very different way. In fact, the practicum writing was very much like that of the workplace:

in the social roles taken on by the students and instructor, in the writers' sense of audience, in its textual features (e.g., shared information, surplus of corroborating detail), and most markedly in the responding and collaborative reading practices of its first reader—the instructor (see Figure 5.3).

What is significant about the practicum writing, however, is the degree to which it differs from typical university writing and the degree to which it is tolerated within that context only as long as it remains an exception. One such course is tolerated, and then only because the best students were allowed entry.

In the end, our investigation of the processes and products of this practicum course produced findings much like those in our analysis of case-study writing. There exists an inevitable, and necessary, gulf between the writing contexts of the workplace and the context of the university. The practicum course provides evidence for this gulf by the

INSTITUTIONAL
CONTEXT—
UNIVERSITY

RHETORICAL
EXIGENCE
Socially constructed by
the university

Academic Essays

Case Studies

Practicum Reports

Co-op Writing

Professional Genres

INSTITUTIONAL
CONTEXT—
WORKPLACE

RHETORICAL
EXIGENCE
Socially constructed by
the workplace

Figure 5.3. Transition from university to workplace discourse

nature of its success in bridging it—that is, by the fact of its exception-
ality. The practicum course *is* the exception that proves the rule.

REFERENCES

Anson, C.N., & Forsberg, L.L. (1990). Moving beyond the academic
community: Transitional stages in professional writing. *Written
Communication, 7*(2), 200-231.

Bakhtin, M.M. (1986). *Speech genres and other late essays.* (C.
Emerson & M. Holquist. Eds., V.W. McGee, Trans.). Austin:
University of Texas Press.

Bitzer, L.F. (1968). On the classification of discourse performances.
Rhetorical Society Quarterly, 7, 31-40.

Dias, P., Freedman, A., Medway, P., & Paré, A. (1999). *Worlds apart:
Acting and writing in academic and workplace contexts.*
Mahway, NJ: Erlbaum.

Duxbury, L., & Chinneck, J. (1993). *The practicum approach to the
teaching of systems analysis and design: A view from the trench-
es.* Paper presented at Administrative Sciences Association of
Canada, Lake Louise, AB.

Freedman, A., & Adam, C. (1996). Learning to write professionally:
"Situated Learning" and the transition from university to pro-
fessional discourse. *Journal of Business and Technical
Communication, 10,* 395-427.

Freedman, A., Adam, C., & Smart, G. (1994). Wearing suits to class:
Simulating genres and simulations as genre. *Written
Communication, 11,* 192-226.

Giltrow, J., & Valiquette, M. (1994). Genres and knowledge: Students
writing in the disciplines. In A. Freedman & P. Medway (Eds.),
Learning and teaching genre (pp. 47-62). Portsmouth, NH:
Boynton/Cook Heinemann.

MacKinnon, J. (1993). Becoming a rhetor: The development of on-the-
job writing ability. In R. Spilka (Ed.), *Writing in the workplace:
New research perspectives* (pp. 41-55). Carbondale: Southern
Illinois University Press.

Miller, C. (1984). Genre as social action. *Quarterly Journal of Speech,
70,* 151-167.

Schryer, C. (1994). The lab vs. the clinic: Sites of competing genres.
In A. Freedman & P. Medway (Eds.), *Genre and the new rhetoric*
(pp. 105-124). London: Taylor & Francis.

Willard, C.A. (1982). Argument fields. In J.R. Cox & C. A. Willard
(Eds.), *Advances in argumentation theory and research* (pp. 24-
77). Carbondale: Southern Illinois University Press.

CHAPTER 6

Writing as a Way into Social Work: Genre Sets, Genre Systems, and Distributed Cognition

Anthony Paré
McGill University

This chapter explores how university social work students fare in the transition from school to the workplace. By examining the subtle, complex process of situated learning in the workplace, it demonstrates how newcomers become encultured through participation in institutional genres. In addition, the chapter describes the conflicts operating within what Bourdieu calls a "linguistic marketplace" (1984/1993): the arena in which competing discourses vie for dominance. Finally, it examines the effect of those conflicts on student newcomers.

My argument is this: by engaging in the production of institutional texts, the social work students described in this chapter participate in what Dorothy Smith (1974) calls "the social construction of documentary reality"—or, more appropriate to this discussion, the documentary construction of social reality. Participation in institutional practices, particularly regular discourse practices, draws the students into the collective reproduction of organizational ideology. As de Montigny (1995) puts it, "Textual practices carve out ideological spaces, domains, and symbolic terrains where social workers can generate a professional corpus, identity, and practice" (p. 61). In the setting described below, however, the ideological space carved out by the textual practices of social work must contend with, and at times acquiesce to, the space created by other, more powerful discourses. The student new-comer seeking professional status must learn to negotiate the various and at times conflicting discourses and the ideologies they enact.

First, some background. The school of social work referred to in this chapter offers three degrees: an undergraduate Bachelor of Social Work, a one-year, post-baccalaureate Certificate in Social Work, and a Master of Social Work. Students in the Bachelor and Certificate programs complete 700 hours of supervised field educa-tion, and the Masters students spend 500 hours in the field. The duration of this internship is a condition of accreditation determined by the profession's national association.

Typically, students are placed in institutional settings such as hospitals, group homes, or government-funded programs of vari-ous sorts for half their internship hours and, for the other half, in community-based settings such as drop-in centers, shelters for bat-tered women, or cooperatives. For the most part, I have followed stu-dents into agency placements, and it is one such setting, a hospital, that I will refer to most often in this chapter.

Large hospitals display what Engeström (1993) refers to as "rationalized activity": "The machinery and size of the organization entail complex interactions. In the name of efficiency, division of labor and centralization are brought to the utmost" (p. 70). In a hos-pital division of labor, social service departments carry a heavy load. They are called in if patients show signs of physical or sexual abuse; they frequently conduct cross-cultural (cross-racial, cross-gender, cross-creed) negotiations between patients and hospital staff; they ensure that patients will be discharged into secure settings; and they often continue seeing patients after they have been discharged. They share the labor with doctors, nurses, psychologists, psychiatrists, physical and occupational therapists, lab technicians, and others. Increasingly, they work with some of these others in multiprofession-al teams, so that medical, psychological, and social issues (and the discourses that embody them) must compete for attention. And, as elsewhere, they work under ever-tighter financial constraints. Over the course of their transition into such a complex setting, I inter-viewed students, as well as the practitioners and managers who served as their guides. In what follows, I draw on their words.

INTERNSHIPS: FROM OBSERVATION TO LEGITIMATE
PARTICIPATION

Internships last for approximately eight months and are concurrent with course work, so that students spend half of each week in school and half in a workplace setting. In the workplace, they are teamed with a supervisor who is a professional and usually veteran social worker—or, in Lave and Wenger's terms, an "oldtimer" (Lave, 1988; Lave & Wenger, 1991). The student newcomer works very closely with the oldtimer, who typically orchestrates and monitors a gradual increase in the student's activities until the student is carrying an approximate equivalent of a social worker's full case load.

Initially, however, students may simply be "sitting by Nellie," as early industrial apprentices called the act of observing veteran factory hands (Clews & Magneson, 1996, p. 1). Students sit in on staff meetings, watch supervisors conduct interviews, and accompany them onto the wards. A second stage in the transition occurs when students begin to perform actual workplace tasks, or parts of tasks, under the direct guidance of and in collaboration with supervisors. With a nod toward Lave and Wenger (1991), Freedman and Adam (Chapter 2, this volume) refer to this phase of transition as "attenuated authentic participation." Learning here is in the context of, and secondary to, the performance of real work required by the community. The collaboration allows for an exchange: oldtimers help newcomers participate appropriately in communal activities, and newcomers contribute viewpoints from outside the community (often in the form of current theoretical perspectives gained in their academic reading). Typical attenuated authentic participation for social work students would include co-interviewing clients with supervisors, interviewing one member of a client family, contributing to meetings by offering assessments of clients or recommending interventions, and engaging in frequent discussions with supervisors about the work they are doing together. One supervisor describes this movement from observation to the beginnings of participation:

> In many respects, at the beginning it's kind of informal; you sort of just throw them into the situation and then answer questions and clarify terms and identify people. . . . There's standard staff meetings that she's involved with. . . . She's gone to activities the patients are involved in to try to get a sense of what the population is like. She has now two clients who she's begun to work with on specific kinds of discharge planning issues.

Eventually, once they go beyond "sitting by Nellie" and collaborating with supervisors, students' involvement in workplace activities enters a third stage that looks very much like what Lave and Wenger (1991) call "legitimate peripheral participation." By "legitimate," Lave and Wenger mean authentic; by "peripheral" they do not mean marginal or trivial but, rather, not central or critical; by "participation" they mean engagement, as opposed to observation only or instruction separate from activity. Here, unlike during the previous stages of transition, newcomers achieve a degree of autonomy. For example, among Liberian apprentice tailors Lave has studied, legitimate peripheral participation includes setting out the materials and tools for the master tailor's work, using a pattern to cut the sleeves for a jacket, or doing finishing work on a garment. This is how Lave (1991) describes the evolution of apprenticeship:

> [N]ewcomers become oldtimers through a social process of increasingly centripetal participation, which depends on legitimate access to ongoing community practice. Newcomers develop a changing understanding of practice over time from improvised opportunities to participate peripherally in ongoing activities of the community. Knowledgeable skill is encompassed in the process of assuming an identity as a practitioner, of becoming a full participant, an oldtimer. (p. 68)

For social work apprentices, then, legitimate peripheral participation means an approximation of full participation. They may begin by conducting initial client interviews without their supervisors present, contacting government or community services, leading small group sessions with clients, or presenting a case at a meeting; finally, toward the end of their placement, they could be responsible for up to fifteen clients, perhaps one fourth or one third of a professional social worker's case load. (Social work case loads vary from setting to setting.)

Early on in this stage of the transition, legitimate peripheral participation begins to encompass the reading and writing of texts. Social work newcomers to the hospital consult the medical chart (actually a file containing reports from the many professionals involved in patient care), sit in on interviews that provide the information for social work records, write letters to clients' families, take minutes at meetings and, eventually, write the social work records that are placed in client files. Typically, when they begin to prepare those documents, students go or are sent to the files to consult the records written by their supervisors and other workers. These files serve a modeling purpose, as these three students attest:

Q: How did you learn how to write [assessment reports]?

A: Um, I think I made copies of . . . [reports], and my supervisor gave me a big file of things she had. . . . And then you learn by reading, and really you sort of crib material from other assessments.

*****

Q: How is the format provided to you?

A: There are headings and then some of the sections have, you know, for example, "include data about home, community, neighborhood, religion," and so forth. And then, you know, you plough through somebody else's file, somebody else's assessment, to see what kind of information they included. . . . I was told, "This person writes wonderful assessments, go read them."

*****

Q: Are you writing documents that go into client files?

A: Yes. I'm actually, right now, trying to write up an assessment. . . . I looked at some old assessments to see how I'm supposed to write it up. . . . [My supervisor] found three that she thought were really good that would give me a good idea how to write them.

This use of filed records as models performs a number of functions, of course, including the conservative one of maintaining the community and its activities (of which, more below). But for the student moving toward membership, models are "embodiments of some of the social knowledge the student lacks. The models provide guidance on what people in a given environment think is worth writing about and on the way they think that writing should be done" (Winsor, 1996, p. 169). Models allow students, literally and figuratively, to speak the same language as oldtimers, to join in the group's sociolinguistic "typifications," as Bazerman (1994a) explains:

> The words, registers, phrases, genres, forms, and other sociolinguistic types provide the basis of symbolic interaction and become the grounds of intersubjective orientation as they are deployed in the course of interaction. Each individual must learn to cope with these typifications, as the individual is socialized into different groups of people; that is, socialization is not indoctrination so much as learning the orientations and resources and practices that allow one to interact with a group. (p. 29)

Although students have considerable autonomy at the stage of legitimate peripheral participation, they still receive close supervision
while they are "learning the orientations and resources and practices" of the group (a learning that may or may not be "indoctrina-
tion," depending on one's definition of the term). All the texts they
produce must be co-signed by their supervisors, and when students
begin to write reports, regular supervision meetings become focused
on those texts and their place and function within the community. A
cycle of revision ensues, which provides the type of essential feedback
to novices that others have described in different circumstances (see
various chapters in this volume; MacKinnon, 1993; Winsor, 1990).
The process is very similar to institutionally organized "document
cycling" routines (Paradis, Dobrin, & Miller, 1985; Smart, 1993), in
which texts go through revision loops—from writer to supervisor and
back—with supervisors offering criticism and suggestions, and subordinates rewriting. The assumption guiding such collaborative routines is that supervisors, usually oldtimers of long standing, can better understand and interpret the needs of the organization. Likewise,
social work supervisors school their apprentices by helping them
shape texts that are appropriate, as these students explain:

Q: Has your supervisor helped you to write?

A: My supervisor was very good about correcting everything, giving it back to me. I often wrote reports 8 times over because she
wanted me to understand what I was doing. She was really wonderful about . . . explaining if I was in a different setting how my
writing style would change.

*****

Q: And how did you learn [to write]?

A: Trial and error. By practice. By reading other people's material, and by doing your own, and having your own processes edited.
. . . I would give it to [my supervisor] to read and then she would
say "Well the language here is a little too strong. You might want
to change the way you've phrased this. This is good but I think
you should include something else which you haven't said."

*****

A: I go over it with [my supervisor]. We go over basically what's
the reason for writing the report. And at the end of it, we make
that clear. So it's been a process of doing and redoing and often
times redoing again, until we have something that's acceptable.

A: It's frustrating when you come with a [draft] you've written which you think is okay, and then leave and there's pencil all over it and these are the things you have to change. But it teaches you about writing in a new language and how to learn how to use that.

*****

A: I think I've learned how to write the way [my supervisor] wants me to write, because now I go and she says, "Yep, that's fine."

Clearly, supervisors do more than surface editing, and students learn more than a superficial "style." They learn how texts represent the varying demands of setting and circumstance, what stance to take toward clients and colleagues, and what should and should not be included; in short, they learn what is "acceptable." We can recognize this process as the gradual initiation of newcomers into genre—that is, into the texts and contexts that the community has organized in order to produce the knowledge necessary for its enterprise. As Carolyn Miller (1984) puts it: "for the student, genres serve as keys to understanding how to participate in the actions of a community" (p. 165). In this way, for good and ill, communities perpetuate themselves through the conservative force of their habitual textual practices. In the present, genres create (or suggest by anticipation) patterns of similarity in situations, events, and individuals, thus ensuring continuity; and in the future, as records are the "rhetorical organization of remembering and forgetting" (Middleton & Edwards, 1990, p. 9), genres will eventually serve to shape a collective memory, a shared history (see also Douglas, 1986, and Engeström et al., 1990). As de Montigny (1995) explains, "records brought forward from the past allow social workers to meet clients as already discursively organized. The client is a textually mediated case marked by continuity between the past and the present" (p. 72).

As social work students move toward full, professional practice, they become increasingly engaged in the activity system that supports the production of social work texts: the interviews, consultations, telephone calls, record searches, assessment meetings, case presentations, drafting, and so on. In so doing, they join a larger, intricate system that incorporates the complex "rationalized activity" of the whole hospital.

GENRES AND DISTRIBUTED OR SOCIALLY SHARED COGNITION

This centripetal force of gradually increasing, guided participation in the community's activity system, particularly its genres or text-making activities, draws students into what has been called "socially shared" or "distributed" cognition (see Cole & Engeström, 1993, for a discussion of the concept of "distributed cognition"). The notion that human cognition is best conceived of as a social phenomenon embedded in activity parallels the view of writing as a social activity that has evolved in composition studies. Proponents of this broader perspective on cognition (e.g., Salomon, 1993) believe that cognition—like writing—cannot be understood out of context. Moreover, cognition—again like writing—is always social; even when "thinking alone," the individual is cognitively enabled, constrained, inspired, and influenced by situation and history, by increasingly wider circles of collectivity: family, friends, school, religion, race, society, culture. Critiques of a psychology focused on isolated individual cognition are similar to those leveled against the cognitive process theories prevalent in composition studies in the 1970s, as this comment by Hutchins (1993) suggests: "when the context of cognition is ignored, it is impossible to see the contribution of structure in the environment, in artifacts, and in other people to the organization of mental processes" (p. 62). (In the literature on socially shared cognition, this parallel with composition and rhetoric has been made explicit with references, first, to Bakhtin [e.g., Wertsch, 1991] and, more recently, to Kenneth Burke [Wertsch, 1995; Wertsch, Del Río, & Alvarez, 1995]).

Under the influence of Vygotsky and the Soviet activity theorists, some psychologists have begun to argue that "the nature of individuals' mental functioning can be understood only by beginning with a consideration of the social system in which it exists" (Wertsch, Tulviste, & Hagstrom, 1993, p. 340).[1] Or, as Michael Cole (1991) puts it, echoing Bateson (1972), "the border of the mind cannot reasonably be drawn at the skin" (p. 412). According to Cole, this notion that the mind is distributed outside of the individual skull has caused "a shift in the psychological unit of analysis away from the organism in an environment to two or more human beings acting in a culturally mediated setting" (p. 413). This sociocultural approach seeks to

---

[1]Douglas (1986) refers to "the claim that psychologists are institutionally incapable of remembering that humans are social beings. As soon as they know it, they forget it" (p. 81). Contributors to Middleton and Edwards' (1990) collection explore this charge.

understand how sharing in a community's activities and artifacts works to initiate individuals into the shared knowledge and common ways of knowing that characterize groups. A key concept here is "artifact," which is defined broadly enough to include physical tools such as computers, and collaborative arrangements such as meetings, and the "master tool" (Cole) itself—language:[2]

> On close inspection, the environments in which humans live are thick with invented artifacts that are in constant use for structuring activity, for saving mental work, or for avoiding error. . . . These ubiquitous mediating structures that both organize and constrain activity include not only designed objects such as tools, control instruments, and symbolic representations like graphs, diagrams, text, plans, and pictures, but people in social relations. (Pea, 1993, p. 48)

The texts that social work students read and write during field placement are physical artifacts; they are "mediating structures that both organize and constrain," as these students discovered when supervisors helped them develop new categories:

Q: How have you learned to write?

A: I learned mostly by . . . I wrote it, and I showed it to my supervisor and, I mean, all the information was right but it was all under the wrong headings and so I had to end up shifting things around and then I redid it and it was fine, I guess.

*****

Q: What does your supervisor say?

A: Well, she'll just point things out, like headings she mentioned that all students have trouble with. Like I would mention that this woman has a history of depression—"This should go under this heading and not this one. Why did you put it there?"

---

[2]Engeström (1997) argues that in practical activity the traditional separation between *signs* and *tools* does not hold, and that "the demarcation line between these two types of mediational means is fluid and they are continuously intertwined or merged" (p. 2). He further suggests that records are "good examples of this merger" (p. 2).

As Cole (1991) says, "the precise ways in which mind is distributed depend crucially on the tools through which one interacts with the world" (p. 412). By learning to use these texts—that is, by learning the questions to ask during interviews, by learning the appropriate stance to take toward information and readers, by learning how to organize their observations of the world under the categories offered by the texts—students are joining in socially shared cognition; they are thinking "in conjunction or partnership with others and with the help of culturally provided tools and implements" (Salomon, 1993, p. xiii). Bazerman (1994a), like Douglas (1986), uses the term "thought style" in describing this process:

> Insofar as each discursive system identifies certain discursive activities to be carried out in a particular form, employing various materials to be displayed and intellectually acted upon in various expected forms, that discursive system develops a characteristic thought or representational style, consisting of the genres, registers, and other sociolinguistic typifications held to be appropriate and part of the decorum. The thought style influences not only the shared public deliberations but also the individual thought of the participants insofar as their thought is aimed at preparing comments for the public discursive field and insofar as individuals employ the public discursive symbols in their private thinking (for example, thinking through a problem in physics by puzzling over the kind of graph that is likely to appear in a physics article). (p. 33)

By adopting the "thought style" of hospital social workers, the students moved toward membership in what Lave and Wenger (1991) call a "community of practice": "a set of relations among persons, activity, and world, over time and in relation with other tangential and overlapping communities of practice" (p. 98). And it was clear that students were not only learning to think *with* others in the social service community, they were also learning to think differently from others: those "tangential and overlapping communities of practice" represented by the many professional groups that comprised the larger hospital community.

As Michael Cole (1991) points out, the concept of sharing has a "Janus-headed nature": "On the one hand," he says, quoting from *Webster's,* "*sharing* means to 'receive, use, experience in common with another or others'. . . . On the other hand, *share* also means to divide or distribute something" (p. 398). Within a hospital setting, social work students learn to make sense of the world in common with other social workers in the social service department. Cognition is, to a large extent and by design, done in partnership: the same mediating tools or artifacts—including texts, genres, interview protocols, standard procedures of various sorts, and collaborative arrangements (e.g., meetings, revision cycles)—are used by all.

However, hospitals, like other large institutions, are organized in disciplinary units, so there are many different communities of practice within a single site, and sharing—in the sense of division—is required as well. Nurses, doctors, psychiatrists, physiotherapists, lab technicians, and others all think about patients, but they think about them in different ways. Cognition is shared by parceling it out, by specialization. The hospital, which has what is sometimes called a "bio-psycho-social" focus, must take deliberate steps to integrate the separate communities of practice and their shared cognition into one rationalized activity, and that is done in large part by organizing the institution's many records and reports into a system of genres. (See Dias, Freedman, Medway, & Paré, 1999, for an analysis of bank writing that draws on distributed cognition.)

GENRE SETS AND GENRE SYSTEMS

Genres, according to Giltrow and Valiquette (1994), are "a system for administering communities' knowledge of the world—a system for housing knowledge, producing it, practising it" (p. 47). Within a hospital, each separate community has its own genre set (Devitt, 1991), which is the repertoire of regular texts and text-related activities that allows each community to deploy its particular knowledge of the world. The whole collection of genre sets in the hospital constitutes what Bazerman (1994b) calls a genre system: "interrelated genres that interact with each other in specific situations . . . the full set of genres that instantiate the participation of all the parties" (pp. 98-99). At the center of this constellation of genres is the medical chart—the file that contains the pertinent texts from each community of practice. Within this file may be found reports from doctors and nurses, psychiatrists and psychologists, social workers, occupational and physical therapists, lab technicians, and others.

According to Amy Devitt, "In examining the genre set of a community, we are examining the community's situations, its recurring activities and relationships. The genre set accomplishes its work" (1991, p. 340). Within hospitals, the social work genre set looks something like this:

- Referral form
- Initial assessment
- Ongoing assessments (progress reports)
- Closing/transfer report

In one of the hospitals I have studied, each of these texts has a set format, with a standard layout and headings. All are one page long, but extra pages can be added. The sequence from referral form to closing report both describes and prescribes the evolution of social work rhetorical activity. The referral form marks the beginning of a worker's contact with a client. Fill-in-the-blank spaces are provided to identify the source of the referral (the department and/or individual asking for social work intervention), the name and medical condition of the patient, and other factual details.[3] Under two headings, larger space is provided (approximately three inches for each heading). One heading asks for "Reason for Referral," the other invites a "Social Work Note." The more detailed assessment that follows must be completed within a specific time and requires workers to write about the "Presenting Problem," the "Psycho-Social Situation," the "Reaction to Health Problem," the "Clinical Impression," and the "Plan." Ongoing assessments or progress reports follow at regular intervals and offer similar headings. The closing/transfer report represents the last contact with and comment on a client; it seeks information concerning "Nature of Contacts" between worker and client, the "Current Psycho-Social Situation," and "Reason for Transfer/Closing." Such a genre set shapes a unity of approach and conceptualization within the community of practice; it shapes in large part the development of the individual's thinking *with* others *about* the client *through* the mediating structures of the genre set.

Learning to complete such records involves considerable collaboration, not just between supervisor and student, but among the many members of the larger community. Consider the following descriptions of learning to write assessments in residential centers

---

[3]In fact, a patient's medical condition and the source of the referral may well require a far more complex explanation than a mere blank line allows, but forms are designed to discourage complexity, or at least elaboration. Moreover, although the forms indicated that a patient was the object of social service attention, many of the workers I interviewed reported that their work was often with hospital staff rather than with patients. For example, they frequently found themselves educating nurses about cultural issues or explaining the patterns of sexual abuse to doctors eager to discharge "healthy" patients into potentially dangerous home situations. Naturally, this important work goes unacknowledged, much less reported.

for adolescents, settings where social work interns must collaborate with members of their own and other professional communities on multidisciplinary teams:

Q: How did you learn to write [initial assessments]?

A: We would have assessment team meetings, and there were various aspects within the assessment process that needed some clarification. Besides, I did the first couple of them with [fellow student]. . . . We basically shared a lot of ideas. . . . And we would pull our supervisor aside, too, and bounce off ideas, and other colleagues. So we had resources. We could access our team. We could access our supervisor. . . . I was put . . . in a situation where we have to respond . . . not only to the family but . . . to the Director of Assessment—what the requirements, policies, and things of that nature need to reflect. We have to respond to the Director of Professional Services. . . . I think it's very important to respond to what the social worker needs to know and what the child care worker needs to know. So, we're writing basically to a family of professionals that need to know where to go with this case.

*****

Q: How do you know what to put into those [ongoing assessments]?

A: . . . basically we take a team approach and so we try to build a consensus in terms of how we work with these families. . . . there's a great deal of consultation in this program because unlike other situations where you're pretty well on your own, we do stress the team approach. It's not a one person show. So there's a lot of consultation and that consultation is kind of sifted down into the [ongoing assessments]. Like we have a team meeting today, and we have discussions, and out of those discussion arrive certain kinds of interventions for certain clients

By participating in the activity system that regularly produces, reproduces, and applies the community's knowledge, the newcomer joins the team, or "family of professionals," and shares in the social distribution of cognition. However, the social work "family" often finds itself in the company of other, more powerful "families": bureaucrats, police officers, lawyers, psychologists, and doctors, for example. That is, social workers rarely practice alone; their activity occurs in concert (and in conflict) with the activity systems of other communities of practice.

Hospitals are particularly crowded sites. According to the director of a social service department in a hospital I visited, the purpose of her unit's texts

> is to document what our professional contribution is to the treatment plan . . . so that other health care professionals can work in concert with us and carry through the best treatment, the most comprehensive treatment plan possible, for the patient and/or the family. And so the psycho-social is one piece of the bio-psycho-social plan, to use current lingo, that would enable the other health professionals to understand what our contribution is.

In the larger context, then, cognition is shared by parceling it out: a social division of cognitive labor. Though the patient's well-being is a common purpose, each community of practice within the larger community has its own focus, its own activities, its own genre set. A "community of practice," to recall Lave and Wenger's (1991) definition, is "a set of relations among persons, activity, and world, over time and in relation with other tangential and overlapping communities of practice" (p. 98). The various genre sets form a genre system that operates to keep the work of the various, overlapping communities in concert.

THE UNEVEN DISTRIBUTION OF COGNITION

The overall picture of the hospital is not unlike the example of distributed cognition that Edwin Hutchins (1993) provides in his description of ship navigation. When a large ship is operating in constrained circumstances—docking, for example—navigation is performed by a team; in the case Hutchins describes, the team has six people. Although all six share a purpose, each is focused on quite different aspects of the task, each has unique activities, each employs task-specific tools, and each passes "pertinent" information on to the team member who is next in the team's communication chain. Pertinence is determined by the task of that next person, which means that team members must know something about the job performed by the person to whom they pass information. The navigation team has a hierarchy of expertise, and a consequent chain of command: the team member at each level of the chain knows much about the jobs below him or her (and has usually performed that job while rising through the ranks). As Hutchins says, "this movement through the system with increasing expertise results in a pattern of overlapping expertise, with knowledge of the entry-level tasks most redundantly represented and knowledge of the expert-level tasks least redundantly represented" (1993, pp. 52-53).

Hospitals, too, have a hierarchy, but one not so clearly tied to expertise, length of service, or difficulty of task, as in Hutchins' navigation example; rather, prestige and power in the hospital is a matter of disciplinary status. No matter how expert or veteran the social worker, no matter how complex the patient's psychosocial circumstances, medical concerns are paramount. The social work newcomer must learn how to participate in the social work community's genre set and learn how that set is influenced by and fits into the larger institution's genre system. In particular, the newcomer must learn to participate in the activities that produce the knowledge that medical personnel want to know. This is how two senior social workers see it:

> this is a medical chart that we're writing in. We're invited to give our opinion. We should give it and thank them. . . . More than that, I don't think is expected.

*****

> I find . . . that in talking to medical people, especially now when everybody's so pressed, that if I can't give it to them in twenty-five words or less, then they tune out.

A student newcomer describes how, early in her internship, she adopted the required brevity of hospital discourse:

> I think [reading the files in the chart] just gave me an idea of what really is included in the chart. That in the medical chart it's more concrete, very clear and concise. And I think it's better to be brief in the report, I mean, that's what I've learned from reading the charts. I've seen other reports that have been brief and concise and so I figured it's probably better to write in a briefer more clearer way.

But her supervisor is less enthusiastic:

> I find the [recording] is useful for a doctor who may be ready to discharge someone. It's useful for the organization. I don't find it useful for social workers.

When hospital social workers are called in for consultation, the situation is almost always severe: the very young or very old in desperate straits, critically ill children and distraught parents, physical and sexual abuse, poverty, and other extreme conditions; in fact, the patient's medical needs often pale in comparison. And yet, the social workers above acknowledge the primacy of medicine.[4] A social work student describes this tension:

> Doctors have in their mind one idea, one suggestion for someone, and you have a different idea and the length of time that it takes you to implement your idea might not fall in conjunction with the doctor's. So if the doctor wants a discharge but the patient has nowhere to go, then it becomes time for you to advocate on their behalf. But it becomes also very difficult because you're dealing with a structure, an institutional structure where there are rules and regulations about how long a patient can stay, etc. So it puts pressure on your job. . . . I think you're constantly battling with the structure and I think you're battling with doctors who don't want to agree with the recommendations that you've made if it hinders a patient's medical progress.

Within the genre system of the hospital, social work texts are important insofar as they provide knowledge to the hospital's more prestigious communities of practice. Social work newcomers learn to collaborate in community knowledge-making activities, or genre sets, that are shaped by levels of power and status within the larger genre system. Their disciplinary inclinations and their training may well be in conflict with medicine or psychiatry, but they must obey the laws of what Bourdieu (1984/1993) calls the "linguistic market": "There is a linguistic market whenever someone produces an utterance for receivers capable of assessing it, evaluating it and setting a price on it" (p. 79). And, as Bourdieu continues, "Linguistic capital is power over the mechanisms of linguistic price formation" (p. 80). Merely by

---

[4]In other settings, law predominates over social work (Paré, 1993). Social work, like other relatively low-prestige disciplines, has a history of struggle with its professional identity and discourse, and frequently either accedes to the authority of or appropriates the discourse of more powerful fields (see Flynn, 1995, for an example of this phenomenon in composition studies). A single, telling example from social work is the conflict over the proper term for the user of social services. "Client," the most frequently used term, suggests a legal relationship; "patient" transforms social or familial difficulty into pathology; "customer" implies a voluntary consumer. In many workplace settings, social workers are torn between two conflicting roles (and their attendant discourse and ideology): agent of the state (institution, hospital, agency) and advocate for the client.

ignoring social work records, medical doctors and psychiatrists could put social workers out of business. For newcomers, this struggle over discourse (and, therefore, cognition) can be difficult:

> My first assessment that I wrote . . . I worked closely with my supervisor on and . . . she really reworded a lot of it. And then the child psychiatrist said to me, "I can't sign this!" So it was quite a shock. And he had different expectations in terms of how information should be organized than she did. . . . So she was speculating in a way or drawing links throughout the write-up of the assessment. And what the psychiatrist wanted was fact, fact, fact, fact, fact. . . . So he had a couple of categories which she didn't have. . . . I understand where they're both coming from and sometimes I feel like I'm between a rock and a hard place.

There is a long tradition in social work of exploiting the heuristic power of writing, of "speculating . . . or drawing links throughout the write-up"; but institutional demands (the struggles among competing interests) suppress narrative, speculation, elaboration—all the lengthy and messy uses of language that promote exploratory thought. The "scientific" fields of medicine and psychiatry want "fact, fact, fact, fact, fact"; they want categories that are different from social work categories, they want a different cognition. They want ways of thinking that sanitize discourse, remove the troubling human elements that cloud reason, as this student discovered:

> the tone of your writing and the way in which you say something . . . can reflect your emotions and your feelings about a certain person. And you have to be very careful to be unbiased and unjudgemental.
>
> Q: Why?
>
> A: Why? It's professional, and I think it's about learning to separate yourself and that's been a very hard lesson to learn. It's that you can't let yourself get emotionally attached or involved with your clients; and there has to be a point where you remove yourself . . . from becoming involved in their problems and sympathizing with them. You can sympathize with them, but no, wait. You can empathize with them, but you can't sympathize with them. You have to harden yourself to some degree.

The positivist sleight of hand that separates the knower from the knowledge in order to create a reality outside human experience, and

thus the pretense of "objectivity," requires collaboration. It demands
a kind of cognitive consensus, an agreement on "the way things are."
As Bourdieu (1972/1977) explains, "One of the fundamental effects of
the orchestration of habitus is the production of a commonsense
world endowed with the *objectivity* secured by consensus on the
meaning of practices and the world, in other words the harmoniza-
tion of agents' experiences and the continuous reinforcement that
each of them receives from the expression, individual or collective (in
festivals, for example), improvised or programmed (commonplaces,
sayings), of similar or identical experiences" (p. 80). Douglas (1986)
echoes this: "Constructing sameness is an essential intellectual activity that goes unobserved" (p. 60). To achieve any degree of sameness,
communal habits of mind and meaning-making are essential—habits
developed in the individual in the process of joining activity systems.[5]
In Douglas's dramatic pronouncement: "Institutions have the pathet-
ic megalomania of the computer whose whole vision of the world is its
own program" (p. 92). In this final interview excerpt, a social work
student explains the tension between the disciplinary perspective he
has gained at school and the perspective shaped by his participation
in the hospital's overlapping communities of practice:

> [The doctor] said to me, "your writing is very literary and you are
> writing in a medical context." So I think that's part of what it's
> about, that it's medical and scientific and so in science we want,
> well, Western science is very much like categorization wouldn't
> you say? So I think that's the justification. Basically what I see
> I'm learning is how to practice an art, an art of working with peo-
> ple's lives, an art of helping people get unstuck and heal them-
> selves and their families through communication and various
> other things. But it takes place within a scientific domain. So
> that you can write up a report as artistic and literary and that
> doesn't fly. Or you can write it up in a way that looks more scien-
> tific and closer to objective.

I am curious about the conflict between the "art" of social work and
the "science" of medicine, a conflict played out in the hospital's genre
sets and genre system. I suspect that a similar friction is felt by all

_____

[5]Of course, it is possible for the individual to resist the institutional habits of
mind and the discourse they promote, and I have met veteran social workers
who were adept at subverting and/or changing activity systems. Here, however, I am concerned primarily with newcomers to social work, who are usually not so able or prepared to resist.

newcomers as they join institutional activity systems and experience the conflicts and contradictions that characterize the intricate ideology of collective enterprise. As a writing teacher, I am puzzled by how we can prepare students for this experience, since linguistic marketplaces are local, contingent, and ever-changing; as a researcher, I am intrigued by this complex process of situated learning by which newcomers join institutional systems of distributed cognition. But finally, I am troubled by the loss reflected in these students' experiences. I am troubled by a professionalism that requires you to "separate yourself," to "harden yourself." I am troubled by what happens when individuals uncritically adopt, or are forced to adopt, discursive systems, the socially shared cognition they encourage, and the ideology they enact.

ACKNOWLEDGMENTS

I would like to thank Dawn Allen, Patrick Dias, and Graham Smart for helpful comments on drafts of this chapter.

REFERENCES

Bateson, G. (1972). *Steps to an ecology of mind: A revolutionary approach to man's understanding of himself.* New York: Ballantine Books.

Bazerman, C. (1994a). *Constructing experience.* Carbondale: University of Southern Illinois Press.

Bazerman, C. (1994b). Systems of genres. In A. Freedman & P. Medway (Eds.), *Genre and the new rhetoric* (pp. 79-101). London: Taylor and Francis.

Bourdieu, P. (1977). *Outline of a theory of practice* (R. Nice, Trans.). London: Cambridge University Press. (Original work published 1972)

Bourdieu, P. (1993). *Sociology in question* (R. Nice, Trans.). London: Sage. (Original work published 1984)

Clews, R., & Magneson, H. (1996, June). *Theory and practicum: Bridging the gap.* Paper presented at the meeting of the Social Work Field Education Conference, Hamilton, ON.

Cole, M. (1991). Conclusion. In L. Resnick, J. Levine, & S. Teasley (Eds.), *Perspectives on socially shared cognition* (pp. 398-417). Washington, DC: American Psychological Association.

Cole, M., & Engeström, Y. (1993). A cultural-historical approach to distributed cognition. In G. Salomon (Ed.), *Distributed cognitions: Psychological and educational considerations* (pp. 1-46). London: Cambridge University Press.

de Montigny, G.A.J. (1995). *Social working: An ethnography of frontline practice.* Toronto: University of Toronto Press.

Devitt, A. (1991). Intertextuality in tax accounting. In C. Bazerman & J. Paradis (Eds.), *Textual dynamics of the professions* (pp. 306-335). Madison: University of Wisconsin Press.

Dias, P., Freedman, A., Medway, P., & Paré, A. (1999). *Worlds Apart: Acting and writing in academic and workplace contexts.* Mahwah, NJ: Erlbaum.

Douglas, M. (1986). *How institutions think.* Syracuse, NY: Syracuse University Press.

Engeström, Y. (1993). Developmental studies of work as a testbench of activity theory: The case of primary care medical practice. In S. Chaiklin & J. Lave (Eds.), *Understanding practice: Perspectives on activity and context* (pp. 64-103). London: Cambridge University Press.

Engeström, Y. (1997, March). *Talk, text and instrumentality in collaborative work: An activity-theoretical perspective.* Paper presented at the annual meeting of the Conference of College Composition and Communication, Phoenix, AZ.

Engeström, Y., Brown, K., Engeström, R., & Koistinen, K. (1990). Organizational forgetting: An activity-theoretical perspective. In D. Middleton & D. Edwards (Eds.), *Collective remembering.* London: Sage.

Flynn, E. (1995). Feminism and scientism. *College Composition and Communication, 46*(3), 353-368.

Giltrow, J., & Valiquette, M. (1994). Genres and knowledge: Students writing in the disciplines. In A. Freedman & P. Medway (Eds.), *Learning and teaching genre* (pp. 47-62). Portsmouth, NH: Boynton/Cook Heinemann.

Hutchins, E. (1993). Learning to navigate. In S. Chaiklin & J. Lave (Eds.), *Understanding practice: Perspectives on activity and context* (pp. 35-63). London: Cambridge University Press.

Lave, J. (1988). *Cognition in practice.* New York: Cambridge University Press.

Lave, J. (1991). Situated learning in communities of practice. In L. Resnick, J. Levine, & S. Teasley (Eds.), *Perspectives on socially shared cognition* (pp. 63-82). Washington, DC: American Psychological Association.

Lave, J., & Wenger, E. (1991). *Situated learning: Legitimate peripheral participation.* New York/Cambridge: Cambridge University Press.

MacKinnon, J. (1993). Becoming a rhetor: The development of on-the-job writing ability. In R. Spilka (Ed.), *Writing in the workplace: New research perspectives* (pp. 41-55). Carbondale: Southern Illinois University Press.

Miller, C. (1984). Genre as social action. *Quarterly Journal of Speech, 70,* 151-167.

Middleton, D., & Edwards, D. (Eds.). (1990). *Collective remembering.* London: Sage.

Paradis, J., Dobrin, D., & Miller, R. (1985). Writing at Exxon: Notes on the writing environment of an R and D organization. In L. Odell & D. Goswami (Eds.), *Writing in nonacademic settings* (pp. 281-308). New York: Guilford.

Paré, A. (1993). Discourse regulations and the production of knowledge. In R. Spilka (Ed.), *Writing in the workplace: New research perspectives* (pp. 111-123). Carbondale: Southern Illinois University Press.

Pea, R. (1993). Practices of distributed intelligence and designs for education. In G. Salomon (Ed.), *Distributed cognitions: Psychological and educational considerations* (pp. 47-87). London: Cambridge University Press.

Salomon, G. (1993). Editor's introduction. In G. Salomon (Ed.), *Distributed cognitions: Psychological and educational considerations* (pp. xi-xxi). London: Cambridge University Press.

Smart, G. (1993). Genre as community invention: A central bank's response to its executives' expectations as readers. In R. Spilka (Ed.), *Writing in the workplace: New research perspectives* (pp. 124-140). Carbondale: Southern Illinois University Press.

Smith, D. (1974). The social construction of documentary reality. *Sociological Inquiry, 44,* 257-268.

Wertsch, J. (1991). A sociocultural approach to socially shared cognition. In L. Resnick, J. Levine, & S. Teasley (Eds.), *Perspectives on socially shared cognition* (pp. 85-100).Washington, DC: American Psychological Association.

Wertsch, J. (1995). The need for action in sociocultural research. In J. Wertsch, P. Del Río, & A. Alvarez (Eds.), *Sociocultural studies of mind* (pp. 56-74). Cambridge: Cambridge University Press.

Wertsch, J., Del Río, P., & Alvarez, A. (1995). Sociocultural studies: History, action, and mediation. In J. Wertsch, P. Del Río, & A. Alvarez (Eds.), *Sociocultural studies of mind* (pp. 1-34). Cambridge: Cambridge University Press.

Wertsch, J., Tulviste, P., & Hagstrom, F. (1993). A sociocultural approach to agency. In E. Forman, N. Minick, & C. Stone (Eds.), *Contexts for learning* (pp. 336-356). New York: Oxford University Press.

Winsor, D. (1990). Joining the engineering community: How do novices learn to write like engineers? *Technical Communication, 37*, 171-172.

Winsor, D. (1996). Writing as a form of social knowledge. In A. Duin & C. Hansen (Eds.), *Nonacademic writing: Social theory and technology* (pp. 157-172). Mahwah, NJ: Erlbaum.

CHAPTER 7

What Do We Learn From the Readers? Factors in Determining Successful Transitions Between Academic and Workplace Writing

Christine Adam
Carleton University

In recent years, complaints that universities are not adequately preparing their graduates for the writing they will have to do in the workplace have been common in both the media and among employers (Aldrich, 1982; Andrews & Sigband, 1984; Gilsdorf, 1986). Accompanying these complaints are the voices of recent university graduates, frustrated and disoriented by the inadequacy they often feel as they attempt to write in their new jobs (Anson & Forsberg, 1990; Bataille, 1982; Bednar & Olney, 1987; Faigley & Miller, 1982; Radar & Wunsch, 1980). Complaints such as these may be perplexing to those of us who teach writing and/or conduct writing-related research in the university, because they do not resonate with what we know about writing at university: students do write a great deal and on subjects similar to those in their chosen fields of work. We also know that they apparently write well enough to graduate from academic institutions. At the same time, the explanations offered for this phenomenon tend to be ill-formed ("students are illiterate," "they don't know grammar," "they can't get to the point"), often because public understanding of rhetorical competence is relatively unsophisticated, and because understanding of the rhetorical competence necessary within disciplinary contexts is only now beginning to reach any kind of elaboration.

As I have argued elsewhere (1994a, 1994b), veteran members of communities of practice can offer insights into beliefs about what constitutes rhetorical competence within their particular environments. Understanding these beliefs is important to our work as researchers and teachers in at least three respects: first, they shape writing and reading practices; second, they are the basis for the value system that determines the success (i.e., effectiveness, appropriateness) of texts; third, they must be understood and adopted by newcomers who wish to write appropriately within a given context. As we go about looking for ways to help university graduates move from writing in an academic environment to writing in a workplace, the voices of veterans (or "oldtimers"; see Lave & Wenger, 1991) offer valuable insight into how both writing and learning differ in the two settings.

When oldtimers are asked to respond aloud to community texts, their commentary provides a window onto the norms, processes, and evaluation of writing within the community, and gives us useful insights into the differences between writing at school and writing on the job. In what follows, I outline some of those differences, drawing on both my own earlier study (1994a, 1994b) and those done in collaboration with others (see Chapters 2 and 5, this volume; Freedman & Adam, 1996; Freedman, Adam & Smart, 1994). I then move from these differences to suggest factors that should be taken into account in the design and evaluation of programs that attempt to help university graduates make a successful transition to writing in the workplace.

THEORETIC BACKGROUND

Social theories of writing provide a theoretic framework for this discussion. Within this framework, the reconceptualization of genre has become central. Carolyn Miller (1984) proposes that we view genre as a recognizable, typified rhetorical response to situations that those involved construe as being recurrent. By relying on the notion of recurrence in rhetorical situations, Miller's definition of genre allows us to see regular patterns in the surrounding or ambient dynamics of textual activity—how the text is initiated, the social roles it implies, the social motives that elicit it, and the composing and reading practices it entails—as constituents of a particular genre. Miller claims that individuals are able to recognize a rhetorical situation as being recurrent, as being of a particular type, by understanding and adopting the social motives that shape and constrain it.

John Swales (1988, 1990) locates genre within the "discourse community," which he defines as any group of people that create and use specific written genres in response to the group's own recurrent rhetorical situations and in order to accomplish common goals. Study of the responses of experienced members to texts written within a particular discourse community should thus be able to identify some of the motives that shape the community's genres. In particular, the reading practices and responses of individuals who fill authoritative roles within specific settings, and whose roles require them directly or indirectly to communicate the norms of the communities to novice writers, furnish a window onto some of the socially constructed exigences that define and characterize those communities, their recurrent rhetorical settings, and their characteristic genres.

As we have noted in other accounts of our research (see Chapter 2, this volume; Dias, Freedman, Medway, & Paré, 1999), the field of situated learning has contributed a great deal to our understanding of how it is that a community's genres are learned and mastered. Petraglia (1995) defines "situated learning" or "situated cognition" as "the ways in which educational contexts shape learning rather than merely furnish a site for it" (p. 84). A central tenet of situated learning is that learning is not something that goes on solely in the head of the learner or as the transference of "knowledge" from one head to another. Rather, learning is understood to take place through activity in communities of practice and among members of those communities. Within communities of practice, there are relative oldtimers, or "guides," and newcomers, or "learners," so the community of practice is always in a state of flux. The guide very often models and then gradually gives over more and more of a task to the learner.

WHAT DO THE READERS TELL US?

There are a number of tools that can be used to access the generic expectations and practices of oldtimers. One of the most powerful methods is the respond-aloud protocol. Deborah Brandt (1990) asserts that "any truly comprehensive and realistic definition of literacy must take into account the actual acts of reading and writing, must take into account, in other words, how literacy is actually accomplished by everyday readers and writers in everyday life. While intrusive and incomplete, writing- and reading-aloud protocols still provide a singularly rich record of minute-by-minute meaning making and thus stand to enlarge existing conceptions of literacy and literate ability" (p. 34). And again, in a 1992 article in *Written Communication,* she describes how respond-aloud protocols can indeed provide a wealth of information about how writers and readers "do writing and reading," and how a social approach to protocol analysis can provide access to the ways in which people do everyday things—their "know-how." Respond-aloud protocols furnish us with a window onto some of this know-how and onto some of the exigences that shape genres within each of the two settings discussed here.

In order to illustrate some of the differences in the exigences that shape academic and workplace writing, I will draw on my earlier study (1994a, 1994b), which looked at these two rhetorical settings through the eyes of experienced members of each of the two communities (professors and managers) as they responded to texts written for them by less experienced members of the communities (students and junior employees). The academic and workplace institutions in that study require the acquisition of particular forms and styles of written expression in order to move vertically (toward graduation and accreditation, or toward promotion) within the organization. In fact, although the two institutions differ in the nature of their daily activities and corporate mandates, they are similar in the degree to which they use, produce, and value written texts. The academic setting was the school of business at a Canadian university. Students who wish to obtain a Bachelor of Commerce must successfully complete a number of core courses in such topics as organizational behavior, finance, private and public policy, accounting, marketing, and economics. The corresponding workplace setting was a major government financial institution. The participants, professors in the academic setting and middle and senior managers in the government agency, fill authoritative roles within their respective communities. They are oldtimers: experienced members who are aware (tacitly, at least) of the exigences that shape rhetorical activities in their organization. Their roles require both the professors and the managers to respond to writing produced for them by less experienced members of their communities. These responses become an important means by which the norms and expectations of the institution are communicated and through which subsequent writing may be shaped.

The discussion below highlights a number of differences between reading practices in the two settings, including when texts are read, why they are read, how they are read, and how they are responded to. These observations provide a useful starting point for determining how to provide students with relevant assistance as they move into worlds of work. The section following this one will suggest factors that ought to be considered in helping writers make that transition.

Texts Are Read at Different Points in Time

Reading in both settings is determined by institutional timetables. In the university and in the workplace, there are specific divisions of time (e.g., semesters, quarters), with their corresponding texts (e.g., term papers, quarterly reports). The primary difference between the two is that the reading of student papers is almost always a predictable event tied closely to academic units of time, whereas much of the reading in the workplace, although somewhat routine, is often unpredictable and responsive to changing circumstances. At midterm and at the end of the semester, when the course is over, professors read and grade student papers. Deadlines are known well in advance and synchronized with other course-related activities, such as lectures and course readings. In most cases, there is no opportunity for the writer to revise and resubmit an essay after it has been graded as inadequate.

In the workplace, however, written texts are not always produced within predictable institutional timetables. Certainly, there are formal procedures for reporting on institutional activities at certain points in the year, providing a degree of stability and predictability to the organization as a whole; however, much workplace writing responds to unforeseen factors, such as changing economic realities that entail policy directions, research, or administrative decisions. Because written texts in the workplace are intended to recommend and support such actions (Freedman, Adam, & Smart, 1994), an important role of the manager is to identify where a text does not meet the expectations of the institution and to indicate where revisions must be made by the writer. This process of document cycling is a primary characteristic of writing in the workplaces my colleagues and I have studied, as well as in many others (Paré, this volume; Smart, 1993). Generally, it involves writers, texts, and readers in a carefully monitored schedule of revision. The manager's response is often the first step in a chain of collaborative textual production.

This difference has important consequences for the readers in the two settings because it means that they work under very different sets of constraints. Observe the differences between two different readers' reactions to the texts they have been given:

> University professor grading student paper: "It's too big a topic. His writing is highly condensed. It's well done—this is the kind of writing you'd expect for a briefing report to some big-shot. . . . I'm going to have to—the criteria are going to have to be a little bit different. But that's O.K. I don't mind that."

> Upper-level manager reading draft of proposal: "I think he's left
> himself open to several logical criticisms. One, the whole question
> of why it is that we can't cut down existing secretarial staff—par-
> ticularly that one of the alternatives suggests implicitly that we
> will cut it by sending them to spend additional time elsewhere.
> That's got to be tightened up."

Rather than dismissing the student essay as inappropriate, the professor is obliged to read and evaluate the student text and even to modify
the criteria that he had originally set out for the class because of the
imperatives of the university schedule. It is completely legitimate for
the professor, within his institutional role, to change those criteria.
The manager, on the other hand, views the text before him as an initial stage in a process: it is the text itself, and not the criteria, that
must be revised. When the text does not meet expectations, time, his
institutional role, and the text's function in ongoing institutional activity do not permit him to modify criteria; rather, he determines how the
text ought to be revised so that it does meet expectations.

The Purposes for Responding to Texts Are Different

As indicated above, the two institutional contexts provide very different purposes for reading and responding to texts. The purpose for
responding to texts in the academic setting is primarily evaluative.
In fact, as Aviva Freedman and I have pointed out elsewhere (1996;
Chapter 5, this volume), any attempt to reshape university writing
away from "evaluation" is always seen as an exception. In the academic setting, response to student writing takes on two forms: the
grade itself and discursive comments. In general, the discursive comments serve to justify or explain the grade. Academic readers are
aware that, for the most part, the response they write on student
texts will not be used directly by the student for revision. A professor's response may, however, be regarded by the student as an indication as to where she succeeded and/or failed in comprehending certain key ideas presented in the course. Consequently, the response
often relates back to aspects of the course or refers to sources that
the student might have used. In the respond-aloud protocol excerpt
below, we see how the reading processes of an academic reader are
shaped by a continual referencing back to a context which was established in the classroom:

> And then [the student writer] goes to show that you have to think
> of what are the alternatives. Now that's something that I stress

very much—don't judge things until you've looked at the alternatives. "For an action to be considered ethical, it should not be
done out of self-interest." Well, he's picked up on one of my preju-
dices. . . . Well, that's my claim, but a lot of business ethics people
say that long term self-interest is ethical. . . . Anyhow, but I do
concern myself with have they learned what I thought I was
teaching them.

We witness this professor looking for references in the student texts to
comments made in class, for echoes of his own voice (comments he has
made about the suitability of essay topics, biases he has in regard to
methodology or ideology), as well as for echoes of the voices of others
(articles or books he recommended, invited speakers). Student writing
is highly contextualized in this way. Not only must students demonstrate their own learning, they must also show how their learning
"fits" within the evolving conversation of the classroom.

In the workplace, texts are usually action-oriented—for
instance, toward making policy changes or making administrative decisions—and intermediate readers typically respond to a text by providing feedback for revisions that will make the text more useful to primary readers. These intermediate readers are not only familiar with the
contexts in which the texts may be used higher up in the institutional
hierarchy, they are also ultimately responsible for texts that go out of
their department (usually under their signature). Consequently, the
workplace reader's response to what he reads reflects the vested interest he has in the production of the best possible text:

> The only kind of things it really needs to bolster [that claim] are
> these kinds of comparative statistics. You see the problem too is
> that even if we were only sending it to Nelson [the department
> chief], he would have an impression of what those statistics
> would be for other departments, but supposing that his impres-
> sion is off by five percent? By presenting only your own [statis-
> tics] you're going to get screwed.

In contrast to the way in which the professor's response looked to
past contexts (the classroom), this workplace reader refers forward to
future contexts in which he envisions other readers responding to
what has been written.

The Processes of Reading Texts Are Different

An important difference between the reading processes in the two
settings is the degree to which the reader is willing to work with the

text as is. The university professor reads a student paper to determine what it reveals about the student's learning in the course. Consequently, he is obliged to examine the text from beginning to end; however, if the text does not match with the student's performance in class, the professor may question whether the text is an appropriate indicator of that student's academic achievement (hence, concerns about plagiarism).

Additionally, the reading process in the university is characterized by the reader's attempts to determine what the writer's intentions may have been, recognizing that the text might not always reflect those intentions. It is the *learning* exhibited both in the text and in the classroom that is the paramount concern, not the text alone. Observe, in the excerpt below, a professor's shifting of focus from the reality of the text to the classroom context, and back again to the text:

> This should be an excellent paper. It's the best student in the class. He speaks better than most people write. Now he's didactic. Factual stuff—good. Well, I would certainly expect him to write a good paper like this. So, you know, this guy has done a number of things that I expected fourth-year students to do.

The professor situates the student writer, and consequently the text, according to a number of criteria: his standing in the class, his oral proficiency, his year of study. All of these serve to form expectations for the student essay. In fact, the academic reader may be willing to overlook deficiencies or confusing segments in the student text if these problems do not match his expectations for that student. Likewise, the professor may question the authenticity of a text that exceeds his expectations for a particular student.

By contrast, it is the text itself that is the primary concern of the workplace reader. Workplace readers, as "intermediate" readers, are charged with the responsibility of ensuring that papers that ascend through the institutional hierarchy facilitate institutional decision making and operations. The workplace reader must therefore take on a collaborative role in reading texts that are written by the employees he supervises. This collaborative role is played out in two ways. First, the workplace reader may act as "surrogate reader," reading the text as though he were the primary reader—usually a higher-level manager. In this way, he is required to determine whether and how the expectations he (or others in the organization) have for the text are met by the text. Second, the reader determines how the text must be revised so that it does meet those expectations and then writes directives on the draft to that effect. The reader's own membership in the workplace community enables him to recognize when the paper does and does not meet the exigences that elicit and shape that community's genres. Consequently, he is able to fulfill his role as collaborator, indicating where there is "one other thing that this paper is missing," or "where there's a point [that] could be brought out." The supervisor shapes his response in a way that requires, without question, a particular response by the writer.

The Comments Written on Texts Are Different

The reader in the workplace has a very different notion of what his response means for the writer than does the professor. The former expects that his response will be incorporated into the text. As a consequence, the response we hear in the protocols is not dissimilar from the comments he writes on the paper itself. It is for this reason that he reads the paper once and with pen in hand. As discussed above, the workplace reader may in fact simulate the reading practices of the primary reader who he acknowledges has little time and is looking for particular arguments. When the text does not meet his expectations (those he anticipates from the primary reader), his response is accompanied by a written annotation, a crossing-out, a directive. When the text does meet the expectations he anticipates, he simply continues to read. There is no necessity for a written response, even a check-mark or "good" in the margin.

As indicated in the previous section, the response written on a workplace text demands its own response: specific revisions to the text. Rather than responding to the achievement of learning, these written comments can provide useful information about the contexts in which the text will operate within the institution, how others will read it, and the decisions that it may facilitate. The newcomer's ability to use these written comments will determine the speed and facility of her initiation into the workplace culture.

Because the primary motive underlying student writing is epistemic, such writing is governed by the need to show that one knows the appropriate arguments (their warrants, claims, and grounds) within the context of the course. It also inevitably means that the student must demonstrate, through her text, *what* she knows and *that* she knows (Freedman, Adam, & Smart, 1994). The text is an end in itself and is rarely used for any other purpose beyond the evaluation of learning. Student writing becomes the tangible means by which the professor can assess the degree of learning achieved by each individual student.

The respond-aloud protocols from one academic reader in my earlier study are peppered with references to his awareness of his role as evaluator, such as this: "I do concern myself with [whether they have] learned what I thought I was teaching them." In no way, however, does he see himself as a collaborator in the student text. His collaborative role ended before the reading of the text—it was accomplished during class time, through his office hours, and on his response to the essay outline submitted a couple of weeks before the final draft. The task now is to determine the degree to which the student has benefited from those collaborative efforts. In the respond-aloud protocol, the professor does not come up with suggested revisions—except to say that the student "could have" or "should have," but not that he "will have to."

University readers render evaluative responses to the student texts they read. As mentioned above, this response takes two forms: the grade itself and discursive comments (typically found in margins or at the end of the paper). In general, the discursive comments serve to justify or explain the grade given. In observing professors respond to student papers, it is clear that they are aware that the response they write on student texts will not be used directly by the student for revision. In fact, the reader's response to the text marks the completion of the rhetorical activity. Consequently, the response often relates back to aspects of the course or refers to sources to which the student might have referred.

WRITING ACROSS THE DIVIDE

In this section, I discuss considerations that should be taken into account when students are offered help with their writing before they move to the workplace (i.e., within university courses or internship programs), or as they begin to write at work. I cannot stress enough the important role that workplace oldtimers can play in helping us understand and facilitate this transition. For the researcher they are an excellent source of insight into the differences between written discourse in the two settings, but they can also provide considerable pedagogical support to students and workplace newcomers.

The Reality of Institutional Roles

Both academic and workplace readers have institutional power over the education and careers of the writers we seek to help, and that power is precisely what shapes much of the literate interaction between them and the writer-newcomers. It is because the professor has the power to give a grade to a paper (and, more often than not, to insist that rewrites are not allowed) that the student must submit a text that demonstrates that she has learned what has been taught. Similarly, it is because the workplace reader has the power to determine whether a written document is finished (ready to be read by others) that the writer must make the revisions that reader requires. It is difficult to see either of these institutional roles played out authentically in the other context. (See Chapter 5, this volume, for an example of a situation in which this does take place successfully.)

When we look at academic and workplace readers, we see that their roles and their institutional contexts elicit specific, "generic" responses. They are not free to respond in other ways, as other types of readers, or they would be denying their institutional roles and thereby redefining the rhetorical situation. Certainly, the authoritative role of the workplace reader, and its difference from that of the professor's role, must be carefully considered in any transitional program. Freedman, Adam, and Smart (1994) show how, even when the professor reads case studies that are prepared and presented in what seems to be carefully simulated workplace conditions, his response is still shaped by the exigence present in the university, namely that he determine if the students have learned what has been taught, compare their texts to others in the class, and give the assignments appropriate grades. When students reach the workplace, they must be helped to see how their new readers' roles and contexts shift their responses.

The Iterative Process

The writer making the transition from the university to the workplace moves from a setting in which her writing is regarded as a final product that demonstrates what she has learned and her ability to participate in the discourse of the classroom to a setting in which her writing is regarded as a first go: a text that will need to be revised before it will be seen as ready for its ultimate audience. Although we assume that the student writer goes through a number of drafts in producing her essay, it will usually be the case that revisions will be made in response to her own developing sense of the assignment and understanding of the course content. On occasion, she may have a classmate, roommate, teaching assistant, or even the professor look over what she has written, but ultimately she decides what will be changed and how. The workplace reader clearly expects that the writer will revise *after* submission of a text, and his role as reader is to provide guidance for that revision. The newcomer, however, may not recognize this subtle shift in the power relationship: the workplace reader, although in an authoritative position, is also her collaborator. In the worst-case scenario, the writer continues along the path that was successful in university, incorporating those suggestions she agrees with but maintaining control over textual revision. The writer misinterprets the writing task as being hers alone. An equally inappropriate response occurs when the writer fully incorporates the readers' comments and later complains when changes need to be made on later drafts. She does not recognize that workplace documents are in a constant state of revision as institutional goals and activities change. As the reader-collaborator works with the writer toward the best possible text for the institution at a given point in time, revision is a necessity.

Writing programs both in the university and in the workplace can assist writers in better understanding the iterative process in workplace writing. University writing programs have long recognized the role that the revision process plays in learning. A key difference here, however, is that learning in this case has primarily been directed toward course content. For the workplace, revision plays a key role in a very different type of learning: learning about the institution itself. In revising an academic paper, a writer clarifies ideas and negotiates various ways of presenting information. In revising a workplace document, a writer indeed gains a fuller understanding of the content, but more important to his success in the workplace, he learns how to make his text fit within a web of institutional activities, values, roles in a broader community, internal politics, previous documents, future documents, and personalities.

The university classroom cannot simulate such complexity; it can, however, provide explicit guidance to students in internships and co-op work terms in contexts where this complexity exists. Such guidance could involve group or classroom analysis of reviewer comments, student discussion of revisions made, the keeping of journals about what one has learned through revising. Within the workplace, a program of sheltering or coaching for new employees can be used to make explicit the role of revision in learning about how the workplace operates. The use of a writing coach permits the new employee to feel free to be a learner (something not always endorsed in the workplace), while still drawing on the experience of an insider who can make explicit much of what may be mysterious to the new employee.

The Contextualization of the Text

The temporal context of discourse is one of the most salient differences between reading and writing in the two settings studied. Texts in school and work respond to and operate within quite different time constraints. Student writing in the university responds retrospectively to a context that has unfolded during course lectures and discussions, office hours, and the reading of texts and other course materials. The student writer is expected to respond to these past utterances. By contrast, the contextualization of writing in the workplace is almost always prospective—anticipating the response of future readers and potential activity. This is not to say that writing in the workplace is not based on prior utterances. Indeed, written texts provide essential links between established policies and practices and future institutional actions; however, the rhetorical situations that shape many workplace texts are anticipated or potential situations.

University writing programs designed to address the needs of the student moving to the workplace must address this difference. Assignments that are intended to give the student workplace writing experience must have an orientation toward future action or response; they need to have consequences beyond the classroom (and the student's grade) in order for the student to fully appreciate the prospective aspect of workplace writing. An example would be requiring students to submit a briefing document for an upcoming meeting on campus environmental issues and for them to attend the meeting. In such a task, students would have to anticipate response at the meeting and shape the document accordingly. Admittedly, design for such a course would always be difficult, as it requires the instructor to continually seek out authentic, and manageable (within the time constraints of the course), writing tasks.

Response to the Text

In making the transition from the university to the workplace, the writer leaves a setting in which her overall performance within that context shapes how a given reader might respond to, and evaluate, what she has written. Her class participation and overall progress might be considered when her term paper is graded. Once in the workplace, however, the writer finds that the halo effect (and, contrarily, the pitchfork effect) no longer applies. In the workplace, it is what is written that counts. Her reader is no longer concerned with what she *might* have said or where she *could* have inserted more statistics to back up this claim; she is now obliged to find a way to collaborate with her supervisor/reader to ensure that her text says exactly what is intended and reflects exactly what is expected.

Complicating the new employee's initiation into the written discourse of the workplace is the nature of the written comments she receives from the reader, usually her direct supervisor, to the texts she produces. The writer has recently experienced years of writing in an environment in which the purpose of the reader's written response to her texts was to indicate her effectiveness in participating in the conversation of the course, to judge the degree of learning, to indicate sections which were particularly effective or ineffective, and/or to justify a grade given. These written comments were necessary aspects of the closure of the writing event: the evaluation. The intention of these written comments would rarely have been to provide directives for future revision. The text the student had submitted was, after all, a "final" draft.

Upon entering the workplace, the writer needs to learn to use a very different type of written response for a very different purpose. The written comments provide the initial content of his institutional learning. They may instruct him, for example, to insert information from other documents (which he may or may not have already read), to get information from other employees, to relate information in one paragraph to another program being proposed, to change a word because it has loaded meanings within that context, and so on. If the new employee is aware of this difference, the reader's comments (the imperative for revision) will guide workplace learning.

CONCLUSION

Studying readers' responses in university and workplace settings allows us to identify and articulate many of the underlying and fundamental sociocultural differences that distinguish their rhetorical activities. These differences are significant because the writing produced in the two settings often appears to be similar on a textual level. Written discourse in a government agency and in a university business program, for example, includes similar disciplinary content, evidenced in both its substance and its lexicon. The writing at the government agency is often characterized by its similarity to academic discourse, in its length and its orientation toward analysis. Likewise, writing in business courses is often based on "real world" contexts: analysis of real events, case studies based on real events, application of theoretical constructs to real events. Given these textual similarities, it is significant that the rhetorical activities surrounding texts in the two settings, in this case the reading practices, are markedly different.

Although the nature of written discourse in the two settings appears similar, written genres arise out of very different social settings and are the result of very different social and rhetorical goals and activities. The practices and response of readers to texts in the two settings differ significantly, just as the processes of composing and revising them do.

For the university graduate moving into the workplace, there is a great deal to learn about how writing as a workplace activity differs from writing in the university—learning that the new employee and her supervisor rarely acknowledge needs to take place (see Chapter 2, this volume). The findings described in this chapter could help that graduate make the school-to-workplace transition, because they provide insight into an important perspective—that of the oldtimer whose comments reflect and maintain the norms and activities of the community that the newcomer is entering, and whose position of institutional power also can be used to determine the extent to which the newcomer has met expectations.

REFERENCES

Adam, C. (1994a). *Exploring the exigencies of institutional reading practices: A comparison of reader responses in two settings.* Unpublished masters thesis. Carleton University, Ottawa.

Adam, C. (1994b). Reading institutional cultures: A comparison of readers in two settings. *Carleton Papers in Applied Language Studies, 11,* 98-122.

Aldrich, P.G. (1982). Adult writers: Some reasons for ineffective writing on the job. *College Composition and Communication, 33,* 284-287.

Andrews, J.D., & Sigband, N.B. (1984). How effectively does the "new" accountant communicate? Perceptions by practitioners and academics. *The Journal of Business Communication, 21,* 15-24.

Anson, C.M., & Forsberg, L.L. (1990). Moving beyond the academic community: Transitional stages in professional writing. *Written Communication, 7,* 200-231.

Bataille, R.R. (1982). Writing in the world of work: What our graduates report. *College Composition and Communication, 33,* 276-280.

Bednar, A.S., & Olney, R.J. (1987, December). Communication needs of recent graduates. *The Bulletin,* 22-23.

Brandt, D. (1990). *Literacy as involvement: The acts of writers, readers, and texts.* Carbondale: Southern Illinois University Press.

Brandt, D. (1992). The cognitive as the social: An ethnomethodological approach to writing process research. *Written Communication, 9,* 315-351.

Dias, P., Freedman, A., Medway, P., & Paré, A. (1999). *Worlds apart: Acting and writing in academic and workplace contexts.* Mahwah, NJ: Erlbaum.

Faigley, L., & Miller, T.P. (1982). What we learn from writing on the job. *College English, 44,* 557-569.

Freedman, A., & Adam, C. (1996). Learning to write professionally: "Situated learning" and the transition from university to professional discourse. *Journal of Business and Technical Communication, 10,* 395-427.

Freedman, A., Adam, C., & Smart, G. (1994). Wearing suits to class: Simulating genres and simulations as genre. *Written Communication, 11,* 192-226.

Gilsdorf, J.W. (1986). Executives' and academics' perceptions on the need for instruction in written persuasion. *The Journal of Business Communication, 23,* 55-68.

Lave, J., & Wenger, E. (1991). *Situated learning: Legitimate peripheral participation.* Cambridge: Cambridge University Press.

Miller, C.R. (1984). Genre as social action. *Quarterly Journal of Speech, 70,* 151-167.

Petraglia, J. (1995). Writing as an unnatural act. In J. Petraglia (Ed.), *Reconceiving writing, rethinking writing instruction* (pp. 79-100). Mahwah, NJ: Erlbaum.

Radar, M.H., & Wunsch, A.P. (1980). A survey of communication practices of business school graduates by job category and undergraduate major. *The Journal of Business Communication, 17,* 33-41.

Smart, G. (1993). Genre as community invention: A central agency's response to its executives' expectations as readers. In R. Spilka (Ed.), *Writing in the workplace: New research perspectives* (pp. 124-140). Carbondale: Southern Illinois University Press.

Swales, J. (1988). Discourse communities, genres and English as an international language. *World English, 7,* 211-220.

Swales, J. (1990). *Genre analysis: English in academic and research settings.* Cambridge: Cambridge University Press.

CHAPTER 8

Revising a Research Article: Dialogic Negotiation[1]

Natasha Artemeva
Carleton University

Studies of scientific research in different disciplines have provided evidence of the profoundly rhetorical and social nature of knowledge making (Barabas, 1990; Bazerman, 1988; Berkenkotter & Huckin, 1995; Blakeslee, 1997; Dias, Freedman, Medway, & Paré, 1999; Latour & Woolgar, 1979; Myers, 1990; Swales, 1990). Journal articles serve as critical moments in this discursive construction of scientific knowledge, as the authors of these articles must collaborate with colleagues, reviewers, and editors in a negotiated effort to produce information and ideas that their disciplinary community will find appropriate and important. This chapter explores that collaborative process by eavesdropping on coauthors engaged in the revision of a research article in the field of metallurgical engineering. The article in question was rejected by one journal and accepted provisionally by a second journal, on condition that the authors make the major revisions suggested by two reviewers and supported by the journal's edi-

[1]This research would not have been completed without the generous assistance of Professor Peter Medway of the School of Linguistics and Applied Language Studies of Carleton University. The author thanks the participants of this study for their insights and Anthony Paré for very useful feedback on an earlier draft of this article.

tor. In what follows, we observe the authors doing the rhetorical work of knowledge making in science.

This case study demonstrates how experienced authors respond to a changing situation and the many cues they receive from different readers in order to revise. In other words, it illustrates the type of transition writers must make within professional contexts as audiences and rhetorical exigences change. A close analysis of this process informed by theories of situated learning (Freedman & Adam, 1996; Lave & Wenger, 1991) and complemented with Bakhtinian (1986) notions of dialogism and Miller's (1984) notion of genre as social action provides insights into the types of transitions that workers must sometimes make between rhetorical situations in workplace settings.

In a Bakhtinian (1986) framework, this process of transition from one audience to another may be presented as a series of dialogues between the authors and their addressees, in which each new draft of the paper, every reviewer's report, each letter from the editor, and any type of written and/or oral communication can be perceived as individual utterances. As Bakhtin (1986) puts it, "Complexly structured and specialized works of various scientific . . . genres, in spite of all the ways in which they differ from rejoinders in dialogue, are by nature the same kind of units of speech communication" (p. 75). Combining this notion with Miller's (1984) view of "genre as a social action," one can consider reviewers' reports in particular as the exigence for the authors' action; that is, the changes made in the text of the article were the authors' "uptake" of the referees' utterances, to use Freadman's (1998) term to describe the dialogic relation between pairs of utterances.

In this chapter, I will describe the review and revision that the research article went through as a dialogue and as a negotiation of knowledge between the writers and their immediate audience (editors and referees). I will show that even experienced writers of scientific papers need to go through a necessary and sometimes painful transition in order to reach a new audience. The reward for a successful transition in this case is publication in the chosen scientific journal. The chapter is divided into five main sections: Setting the Stage; The Response to Referees' Criticism; Types of Collaboration; Letters to the Editor; and Conclusions.

SETTING THE STAGE

This investigation considers two professors at a Canadian university, junior and senior members of a faculty of engineering. The senior professor, whom I shall call Jack, is a researcher and practitioner well known in his field. Recently he and the junior professor, whom I shall call Alex,[2] approached a certain area in computer simulation of metallurgical processes that they had not explored before. The research article in which they discussed their findings presented a new step in the development of an already-known computer model that simulates changes that occur in metal structure during metallurgical processes. The authors claimed that this new modification would enable researchers to use realistic conditions in the simulation and thus to obtain results as close to the real-world picture as is possible with current computer equipment.

The first version of the article was sent to a prestigious European journal that the authors considered most appropriate to the topic of their paper because the main research in the area was published there. The text was prepared according to the requirements of this journal and was intended to address an elite or highly specialized scientific audience. When sending their article to this journal, Alex and Jack were aware that there was a chance of having their manuscript rejected, but they expected the article at least to be reviewed. Knowing that the referees for this journal would be recognized authorities in the field, the authors thought that they would receive constructive feedback. Because in the academic world "prestige is more important than speed or certainty of publication" (Garvey, 1979, p. 79), they took the risk and sent the article to the prestigious journal.

This investigation starts at the point where the first version of the article was rejected by the editor of the prestigious scientific journal without review. The editor justified his decision by saying that a page limit imposed by the publishers forced him "to redirect to other journals papers which, though scientifically sound, deal with a topic or use an approach which is better suited to publication elsewhere" and suggested an alternative international journal. This was not a surprise to the authors because, as Garvey (1979) explains, "in the most prestigious journals a majority of the manuscripts received are not accepted for publication" (p. 72). There are various pretexts for rejection, including page limit. Still, Jack and Alex were disappointed not to get feedback from reviewers.

---

[2]Alex is a newcomer to Canada. When this research started, he had been with the Department of Engineering for about three years. Though he is not a native speaker of English, he has considerable experience writing for European scientific journals; before his arrival in Canada, Alex had published several articles and a scientific book in English.

Though the authors wanted to publish the article as quickly as possible, they did not send it to the journal the editor recommended. Alex explained in an interview that he had looked through some issues of that journal and concluded that the article might not suit it. He also stressed that he would like to publish another paper there, which he would address to the specific expertise and interests of its audience. Both authors were anxious to get their work published and so decided to send it to a less prestigious national journal where the time between submission and publication might be shorter. Even though the first version of the article had been written with the highly competent audience of the prestigious European journal in mind and some routine details of the procedure had been omitted from the paper, Alex and Jack, trying to save time, sent the original text unchanged to the chosen national journal.

The editor of the national journal sent a letter acknowledging receipt of the paper and forwarded the paper to two referees. After some time the authors received two anonymous reviews accompanied by a letter from the editor. As both reviewers requested major revisions to be made in the article, the editor recommended that this advice be taken into consideration and that the paper be revised and sent back to the journal for reconsideration.

After this, the authors started a long process of changing the paper to satisfy the requirements of the two reviewers (I shall call them R1 and R2), clearly understanding that "before any article can reach the diffuse and perhaps distant audience of journal readers, it must pass by the immediate and definite audience of a few referees" (Myers, 1990, p. 63). Because the process of revision was initiated by the reviewers' critical comments, the reviewers' reports can be considered an exigence calling forth an immediate action or uptake: changes in the existing text of the article. R1 and R2 became for the authors their "immediate audience at which the persuasion is directed" (Myers, 1990, p. 63).

THE RESPONSE TO REFEREES' CRITICISM

Though both referees' reports were supposed to be anonymous, neither R1 nor R2 succeeded in concealing his identity. The authors easily understood who R1 was by his use of specific expressions that were very typical of his scientific articles. After having studied the referees' comments in detail, Jack and Alex came to the conclusion that R2 had directed his major criticism towards aspects of the problem that had been considered in an article of his own. R2 revealed his identity by explicitly referring to that article in his report, claiming that the manuscript "may be considered for publication" if the aspects discussed in his article "are considered in the simulation and missing information is provided in the paper." Jack and Alex had not included this article in their literature survey because it had been published after their paper had been sent to the European journal.

Because the authors' first intention had been to have their article published in the prestigious journal, they had referred mainly to the papers previously published there, a common rhetorical strategy in academic and scientific discourse:

> articles published in a journal most frequently cite other articles published in the same journal . . . [though] it is not clear how much such citing is done because of the relationship of citations to the structure of scientific knowledge or how much because an author is trying to infix his article in a particular stream associated with a journal. In any event, an author will be better off if he makes certain he has cited all relevant articles previously published in the journal to which he is submitting his manuscript than concentrating on citations outside the stream of that journal. (Garvey, 1979, p. 84)

Trying to save time, Jack and Alex had not adjusted their bibliography when sending the article to the national journal because the insertion of new references would have required corresponding changes in the text of the article. In effect, they had failed to link up to the journal's intertextual chain, its sequence of utterances, and their article was not recognized as an appropriate uptake. Therefore, after receiving the referees' reports, Jack and Alex had to include new information and references in the revised draft of their article. In addition, they had to refer to R2's paper in the list of references in spite of the fact that, according to Alex, R2's article had made no important contribution to the field and the questions R2 asked in the reviewer's report were "primitive questions that could only be asked at the defense of a Master's thesis but even not at the defense of a Ph.D dissertation" (from an interview). The act of including R2's article in the list of references and of referring to it in the text of the paper was merely a move to satisfy R2's demands.

Discussing R1's report, which was much more negative than R2's, the authors emphasized that some of R1's statements were erroneous because he criticized the method used in the article as "not a proper test for their model" and suggested that another method be used. The authors claimed that their article continued a scientific tradition that routinely used this method for the solution of analo-

gous problems. In the letter to the editor, which they started composing while drafting a new version of their article, they justified their
use of the method:

> Solidification from the supercooled melt is a long standing solidi-
> fication problem. It is the object of intensive studies and is **rele-**
> **vant to** real solidification processes. . . . It is quite natural to use
> the test with one dimensional growth from a supercooled melt to
> test this model. . . . Similar models have been used for the simu-
> lation of different phase transformations. (From the draft letter
> to the editor; emphasis in the original)

They pointed out that if a model is modified, it must be tested in the
framework used in the previous research for the sake of consistency
and comparability of results. The writers insisted both in their final
letter to the editor and in the interviews with me that only by using
the same method consistently could they compare the obtained
results with the data in previous publications. Jack and Alex's claims
for the appropriateness of their method match Gilbert's (1977)
description of a typical organization of a scientific article:

> authors typically show how the results of their work represent an
> advance on previous research; they relate their particular findings
> to the current literature of their field; and they provide evidence
> and argument to persuade their audience that their work has not
> been vitiated by error, that appropriate and adequate techniques
> and theories have been employed, and that alternative, contradic-
> tory hypotheses have been examined and rejected. (p. 116)

Discussing possible sources of R1's criticism, Alex even supposed that
R1 had attacked the method used in the article and suggested an alternative method because he had used this alternative method in his own
research. As Berkenkotter and Huckin (1995) mention, "an author
often encounters reviewers with competing research agendas" (p. 63)
who may use their power as gatekeepers to prevent competitors'
research from being published. R1 also required some technical details
that both Alex and Jack had considered basic knowledge and omitted
from their article. R1 claimed that Jack and Alex "did not try to compare their model results with any form of experimental results and
they did not even bother to check on the numerical accuracy and consistency of their results." According to the authors, however, such a comparison is the first standard step in any numerical modeling and "is an
elementary problem that is taught to second year engineering students" (from an interview). Jack and Alex considered this information

unnecessary because such technical details had not been mentioned in any of the publications originally included in their literature survey.

From some of R1's statements, Jack and Alex concluded that he had not read their article carefully enough to understand the results they achieved in their research because R1 had pointed out their main result as "a critical weakness" (from R1's report) of the paper. The authors guessed that R1's criticism was based mainly on the fact that they had ignored his publications in their article: "[T]he authors do not seem to be aware of the relevant literature in English in the field and therefore did not refer to a few relevant and important papers related to the work" (from R1's report); he did not specify, though, which papers those could be (in contrast to R2, who referred to his own article in the report). The original version of the article, sent to the prestigious journal in February, 1994, and then without changes redirected to the Canadian journal, contained a list of fourteen relevant references published between 1980 and 1993. While revising their paper, in addition to R1's and R2's articles, Jack and Alex referred to several more recent publications of well-known scientists that helped them support their scientific claims. In making the transition to a new audience, the authors had to relocate their discussion, placing it within the relevant chain of utterances.

Responding to R2's criticism, Jack and Alex now included descriptions of technical procedures that, according to Alex, would have been omitted from consideration by any experienced researcher in this field. Alex claimed that such details only made the article "more boring and difficult to read" for a well-prepared, competent audience. However, because the national journal had an audience that differed from the audience of the international journal first chosen by the authors, they were forced to adjust their article to the referees' requirements. As Garvey (1979) aptly puts it,

> [A]s rigid as the journal article style and format may be, there is still considerable room for shaping the content of the manuscript to match the characteristics of the criteria editors and referees use to select manuscripts. Much of such adjusting by the author is simple and straight-forward, e.g., emphasizing applied implications, stressing theoretical implications, and giving more weight to integration of information bearing on a subject. (p. 84)

Jack and Alex made major changes in the description of the procedure and the presentation of the results; the conclusions drawn from the research remained unaltered. Therefore, Alex still thought that new criticism might be brought up by R1, who seemed to be attacking the main conclusions of the study.

Both Jack and Alex thought that R2 would be satisfied by the reference to his article in their revised manuscript, despite the fact that his article (identified below as [26]) had been referred to critically:

> In [26] this feature of a simulation model was considered as a method for modeling anisotropy effects in dendrite growth processes. However, this anisotropy arises from the mesh and it can occur in all computer simulation models. **It does not represent real anisotropy of a physical system.** Modeling of real anisotropy effects should involve the anisotropy of solid-liquid interface properties, i.e., surface energy and kinetic coefficient. (emphasis added)

Because science policy makers and scientific funding agencies use citation-count measures in both the evaluation of funded research and in the determination of which research to fund, as well as in decision making on matters such as tenure (Garvey, 1979), perhaps the authors felt R2 would not mind if his article was cited in a critical context, as long as it was cited.

TYPES OF COLLABORATION

The collaborative research and coauthoring conducted by Jack and Alex are "a functional requirement of contemporary scientific investigation" (Zuckerman, cited in Ede & Lunsford, 1992, p. 75). Single authorship remains typical in the humanities and social sciences, but in fields such as medicine, science, and engineering multiple authorship is common. When revising their article in order to adjust it to the expectations of their new audience, Jack and Alex were making decisions about text alterations collaboratively. Such a collaboration of authors during the process of writing and revising a paper involved different types of written and oral communication.

Thus, Jack would send e-mail messages to Alex with his suggestions about the changes that might be made to improve the paper:

> *I will leave the introduction to the solidification paper in your mailbox today about 1 pm. I think the introduction could be much shorter or at least an introduction to the introduction. A rough draft is suggested below. It contains errors but the idea should be clear enough. . . .*

A rough draft followed. Then a more polished version of the text appeared in Alex's office mailbox. Alex and Jack used another way to communicate through e-mail. They sent to each other the actual text of parts of the article (or of the whole article) with highlighted new or changed paragraphs and/or comments and suggestions so that those paragraphs could be easily recognized in the familiar text and then reviewed and, if necessary, modified. For example, draft 4 had been e-mailed to Jack. It contained the following paragraph:

> In the second group of models with a diffuse interface a phase field (Q) characterizes the phase state of the system in each point, and points in the interphase boundary have phase field values that can vary in some finite interval between values corresponding to the solid and liquid states [22-23]. The free energy of the system (F) is described as a functional of the phase field, concentration (c), their gradients, and the temperature (T) [22].

Jack then e-mailed a new version to Alex with highlighted changes and suggestions (draft 5), including the following comments on the above paragraph:

> I am not sure the [paragraph] is exactly correct. It is standard in differential geometry in 3D to represent surfaces either explicitly or as a level set of a scalar function. An explicit representation of the surface suffers from the topological difficulties you describe [in the paragraph]. The level set of a function does not suffer from the topological difficulties. Both represent a surface as having zero thickness. I agree with your other differences such as solving in two domains.
>
> Of course, there is a difference when you discretize the two formulations. In the first case, the surface is only defined as having zero thickness. In the second case, the surface can be interpreted as having a thickness or uncertainty.

As we see, the text is not intended for insertion in the article. Rather, it constitutes an utterance in an ongoing dialogue. Jack poses questions in connection with the changes Alex had introduced in draft 4. This prompt of Jack's leads to some major changes (italicized below) in the paragraph in draft 6 of the article:

> In the second group of models *the interface boundary is described as a level set* of phase field characterizing the phase state of the system in each point. *A sharp boundary can be described by the level set corresponding to a single value of the phase field. Such*

> *an approximation together with the boundary integral equation*
> *describing the phase field evolution was used in [21] for a thermal*
> *dendrite growth. The solution was obtained on the whole system*
> *and the changes in the topology of the moving interphase bound-*
> *ary did not require any additional efforts. A diffuse boundary is*
> *described by* the phase field varying in some interval between
> values corresponding to the solid and liquid states [22-23]. *In*
> *such phase field models* the free energy of the system (F) is
> described as a functional of the phase field, concentration (c),
> their gradients, and the temperature (F) [22].

Comparing texts of the same paragraphs in draft 4 and draft 6, we
can see how Jack's words and their meanings are not only interpreted and used as a prompt for the changes but are also actually
employed in the new version of the text.

E-mail played an important role in the process of revising the
article by making possible the speedy exchange of several drafts during one working day. Nevertheless, both Jack and Alex continued
printing out versions of the article and worked intensively with the
hard copy of the text as well. This approach helped them to control
the changing text of the article as a whole, whereas e-mail was used
for the discussion of alterations in separate smaller sections (often,
paragraphs) of the paper. Jack and Alex also exchanged written
notes with their ideas and comments while rewriting the article and
discussed new ideas during numerous conferences. Thus, for example, Alex sent one of the drafts of the paper in hard copy to Jack
along with a letter in which he described the changes he had made
and gave his justifications for those changes, stating that he thought
that the introduction should have been written in more detail "to give
information about main previously obtained results, to characterize
main important effects that should be incorporated into simulation
model, and to describe the potential and the limitation of existing
models." Further he claimed that it was

> necessary to keep this analysis as we discussed it first time, in
> particular because one of the negative comments of the first
> reviewer is that an incomplete consideration of the contemporary
> state of the dendrite growth theory is given and the place of our
> model in the whole picture is not shown.

After Jack had received these texts and had read and analyzed them,
he and Alex had a conference together after which new changes in
the draft were made.

LETTERS TO THE EDITOR

Responding to R1 and R2's criticism and anticipating future criticism, Jack and Alex significantly changed some parts of their article by inserting relevant paragraphs in the text. They referred to those changes in their final letter to the editor, which they composed in the course of their revision of the article:

> In a revised version of our paper we have provided information on the selection of **cell size** used in the modeling and on **the effects of cell size on the simulation results** (1). We also give information on **the time discretization** criteria used to avoid instability in numerical solution of heat and solute diffusion problems (2). Possible **anisotropy** effects which can be produced in this simulation model are discussed (3). (emphasis added)

The numbers mentioned in this letter refer to the reviewers' comments: (1) refers to R2's requirement that, "[t]he authors should give the . . . cell resolution, effect of cell resolution on the shape evolution," where terms *cell resolution* and *cell size* are equivalent, and R1's requirement that "[t]he authors must carry out and report grid sensitivity tests of their two-dimensional finite-difference equations," where *grid sensitivity* is equivalent to cell size; (2) refers to R1's requirement that "[t]he authors should report the time step and grid sizes used," where *the time step* and *grid sizes* are equivalent to *the time discretization* and *cell size*, respectively; and (3) refers to R2's requirement that the authors should consider in their simulation that "[d]endrite growth depends on the *crystallographic direction*," where the term *crystallographic direction* has the same meaning as *anisotropy*.

According to Berkenkotter and Huckin (1995), such letters "must convince the editor either that necessary repair of a manuscript has been made, or that a specific request of a reviewer is unwarranted" (p. 63). Jack and Alex in fact wrote three drafts of the letter to the editor emphasizing the changes made in the text of the article in response to referees' requirements, and attempting to express the fact that some essential details of their study had been overlooked by the editor and/or by the reviewers. In revising the letter, they stressed their concern about the audience. Thus, for example, the phrase "We also discussed the selection of initial conditions and the question why it is necessary to introduce the initial nucleus (substrate) of solid phase into the solidification model" was changed into "We also discussed the selection of initial conditions and **explained** why it is necessary to introduce the initial nucleus (substrate) of solid phase into the solidification model" (emphasis in the original); the phrase "In particular, we have clarified the idea . . ." was changed into "In particular, we have **emphasized** the idea" (emphasis in the original). By making such changes the authors afforded more support to the claims and statements made in the article.

Jack and Alex considered their letter to the editor as a part of their response to the reviewers' reports together with the final text of the revised article. The letter to the editor was an essential part of the authors' utterance in the dialogue with the editor and the reviewers. It was "filled with echoes and reverberations" (Bakhtin, 1986, p. 91) of the referees' utterances to which it was closely related. The text of the article and the letter to the editor mutually modified each other and had a specific meaning for the immediate audience (the referees and the editor)—a meaning that would not exist for the ultimate audience, as the referees' reports as well as the letter to the editor would never become known to the readers of the published article. By sending the letter to the editor along with the final copy of the article, the authors not only responded to the reviewers' criticism and to the editor's suggestions for the changes to be made and the article to be resubmitted, but also defended their scientific claims.

Jack and Alex strongly believed that the revised version of their article was going to be published in the national journal, as they had gone through a long process of revising it in negotiation with their immediate audience of R1, R2, and the editor, and they had tried to anticipate the response of the potential audience of journal readers. They perceived this negotiation as directly addressing their claim and the evidence for it and also as focusing on the form of the text. The authors not only had included more information in the article and had been more explicit about certain details of the procedure, but also had employed actual words and meanings used by the referees, both in the text of their paper and in the letter to the editor.

After Alex and Jack had resubmitted the final copy of the article to the national journal, they received a letter of acceptance from the editor. The editor wrote:

> I would like to inform you that your revisions have been accepted and your paper is recommended for publishing. . . . Congratulations and thank you for giving us the opportunity to review your work.[3]

---

[3]This article was published in 1997.

The long and painful process of transition from one journal audience to another was, therefore, successfully completed by Jack and Alex.

CONCLUSIONS

This observation of the process of revision illuminates the social nature and situatedness of the collaborative process of writing a scientific research article. In this context collaborative writing can be considered as an ongoing dialogue between the authors and, at the same time, as the process of knowledge negotiation between the author-researchers and the immediate others (referees and the editor) involved. The authors try to show that the results obtained in the research deserve credit, "while . . . the editors and reviewers try to relate the claim to the body of the knowledge produced by the [scientific] community" (Myers, 1990, p. 67) or try to pursue their own ambitions and interests.

The negotiation of knowledge that the authors went through with the referees and the editor demonstrates that learning and relearning constantly takes place in the scientific world well beyond university years. The cues in the referees' reports that Jack and Alex responded to were quite different from the often explicit cues that guide learning at school (Freedman, Adam, & Smart, 1994; Winsor, 1996). The authors' eventual success in publication shows that they have learned to change or shift their ways of persuasion while negotiating with their immediate audience. This again illustrates that learning and knowing are context specific and that learning is accomplished through processes of coparticipation (Blakeslee, 1997; Dias, Freedman, Medway, & Paré, 1999; Freedman & Adam, 1996; Lave & Wenger, 1991).

All the utterances produced by different participants—both authors, the two reviewers, and the editor—interrelate in this dialogic process of the negotiation of meaning. As Bakhtin (1986) brilliantly expresses it,

> [T]he unique speech experience of each individual is shaped and developed in continuous and constant interaction with others' individual utterances. This experience can be characterized to some degree as the process of assimilation—more or less creative—of others' words. . . . Our speech, that is, all our utterances (including creative work) is filled with others' words, varying degrees of otherness or varying degrees of "our-own-ness," varying degrees of awareness and detachment. These words of others

carry with them their own expression, their own evaluative tone, which we assimilate, rework, and reaccentuate. (p. 89)

Theories of situated learning, combined with Bakhtin/Miller perspectives on genre, provide new insights into the actual process of transition that even experienced writers of scientific research papers go through in the workplace context while trying to meet the expectations of a changing audience. In addition, they allow us to see into the social roles of all participants of collaborative writing, and into motivations for the turns taken in the complex dialogue called "writing and revising a research article."

REFERENCES

Bakhtin, M. M. (1986). The problem of speech genres. In C. Emerson & M. Holquist (Eds.), V. W. McGee (Trans.), *Speech genres and other late essays* (pp. 60-102). Austin: University of Texas Press.

Barabas, C. (1990). *Technical writing in a corporate culture: A study of the nature of information.* Norwood, NJ: Ablex.

Bazerman, C. (1988). *Shaping written knowledge: The genre and activity of the experimental article in science.* Madison: University of Wisconsin Press.

Berkenkotter, C., & Huckin, T. N. (1995). *Genre knowledge in disciplinary communication: Cognition/culture/power.* Hillsdale, NJ: Erlbaum.

Blakeslee, A. M. (1997). Activity, context, interaction, and authority: Learning to write scientific papers in situ. *Journal of Business and Technical Communication, 11*(2), 125-169.

Dias, P., Freedman, A., Medway, P., & Paré, A. (1999). *Worlds apart: Acting and writing in academic and workplace contexts.* Mahwah, NJ: Erlbaum.

Ede, L., & Lunsford, A. (1992). *Singular texts/Plural authors: Perspectives on collaborative writing.* Carbondale: Southern Illinois University Press.

Freadman, A. (1998, January). *"Uptake."* Paper presented at the Symposium on Genre, Simon Fraser University, Burnaby, British Columbia, January.

Freedman, A., & Adam, C. (1996). Learning to write professionally: "Situated learning" and the transition from university to professional discourse. *Journal of Business and Technical Communication, 10*(4), 395-427.

Freedman, A., Adam, C., & Smart, G. (1994). Wearing suits to class: Simulating genres and simulation as genre. *Written Communication, 11*, 193-226.

Garvey, W. D. (1979). *Communication: The essence of science. Facilitating information exchange among librarians, scientists, engineers and students.* Oxford: Pergamon Press.

Gilbert, G. N. (1977). Referencing as persuasion. *Social Studies of Science, 7*, 113-122.

Lave, J., & Wenger, E. (1991). *Situated learning: Legitimate peripheral participation.* Cambridge: Cambridge University Press.

Latour, B., & Woolgar, S. (1979). *Laboratory life: The social construction of scientific facts.* Beverly Hills, CA: Sage.

Miller, C. (1984). Genre as social action. *Quarterly Journal of Speech, 70*, 151-167.

Myers, G. (1990). *Writing biology: Texts in the social construction of scientific knowledge.* Madison: The University of Wisconsin Press.

Swales, J. (1990). *Genre analysis: English in academic and research settings.* Cambridge: Cambridge University Press.

Winsor, D. (1996). *Writing like an engineer: A rhetorical education.* Mahwah, NJ: Erlbaum.

CHAPTER 9

Organizational Cultures as Contexts for Learning to Write[1]

Jane Ledwell-Brown
McGill University

That's how I was taught by the managers here. And it's sort of accepted within the company that that's the way a research report should look.
—Esther B., manager

It is to be expected that university graduates who become members of an organization will not only have to learn job-related tasks and establish workplace relationships, but will also in the process gain an understanding of the organization's way of doing things, what one might call its culture, aspects of which are its particular jargon, the power and political structures within the organization, its tradi-

[1]This article is based on my doctoral dissertation completed in September, 1993 and supported by the Social Sciences and Humanities Research Council of Canada and the McGill Major Fellowships program. In order to maintain the confidentiality I have assured them, I am unable to mention the research participants' names. They contributed valuable information about their experiences as writers and readers at the Health Care Company; they also gave me generous amounts of time for interviews and supported this project with much interest.

tions, rituals, goals and values (Chao, O'Leary-Kelly, Wolf, Klein, & Gardner, 1994). This task is complicated by at least three factors: (1) established members of the organization may not be able to articulate their knowledge about the culture for the newcomer because much of such knowledge is tacit (Sathe, 1989); (2) newcomers may not recognize the need or find it difficult to establish comfortable working relationships with potential mentors (Freedman & Adam, Chapter 2, this volume); and (3) an organization's culture may be enacted in different ways from division to division, so that it would be appropriate to speak of sub-cultures rather than a single culture within an organization (Martin 1992; Morgan, 1986; Paré, this volume; Sackmann, 1992).

Whether universities should be expected to prepare students to meet these complex socio-rhetorical demands of organizational life remains a moot point (see Tebeaux, 1996). Surveys of writers in the workplace (Anderson, 1985; Bataille, 1982; Brown, 1988) have suggested that workers develop their writing ability on the job rather than in the classroom. My own part-time students who are full-time workers confirm this and report that the criteria for successful workplace writing differ considerably from those for successful university writing. Certainly, the research reported elsewhere in this book points to the reasons for this.

Studies of writers and texts in both academic and nonacademic settings clearly demonstrate that learning to write is an ongoing process as writers move into and meet the demands of new situations. The literature on writing often refers to such situations—disciplines, companies, and institutions, for example—as "discourse communities," in which "members know what is worth communicating, how it can be communicated, what other members of the community are likely to know and believe to be true about certain subjects, how other members can be persuaded, and so on" (Faigley, 1985, p. 238). Members' texts are community-specific genres, which Swales (1990) defines as typified rhetorical actions needed to achieve a community's goals, actions that, as Dias (this volume) suggests, are responses to community members' interpretations of situations.

The particular task of this chapter is to look at one such community, a large pharmaceutical company, in order to elaborate on the nature of those cultural demands, specifically insofar as they impact on writers. The data I draw on comes from a larger, comprehensive study of the Health Care Company (HCC), the Canadian arm of a large multinational organization engaged in the research, development, production, and marketing of pharmaceuticals (Ledwell-Brown, 1993). I hope to show from that data how the overall values and attitudes of the organization translate into specific expectations of writers, and how the unique divisional functions and place within the organization determine rhetorical strategies. Because these rhetorical practices remain implicit, we must ask how newcomers may be better prepared to take them on.

Writers and texts rather than readers have been the primary source for understandings of what writers must learn to become members of discourse communities. (The few exceptions include Adam, this volume; Kleimann, 1993; Smart, 1993.) But, because managers in organizations are typically the first readers of employees' texts and responsible for ensuring that discourse conforms to the organization's goals and values, a study of writing from the perspective of such readers should help elucidate why managers respond to writers' texts as they do and the criteria they use when they approve the texts or return them for revision.

When I use the word "culture" in this chapter, I have in mind "the underlying values, beliefs, and principles that serve as a foundation for the organization's management system as well as the set of management practices and behaviors that both exemplify and reinforce those basic principles" (Morgan, 1986, p. 2). Such a culture, as Morgan notes, is rarely a single, unified culture; rather, organizations may have many subcultures based on professional differences (p. 127). Such cultural divisions also occur along hierarchical and functional boundaries (Schein, 1971).

RESEARCH GOAL AND METHOD

As mentioned earlier, I was concerned primarily to understand how the beliefs, goals, and values of the organization, explicitly announced or implicit, were reflected in the managers' stated expectations for written communication and in their responses to writing. To obtain the required information, I conducted interviews, both structured and unstructured, observed on site, and reviewed documents. Over a period of 22 months, I tape-recorded interviews with 22 participants, transcribed the 56 interviews for analysis, reduced the data through recursive cycles of review to discern patterns and themes, conducted frequency counts to determine dominant trends in the categories, constructed case descriptions, and verified my understandings with the participants (Goetz & LeCompte, 1984; Miles & Huberman, 1984).

The introductory interviews included open-ended questions about the organization and about the participants' jobs, careers, and experience with writing and reading. To complement my understanding of the organization's activities, values, and goals gained from interviews, I also tracked many of the organization's events, such as staff promotions and awards, new product launches, and public citations, and reviewed the in-house newsletters, bulletin boards, policies and procedures, guidelines for reports, performance appraisal forms, and training material. In further interviews, I asked participants to relate a *critical incident* (Flanagan, 1954) connected to their writing or reading at work. These narratives usually focused on their best or worst writing experiences and thus helped elicit critical details about writing expectations within the company. Other interviews centered on the writing and reading of specific texts, and included "respond-aloud protocols" (Dias, 1996) in which managers commented aloud as they reviewed texts. From the latter interviews, I was able to learn about the tacit criteria managers brought to these reviews. Finally, I met with the participants after they had read the transcripts of their interviews to verify my understandings of their information.

THE RESEARCH SETTING

HCC is a tightly structured corporation where the lines of authority are clearly delineated, and where internal reports that drive the daily operations must be approved at each level as they move through the hierarchy. Managers cannot approve recommendations that require resources beyond their "grant of authority" (the spending limit associated with their position). The approval procedure is specified in the standard procedures manual, which lists the people who must sign particular reports. Thus, internal reports often have long lists of people to whom the report is addressed and copied. As they review reports intended for other readers in the organization, managers play an important role in helping writers to meet organizational and divisional expectations.

Of the 22 participants in this study (managers, directors, and employees who reported to them), two had less than two years' experience in the company, nine had five years or more, and eleven had more than ten years. Many of the participants worked in the Marketing or Management Information Systems divisions, although many of these, especially those in Marketing, had worked in other divisions such as Research, Sales, and Production during their careers with HCC. Other participants included employees in Human Resources, Medical Research, and Sales.

ORGANIZATIONAL CULTURE AND EXPECTATIONS FOR WRITING

My reading of the goals and values underlying HCC's management system and practices emerges from interviews with the participants, reviews of company texts, and recorded observations. Analysis of this data reveals recurring themes. I refer to these themes as *mottoes* and, because of their recurrent surfacing in the data, I believe they delineate fairly well the overall organizational culture. In what follows I describe these mottoes and how they are reflected specifically in beliefs about writing.

We aim for the highest quality
The company's mission, as quoted by a senior manager, is "to be the preeminent pharmaceutical company in Canada through development, research, productivity, and marketing of the highest quality products to enhance the health and quality of community life." This theme, illustrated by the following quote from a market analyst, resonates through all the interviews with the participants:

> We all pride ourselves in working for a company that has quite a unique status in the industry. It comes from the culture of knowing that The Health Care Company hires the best people and you want to live up to its expectations.

In their stories about legendary company figures, participants suggest that education, experience, and talent are key elements in the meaning of "best people." For example, a company magazine features the story of a retiring vice president who made "the greatest strides in modern [industry] marketing" on his return from company-sponsored studies at the Massachusetts Institute of Technology. Citations in business journals referring to HCC's excellent performance support this claim to its unique status in the industry.

Organizational goals for written texts reflect this drive for quality. Participants believe that HCC has particularly high standards, as illustrated by this comment:

> Everything that is sent out of this company—every word, every comma is scrutinized. The legal department makes sure that everything we say or imply in any way, shape, or form is in accordance with full disclosure and balance. Other companies are very ethical in that sense, but HCC is *particularly*.

We expect dedication to the job

HCC's "culture of pride" (Kanter, 1983) is closely associated with the theme of dedication to the company's work. Stories abound about working long hours, especially when a new product is about to be introduced to the market: "I didn't see my wife and children basically for three months. I was here Saturdays and Sundays—every night."

In addition to the promise of security and attractive monetary rewards, upper management encourages the widespread belief that HCC employees are capable of extraordinary effort: "The sheer number of product launches puts huge demands on marketing, sales, production, and other groups that would have overtaxed virtually any other organization" (presidential message in the Annual Report).

Recommendation reports requiring approval at the vice-presidential level circulate between writer and supervisor many times: "This is the third [revision] and we've probably got to go around at least another four times, I'm sure." This time-consuming revision process between manager and writer reflects HCC belief in working hard to achieve a product that will be acceptable to upper management. Unacceptable reports indicate a certain lack of dedication. As one manager states:

> I try to be very exacting, because I'm answerable to a higher authority, my boss, who is also very exacting. I would hate to be in a position for a report or recommendation to come out of my department and to have my boss call me in to his office and say, "I'm sorry, I don't understand this." Because what it says is I'm not doing my job.

We respect our traditions

As announced in the annual report, the leadership at HCC strongly believes that traditions are important for maintaining the company's success: "The staying power of an outstanding organization is the commitment by generation after generation of its people to hold fast to its founding values." According to the participants, to maintain its market position HCC has created a highly structured organization:

> I think what makes the company successful is the bureaucracy. It's still quite structured compared to other companies. If I suddenly left the company tomorrow, there'd be another person who could come in and the structure would be there that would allow them to pick it up quickly. So, I think the company has a lot of continuity.

Bureaucracy is obviously not a pejorative designation, and may be read as HCC's concern for continuity, illustrated in part by its policies on the use of report formats, some of which are specified in standard procedures manuals. Managers point out that standard formats make reading and responding more efficient because the reader finds certain information in expected places. In some cases, managers note that formats develop certain reading patterns in readers: "People get used to reading this way and they get used to reading what they want to read."

Even when no written guidelines exist for particular reports, unwritten expectations exist for a traditional format: "It's [the format] sort of in their heads." Writers point out that using the accepted format helps to ensure a positive reception:

> [The format] works well with him, because he's very much an HCC man. This is the way we do things here; there's no other way to do it. So if you follow that message, you set the stage in a positive environment for him to read whatever you're publishing.

We are always selling

External markets and competition for resources within HCC focus attention on selling. Externally, the sales force sells the company's products. Internally, participants sell ideas and projects:

> We always find ourselves selling: Product Managers trying to sell a project to the directors, the [product] group selling our strategy to the Vice-President of Marketing, or simply the Product Manager presenting the strategy to the Sales Representatives for the next two months.

This manager's observation about diction illustrates his belief in writing that sells: "It's 'optimizing.' That means there's an effect on the bottom line, I can gain something from it. As a result of using words like that, you pique the reader's interest." HCC values a selling approach when making recommendations, but, as one manager observes, "It can't be salesmanship of the glossy type, because most of us have been through all that before."

What's not on paper doesn't exist

Participants maintain that HCC values writing highly. One manager explains:

> I generate a lot of paper and I think one of the reasons for that is that one of our old vice-presidents said, "What's not on paper doesn't exist." He's retired now, but a lot of people that worked under him still share that mentality.

This former vice-president's motto occurs as a leitmotif throughout my interview transcripts with all the participants. Written texts very often serve documentation rather than decision-making purposes. For example, one writer explains that although a plan for promotion materials is already included in the current market plan and budget, he must write a recommendation report which his manager will review before it goes to upper management for a signature of approval: "He [the manager] will agree on the project, that's not an issue. It's just that we have to agree on the document before it gets to his boss [for a signature]."

Plans are often presented orally to upper management because, as one participant explains, "We're looking at maybe 20 acetates to present to management, because you can't present all this [a very long report] to management, they'll go crazy." In this case, plans may be approved in principle and later ratified through signatures on the written text.

Texts also serve to continue organizational traditions, as one newcomer explained:

> By using these models [reports found in his predecessor's files] and being new to the company, I've perhaps not injected much of my own style into my report writing yet because I'm still just trying to appease everyone and adhere to the culture here.

Thus these texts not only serve the important function of documenting management decisions, they also help establish the ways in which such decisions are inscribed in the organization's memory.

We value a team approach

During this research I observed a growing emphasis on leadership training for managers to help them with both interdepartmental and intradepartmental teamwork. One participant explained that teamwork is essential to the work of his department: "You build confidence, trust, credibility—these are fundamentals. If you don't have that, you can make no progress." On the other hand, despite the apparent stress on working together, there is an element of surveillance that somehow enforces such collaboration. As one participant's explains the carbon-copy list on one of his memos to team members, "You have to copy your boss and you have to copy the supervisor of the person to whom you're sending the memo."

A similar stress on working together, and incidentally a strong element of supervision, is illustrated by the review process, what participants call "dry runs" or "walk throughs" for presentations to upper management: "It's a matter of all of us trying to apply whatever brainpower we happen to possess to put together as good a job as we can."

We learn from our mistakes

Participants report few formal procedures for orientation to new positions; rather they learn about their jobs by doing them. One newcomer to the organization describes his experience:

> The orientation here is not very formal. For someone like myself that wasn't really disadvantageous at all in that I had two days with [the person] I replaced. Imagine a relay race where you're running around and you hand the baton over. That's what it was; I was running right away. And [his manager] worked very closely with me so, if I tripped at all, she was there to catch the fall. So that way you're allowed to learn and make mistakes. It's well buffered and everybody's checking all the way along the lines.

Another newcomer recounts his experience differently:

> There's a lot that you pick up just by being involved, going to meetings and conferences where all you do is sit and listen. It's tough because you're sort of on the outside for quite a while not participating or contributing. So, you just sit and listen and try to keep track of what's important, what the big concerns are to the department.

It may be of some significance that of these two participants, it was the relay runner who received two promotions during his first two years on the job and the observer who resigned after two years in the same position with the company. These two experiences suggest that how newcomers move from the initial stage of observation, the "sitting by Nellie" stage described by Paré (this volume), to the stage of "attenuated authentic participation" (described in this volume by Freedman & Adam, Chapter 2, and by Paré) has important implications for the process of organizational socialization. Orientation is also a concern for established members of HCC who move to another department within the company: "You haven't been in the job long enough to know the right questions to ask. I was bombarded with meetings and meetings and couldn't get things done. So, it was quite stressful trying to learn everything."

Although close monitoring and recycling of documents enforces the organization's traditional style and formats, there is room for experimentation, but only on a small scale. One writer recounts how he learned by trial and error to get action with his memos: "When I started, I used to say, 'If you are free, could you please try to attend this meeting.' Of course, nobody showed up. I changed my style and now I'm saying, 'Please attend'—and everybody shows up." But, however justified by writing-course recommended practices, certain stylistic endeavors are not tolerated. Another writer explains a less successful effort to make a change in style: "If you take the report-writing class here [a company-organized course taught by an external consultant], they tell you to use 'we'—'We suggest we do this.' HCC are still using 'It is suggested,' 'It is recommended.'" This manager went on to say that she tried using "we" in a report once and "I got it scratched out, so I don't bother. I'm more comfortable with the passive tense [voice] because that's what I've been using for a long time."

In one form or another, these seven themes were expressed by each of the research participants, suggesting there is a unified organizational culture, and that employees have been acculturated into it. All the mottoes equate the organization's success with the organization's traditional ways of operating, ways that apply as well to the production and transmission of written documentation. Close supervision is valued as supportive and evidence of concern for putting out the best product; managers as purveyors of the organization's traditional goals of excellence promote teamwork and collaboration. Outsiders may well read such moves as socialization and cultivating dependence.

Interestingly, the conclusions of a communication survey (commissioned by the organization and conducted by an independent consultant a few years before this study) suggested that an attitude of complacency seemed to exist throughout HCC, fostering a kind of child-parent relationship between the employees and the organization. As the survey report states: "Employees often referred to the Company as 'mother [HCC]' . . . a feeling that no matter what happens to the business, the Company can take care of all employee needs and desires." Many of the employees have worked at HCC for their entire careers, gaining responsibilities as they moved from position to position. This trust in the company as a secure environment, managed in the best interests of the employees, is reflected in the participants' strong emphasis on and uncritical acceptance of routines for gaining approval for their texts from various levels of the hierarchy.

ORGANIZATIONAL SUBCULTURES

Generally, the goals and values of the organization appear to be held consistently across the company; however, I focused on two divisions within the company (Marketing and Management Information Systems) to consider how those goals and values play out at the divisional level, specifically how and whether they shape different writing practices and likely create transitional problems for newcomers.

Both divisions place different emphases on goals for writing and on ways to achieve them. As well, managers' responses as they responded aloud to specific texts also reveal differences between the two divisions. In what follows, I shall describe the two divisions and consider how their distinct goals and values apply to writing practices within those divisions.

The Marketing Division

This division is responsible for marketing HCC's products. The product managers plan strategies for the introduction of new products to the market; they also ensure that appropriate strategies are in place to protect existing products against competing interests. They write major reports such as marketing plans, pricing proposals, and promotion plans; they also write frequent memos requesting or sending information and confirming agreements reached at meetings.

Product managers work with a team of experts who provide the services needed to ensure effective marketing of the product. These experts include the market research analysts and others throughout the organization, such as those in sales, promotion, production, and public relations. The market research analysts collect statistical data on product performance and market trends to forecast the performance of HCC's products.

Employees rotate positions about every two years in the Marketing division. For example, one participant charts her six years with HCC this way: market research analyst, sales representative, then manager of Market Research. Some employees begin as sales representatives and then move into market research. This rotation ensures that all members of this division have experience with the organization's clients and with the various marketing functions. Another effect of the rotation is that employees move from a position (manager of Market Research, for example) in which they have people reporting to them to a position (as product manager, for example) in which no one reports to them (and vice versa). One participant notes: "Before he was my boss, I was working very closely [with him].

But it's always different when you're reporting to somebody than when you are just working with somebody."

As I shall argue below, the Marketing division's beliefs about managing its operations by shifting job responsibilities and relationships to facilitate teamwork are reflected in their beliefs about and responses to writing.

The Management Information Systems Division (M.I.S.)

This division is responsible for the company's automated information systems, telecommunications, and office equipment such as photocopiers and printing equipment. Video conference facilities, computer training, in-house voice mail, mail delivery, portable computers for the sales force, and automated project scheduling are all implemented and maintained by this division. A major writing task is the writing of recommendation reports to justify the implementation of information systems, the purchase of new equipment, or the change in a communication system.

The analysts in this division work with other departments to examine their work routines, define problems, and explore solutions: "It's like moving to a new city each time for the analyst, having to learn who's there, what they do and get along with them all." Because the M.I.S. department works in a technical environment, they speak a language that is often unfamiliar to others in HCC:

> [The analysts] are not knowledgeable about marketing, finance, et cetera—necessarily—so they have to learn and then translate that backward into technical requirements. They become the bridge between the technology and the business people; they have to walk the mile in the other guy's shoes and come back and translate that into technology and back-translate that back into the other guy's shoes and explain it to them.

This division's management practices do not include job rotation; for instance, junior analysts become senior analysts only when positions become available. One member of this division explains the situation this way: "The career path basically comes to a stop in our department. You've reached as high as you can go." As with the Marketing division, the M.I.S. managers' beliefs about writing and their responses to their staff's texts are related to the division's hierarchical structure and its role within the company (in this case, its position as a bridge between technology and the users).

Clearly, these two divisions have distinct functions within HCC and operate on somewhat different assumptions about how their work should be carried out. For instance, the Marketing division projects a strong commitment to teamwork as members work closely with others within the division to plan and carry out marketing strategies. This teamwork is greatly facilitated by the division's tradition of job rotation, which ensures that members understand each other's work. Furthermore, their office space is designed to promote communication among the employees. Offices (except for those of the directors) are, in fact, cubicles with low walls and no doors. A major document file in the Marketing division is the chronological record of every memo or report they have issued, "because we all work on various projects, there's a tendency to overlap." Symbolic of their belief in teamwork is the Marketing division's tradition of distributing gifts to all the employees in the organization when a new product is launched. For example, a recent gift of a bathrobe and hot chocolate to all HCC employees recognizes the efforts of the whole organization to launch the product.

No gifts are forthcoming when the M.I.S. department installs a computer system. Moreover, their unfamiliarity with each other's work and with the jobs done by their clients in other divisions makes teamwork difficult. Within the division, small offices are separated by walls, and computer screens are the most obvious feature. Whereas the main document file, the "systems dictionary," documents the technical details of specific automation projects, it also provides justification for specific events. As one participant explains:

> It's very important to recognize that a system's behavior is affected by correspondence. You have to be able to track back through the correspondence to specific dates, because sometimes people— a year and a half out—will say, "Well, how come you're late? How come you're two months late on this project?"

Members of the M.I.S. division view their mandate as responding to requests for technical solutions to organizational problems. However, as one senior manager explains, the division is beginning to perceive its role somewhat differently:

> We are now marketing-people; we market ideas. We build systems around those ideas and we work with others to make it happen. So, interpersonal skills become a very strong asset for people that are generally conservative, generally introverted.

Future plans include reorganizing M.I.S. members into teams who will specialize in various areas of the organization's work. Managers believe this change will not only generate teamwork, but will also increase the employees' opportunity for growth and development.

The next section describes the ways in which both cultural and functional differences shape the divisions' expectations for writing and their responses to texts.

Differences in Attitudes Toward Writing

An analysis of the interview transcripts produced categories of comments that reveal the participants' beliefs about the goals they had for their texts (*desired outcomes*) and the way texts should be written at HCC (*prescriptions*). As mentioned earlier, the process of arriving at the categories began with reflecting on the questions the readers seemed to be asking of the text or the writer, and going on to arrive at a tentative categorization and coding of comments, and later, a refining of the coding scheme and definitions to account for all the comments made by readers as they responded to their subordinates' texts. The occurrence of statements about desired outcomes and prescriptions in the interview data were tabulated, and in the account that follows, the differences in attitudes toward writing between the two divisions are presented as percentages of relevant comments tabulated for both divisions. It is not axiomatic that a frequency count in and of itself is indicative of a specific tendency. Rather one might regard such quantitative differences in emphasis between departments as signaling tendencies also manifested through several interviews, on-site observations, examination of written policies and guidelines, analysis of the writing produced in these divisions, and ongoing verification of interpretations with participants over the two years of the study. Moreover, the differences that emerge accord with participants' perceptions of divisional goals and values.

Participants (writers and readers) from both divisions value texts that produce the following outcomes: approval by upper management, action from the readers, justification of expenses, efficient writing and reading, and credibility of the division. The outcome considered most important in both divisions is approval of their texts by upper management. A typical comment in this category is an explanation of the review process: "The whole concept of it is to make sure that we have our statement precise and accurate enough so that it passes." The ways to achieve these writing goals (*prescriptions*) include understanding the review process, adhering to traditional formats and accepted models, attending to style, ensuring that the information is complete, attending to the reader's situation, establishing authorial credibility, and preparing the readers before they receive the text. In both divisions, the most common prescription for attaining the desired quality in written texts is the traditional review process. One manager explains the benefits this way:

> I had a manager who was very exacting about written reports. I'd spend a lot of time in his office. Something that I thought I did just a bang-up job [on] would be just torn apart. I'd be walking out of there and basically redoing it—but redoing it and getting a better product, ultimately.

The differences in attitudes towards writing between the two divisions are fewer than the beliefs they hold in common, and may be summed up as differing emphases on the *desired outcomes* and *prescriptions* for writing. For example, the M.I.S. participants tend to speak more often (16% of total comments vs. 8%) about actions from intended readers as desired outcomes for writing than do the Marketing participants. The following quote from an M.I.S. participant illustrates this concern:

> You can't use "should" and "could" or "might." You have to be very solid. . . . You can't come off half-baked; otherwise, my reaction would be—I'd go and look somewhere else [because] these people don't know what they're doing.

This emphasis on readers' responses reflects the M.I.S. division's strong belief in the value of establishing working relationships with their readers (users and upper management) in order to carry out their projects.

This concern about readers is further reflected in the M.I.S. tendency to focus on justification (13% vs. 7% for the Marketing division) and credibility as desired outcomes for their texts. A typical comment illustrates this focus:

> You put a number down, saying—"We're going to spend three hours per week doing business cards." Well, how did you get that number? Is this the number that looked good that you picked out of the air?

Perhaps the fact that the M.I.S. division's hierarchical structure and lack of facilitation for collaboration among themselves increases their sensitivity to the necessity of teamwork with the rest of the organization for the success of their projects. This suggestion is supported by the prevailing view in the M.I.S. division that others in the organization, such as Marketing, have priority in terms of resources. Of course, Marketing also requires the cooperation of other departments; but because Marketing is a major part of the HCC mission, it is more likely to gain cooperation.

Compared to the differences in *desired outcomes* for writing between the two divisions, the differences in the *prescriptions* for writing are even less pronounced. M.I.S. seems to emphasize the importance of word choice and the review process as ways to obtain their writing goals more so (17% vs. 12%) than does Marketing. On the other hand, the Marketing participants seem to place more value on formats and models (12.5% vs. 8%) than the M.I.S. participants do. Again, these numbers do not speak as convincingly as do the key documents that accompany the marketing planning process, documents for which report formats are included in their standard procedures manual. Although M.I.S. also has a standard procedures manual, report formats are not included; these writers negotiate formats with the managers or use existing reports (especially those written by the managers) as models.

Considering that Marketing relies on market research information to support its planning of market strategies, I expected more prescriptions about collecting information from the Marketing participants. However, procedures for collecting marketing information are fairly standardized and much of that work is accomplished by external market research agencies; therefore, the marketing division emphasizes the interpretation rather than the collection of this information. For example, a sample Marketing comment in this category is, "It's a question of not just [having] to regurgitate data, but of analyzing. [We have to] produce reasons for numbers being what they are, rather than just saying what they are." On the other hand, the M.I.S. participants' emphasis on information (12.5% vs. 6%) is closely associated with their need to collect enough information to justify their recommendations to upper management. For example, a typical M.I.S. comment in this category is, "We're going to save eight hours somewhere else? What does it mean exactly? I'm sure the question will come up. Because of the freeze on manpower, on hiring, we have to look at that more closely."

These differences in assumptions underlying the two division's ways of operating and in their preferred goals for writing and prescriptions for accomplishing these goals are borne out in an analysis of Marketing and M.I.S. managers responses to written texts. The analysis of the respond-aloud protocols described in the next section underscores the distinct goals and values of the two divisions.

RESPONSES TO WRITING WITHIN DIVISIONAL SUBCULTURES

The respond-aloud protocols were designed to explore the tacit criteria managers bring to their review of writing done by their staff. As Langer (1986) notes, respond-aloud protocols seem to capture the momentary decisions that readers no longer remember after reading (p. 235). Louise Rosenblatt (1978) describes the literary reading experience as having concurrent strands of response: the reading activities of responding to cues in the text, anticipating, and synthesizing are accompanied by the reader's reactions to the text he or she is creating. These reactions include "approval, disapproval, pleasure, shock; acceptance or rejection of the world that is being imaged; the supplying of rationales for what is being lived through" (p. 69). Although Rosenblatt is describing readers' responses to literature, her description seems to apply also to the readers' reactions in this study. The transcripts of these respond-aloud protocols appear to reflect managers in dialogue with the texts (and the absent writer or future readers) during the reading process. They reveal managers posing questions to the writer as they read the text (the writers were not present during the readings), anticipating responses from future readers, agreeing and disagreeing with the writer's ideas, and contributing information to complete the writer's ideas.

In order to understand what the managers were attending to when they reviewed written reports, I focused on the implicit questions these readers seem to be asking themselves as they read, and identified the following categories of comment: *consistency* (the reader's agreement or disagreement with the writer's view of a situation or event); *effects on readers* (comments about the reactions of the present or a future reader); *missing information* (comments about the completeness of the information); *writers' intentions* (readers' attention to perceived writers' intentions); *style* (comments about diction, tone, and clarity); *message* (comments that paraphrase or explain the message in the text); *organization* (comments that address the arrangement of information in the text); *format* (the reader's attention to the writer's use of standard formats); *mechanics* (comments about spelling, grammar, punctuation, and typographical errors); and *visuals* (comments about charts, graphs, or fonts).

The Marketing Division and Response to Writing

I was present at the reading of seven texts in the Marketing division: a marketing plan, two marketing research reports, a meeting report, an information report, a recommendation, and a monthly status report, all destined for readers within the organization. Typically, a manager must sign a report before it leaves his or her department; often, the report is returned to the writer for revision before the manager signs it. The writers alerted me to the time when the managers would read the reports, so I could be present at the first reading of each text to tape record managers' comments.

Certainly, the managers in Marketing commented on such features as missing information and the writer's intentions (12% of the total comments fell into these categories); but the main focus of attention during the readings of these reports was on the consistency of information (32% of the total comments) with the managers' mental models of HCC's market situation. The managers made remarks about consistency almost three times more often than they did about any of the other categories of comment. Typical comments in this category are "It's surprising that this number is so low," or "That makes sense." During the reading, it was obvious that the managers knew a great deal about the information in the reports before reading them. Because the managers work closely with their staff and attend many of the same meetings, they are aware of issues and research results. For example, the market research reports read for this study contained survey results that had been presented by an external research agency at a meeting of product managers, marketing directors, and research analysts. The marketing plan had already been thoroughly discussed at planning meetings within the Marketing division.

Members of the Marketing division place a high premium on information and its relevance, particularly as they plan their strategies for gaining the largest market share possible for HCC's products. As marketing decisions are based on both "soft" (perceptions of clients) and "hard" (numbers of products sold) data, members of the Marketing division tend to compare the data with what they already know from meetings and discussions; in effect, they do a "reality check." This focus on consistency reflects the value of teamwork within the culture of the Marketing division. In most of the Marketing reading events, there were differences between the readers' and writers' intentions for the report, which resulted in the managers' requests for revisions; however, the revisions usually required fairly minor changes. The gap between writers' and readers' intentions was a matter of focus rather than of real differences in goals; that is, the managers' intentions for writing included broad organizational goals, whereas the writers were more immediately concerned with divisional goals and their own job responsibilities.

The M.I.S. Division and Response to Writing

I collected five respond-aloud protocols in this division from managers reading four texts: three recommendation reports, and a report about new features in the computer system, all written for readers within HCC.

Whereas the Marketing managers focused mainly on consistency, the managers in this division attended mainly to the texts' effects on readers in the organization (24% of the total comments in M.I.S.). For example, typical comments in this category are: "He will pick these things up and say, 'Well, what does that mean?'" and "If you put in a lot of numbers, they can relate to that easily."

The M.I.S. managers are acutely aware of the need to translate their technical jargon for upper management and of their relatively low status in the hierarchy. Consequently, to obtain executive approval for their recommendations, they work hard to ensure that their texts provide strong justification for recommended expenditures of the organization's resources.

Managers' comments about the readers reflect this division's changing mandate, from filling requests to marketing their services to in-house "clients." The managers are familiar with the issues and controversies within HCC; as a result, they know how other readers in the organization will respond to the reports issued by M.I.S. The difference between the managers' and writers' knowledge of organizational issues and key players is reflected in comments made about the "writers' intentions" (19% of the total comments); intentions of readers and writers were often in conflict because of the writers' limited knowledge about political issues and their reticence about the increasing emphasis on marketing. The value placed on prompting action from intended readers was clearly expressed by the managers, but difficult for writers to implement without many managerial revisions. Because of the differences in perspective, the review process in this division was often difficult for the writers, many of whom saw the changes required by their managers as managerial idiosyncrasies.

The recurring themes in the interviews, respond-aloud protocols, documents (procedures, policies, newsletters, etc.), and my field notes support the conclusion that the managers' responses reflect the goals and values of their particular division and the organization as a whole. For example, the broader organizational goals and values are reflected in HCC's standard procedures, such as grants of authority and prescribed approval procedures, which are common to both divisions. The procedure of reviewing writers' texts before they are issued is also common to both divisions, a policy that reflects the organization's beliefs in the values of tradition, quality, and dedication. For instance, the review process has been handed down from manager to manager; managers in Marketing and in M.I.S. tell stories about their own experiences as writers. These stories involve accounts of great effort and many revisions suggesting that the participants believe that dedication to the job will produce a quality report, a "better product."

CONCLUSIONS AND IMPLICATIONS

This study of HCC was designed to understand one organization's expectations for writing within the framework of its beliefs, goals, and values. As Sathe (1989) reminds us: "[R]eading a culture is an interpretive, subjective activity. . . . The validity of the diagnosis must be judged on the utility of the insights it provides, not on its 'correctness' as determined by some objective criteria" (p. 393). My reading of the culture at HCC provides a basis from which to understand the managers' expectations for written texts in the organization.

In brief, this community believes that the concerted efforts of their highly expert members in a traditional structure of hierarchical authority are responsible for HCC's success in the marketplace. At HCC, the "common project," the organization's mission to be the industry leader, and beliefs in the value of its traditions are most clearly evident in its procedures for rationalizing and documenting its decisions. Even though decisions may be made at the departmental level, at HCC they must be documented for formal approval by upper management, who have their own mental models of how decisions should be rationalized. As Mintzberg (1990) points out, managers, especially those in the higher echelons, build their own models of reality through frequent verbal interaction with others inside and outside the organization.

Managers at HCC, who consider the review process a standard procedure, approach the process with a belief in the value of working hard to achieve a "quality" product that clearly provides the kinds of justification required to "sell" it to upper management, who must ratify the decisions made at the lower management levels. This standard procedure for providing accountability within the organization is reflected in managers' attention to specific features of texts when they review them. To ensure a "quality" product, managers at HCC respond to writing with particular attention to the goals and values of their own divisions. The divisional differences in emphasis on desired outcomes and prescriptions for writing and on the managers' responses to texts reflect not only differences in their mandates, but also in their assumptions about collaboration. The Marketing division's belief in teamwork and their actions to facilitate it contrast sharply with the M.I.S. division's belief in hierarchy and individual effort.

The work of several researchers (e.g., Barabas, 1990; Bazerman, 1985; Kleimann, 1993; and Smart, 1993) supports this conclusion that readers' responses clearly reflect the organization's goals and values. For example, researchers have noted that readers attend to selective elements in the text depending on their disciplinary interests and work-related goals (Bazerman, 1985), and their mental models of reality (Smart, 1993). Kleimann's (1993) study provides evidence that values of particular subcultures within an organization strongly influence the effectiveness of the review process.

This study of HCC suggests that writers need to know a great deal about the organization and the readers (managers and intended readers) to generate "good" writing, writing that receives managerial approval. Even though much of their cultural knowledge may be tacit, managers' comments on writers' texts and their explanations of the reasons for such comments in discussion with writers, should help to make much of such tacit knowledge explicit. Newcomers have much to learn if they approach the document review process as a process of induction into the expectations and values of the organization. Such a process would reveal:

- the manager's interpretations of both organizational and divisional goals and values;
- the manager's knowledge of other intended readers' expectations and prior knowledge;
- the manager's perception of the writer's role (gained through his or her own experience as a writer whose reports have been reviewed by a manager); and
- the manager's understanding of his or her role in the review process.

However, like the supervisors in the studies reported in this volume by Paré and Freedman and Adam (Chapter 2), HCC managers maintain that their responsibilities do not include teaching writing. As one manager who wished she didn't have to make so many changes on draft reports states: "I mean, I'm not a school teacher."

Clearly, not all managers see value in assisting writers through the review process and, in the long run, prefer to save themselves several rounds of laborious and sometimes painful editorial comments. Instead, the managers' primary goal may be to complete the job rather than to educate the writer. Indeed, many managers may not know how to help writers learn to write (see Blakeslee, 1997; Freedman & Adam, Chapter 2, this volume). These researchers also suggest that writers' prior experiences with learning and writing in university may inhibit them from learning to write in the workplace. However, it may not be just the reliance on successful university experiences with writing and learning that prevents newcomers from gaining knowledge in the review process, but also the transition from the university culture into an entirely different one.

As Schein (1987) suggests, graduate management education may socialize students in ways that run counter to the values and beliefs of the organizations they join when they graduate. He explains:

> Where his education has taught the graduate principles of how to manage others and take the corporate point of view, his organizational socialization tries to teach him how to be a good subordinate, how to be influenced, and how to sell ideas from a position of low power. (p. 97)

This is often the position of writers who are newcomers to an organization, especially when they enter a strongly hierarchical culture. However, gaining an understanding of the culture would help them advance from the role of "good subordinate" to attain the kind of membership that allows them to "achieve common interpretations of situations so that coordinated action is possible" (Smircich, 1983, p. 351, cited in Alvesson, p. 43).

Perhaps the most difficult task for newcomers writing in organizational settings such as HCC is learning to accept comments of their supervisors for what they are: attempts to ensure that written documents conform to expectations higher up the line of decision-making, and moreover, to help subordinates present cases, problems, situations, and arguments in ways that will get the desired results. This is a far cry from the demands placed on writers in school, where writing is hardly expected to change anything, desired outcomes other than grades are not in the balance, and the single reader does not expect to be informed or changed by the writing. Far many more interests than those of a single reader (e.g., the teacher) are involved in writing at work. Until newcomers have learned more about the various interests involved and deciphered the differences in perception and power they represent, it will be their supervisors who will have to guide them, and the organizational guidelines and protocols that appear constricting and controlling may be necessarily so.

Although newcomers may feel initially that independent thinking and creativity are being stifled, they may come to acknowledge that organizational ways evolve from a long history of failures and successes, and the path to exercising initiative may lie in first learning what those ways are and why they might matter. It will turn out that a pattern of learning established in school, learning the ways of a discipline, need not differ fundamentally from learning and acquiring the ways of the community they have newly joined.

REFERENCES

Alvesson, M. (1993). *Cultural perspectives on organizations.* Cambridge: Cambridge University Press.

Anderson, P. V. (1985). What survey research tells us about writing at work. In L. Odell & D. Goswami (Eds.), *Writing in non-academic settings* (pp. 3-83). New York: Guilford.

Barabas, C. P. (1990). *Technical writing in a corporate culture: A study of the nature of information.* Norwood, NJ: Ablex.

Bataille, R. R. (1982). Writing in the world of work: What our graduates report. *College Composition and Communication, 33,* 276-282.

Bazerman, C. (1985). Physicists reading physics. *Written Communication, 2,* 3-23.

Blakeslee, A. M. (1997). Activity, context, interaction, and authority: Learning to write scientific papers in situ. *Journal of Business and Technical Communication, 11,* 125-169.

Brown, J. L. (1988). A survey of writing practices in management. *English Quarterly, 21,* 7-18.

Chao, G. T., O'Leary-Kelly, A. M., Wolf, S., Klein, H. J., & Gardner, P. D. (1994). Organizational socialization: Its content and consequences. *Journal of Applied Psychology, 79,* 730-743.

Dias, P. (1996). *Reading and responding to poetry: Patterns in the process.* Portsmouth, NH: Boynton/Cook Heinemann.

Faigley, L. (1985). Nonacademic writing: The social perspective. In L. Odell & D. Goswami (Eds.), *Writing in nonacademic settings* (pp. 231-248). New York: Guilford Press.

Flanagan, J. C. (1954). The critical incident technique. *Psychological Bulletin, 51,* 327-358.

Goetz, J. P., & LeCompte, M. D. (1984). *Ethnography and qualitative design in educational research.* New York: Academic.

Kanter, R. M. (1983). *The change masters.* New York: Simon and Schuster.

Kleimann, S. (1993). The review process and cultural influence. In R. Spilka (Ed.), *Writing in the workplace: New research perspectives* (pp. 56-70). Carbondale: Southern Illinois University Press.

Langer, J. A. (1986). Reading, writing, and understanding: An analysis of the construction of meaning. *Written Communication, 3,* 219-267.

Ledwell-Brown, J. (1993). *Reader response to writing in a business setting: A study of managers' responses to writing in an organizational culture.* Unpublished doctoral dissertation, McGill University, Montreal, Canada.

Martin, J. (1992). *Cultures in organizations: Three perspectives.* New York: Oxford University Press.

Miles, M. B., & Huberman, A. M. (1984). *Qualitative data analysis.* Beverly Hills, CA: Sage.

Mintzberg, H. (1990, March/April). The manager's job: Folklore and fact. *Harvard Business Review,* 163-176.

Morgan, G. (1986). *Images of organization.* Newbury Park, CA: Sage.

Rosenblatt, L. M. (1978). *The reader, the text, the poem.* Carbondale: Southern Illinois University Press.

Sackmann, S. A. (1992). Culture and subcultures: An analysis of organizational knowledge. *Administrative Science Quarterly, 37,* 140-161.

Sathe, V. (1989). Implications of corporate culture: A manager's guide to action. In L. A. Mainiero & C. L. Tromley (Eds.), *Developing managerial skills in organizational behavior: Exercises, cases, and readings* (pp. 392-407). Englewood Cliffs, NJ: Prentice Hall.

Schein, E. H. (1971). The individual, the organization, and the career: A conceptual scheme. *The Journal of Applied Behavioral Science, 7,* 401-426.

Schein, E. H. (1987). Organizational socialization and the profession of management. In E. H. Schein (Ed.), *The art of managing human resources* (pp. 83-100). New York: Oxford University Press.

Smircich, L. (1983). Concepts of culture and organizational analysis. In M. Alveson (Ed.), *Cultural perspectives on organizations* (pp. 339-358). Cambridge: Cambridge University Press.

Smart, G. (1993). Genre as community invention: A central agency's response to its executives' expectations as readers. In R. Spilka (Ed.), *Writing in the workplace: New research perspectives* (pp. 124-140). Carbondale: Southern Illinois University Press.

Swales, J. (1990). *Genre analysis: English in academic and research settings.* Cambridge: Cambridge University Press.

Tebeaux, E. (1996). Nonacademic writing into the 21st century: Achieving and sustaining relevance in research and curricula. In Duin & Hansen (Eds.), *Nonacademic writing: Social theory and technology* (pp. 35-55). Mahwah, NJ: Erlbaum.

CHAPTER 10

Reinventing Expertise: Experienced Writers in the Workplace Encounter a New Genre

Graham Smart
Purdue University

"I'd heard the stories about it, but. . . ."

For a number of years now researchers in our field have been studying how novices in a discipline or profession learn to participate in its discourse (e.g., Anson & Forsberg, 1990; Berkenkotter, Huckin, & Ackerman, 1988; Freedman, 1987; MacKinnon, 1993; McCarthy, 1987; Paré & Szewello, 1995; Winsor, 1996). In this chapter I explore a neighboring topic: what seasoned, accomplished writers in a workplace experience when they encounter a genre that is significantly different from anything they have done before.

    Looking at such a transition point for individuals within their careers casts light on two closely related issues: first, what expert performance in the specialized discourse practices of a professional community involves; and second, what learning to write in a new workplace genre entails. In turn, these issues prompt consideration of three more general questions: What is the nature of expertise in writing? Which aspects of the expertise acquired by a writer in one domain of discourse can be carried into another? And finally, of those areas of expertise that can come only from enculturation in a new domain, which are the most important and/or most problematic to acquire?

To this point in the development of Composition Studies we have designed and implemented pedagogies *as if* we knew for certain which facets of expertise in writing transfer across different boundaries—what else could we have done?—when actually we have only limited research and theory to guide us. If we are to devise writing pedagogies that are effective in helping people cross discursive boundaries—be they those separating a particular type of school writing from another, school writing from nonacademic writing, or one domain of workplace discourse from a second—we must be able to distinguish between general, transferable aspects of expertise and those that are local and context-specific. One way to increase our understanding in this area would be to study a variety of situations in which experienced writers are engaged in learning new genres in unfamiliar rhetorical territory. This chapter offers one contribution to this projected line of research.

Recently I observed a number of staff economists at the Bank of Canada[1] go about the task of producing, for the first time in their careers, an article for the *Bank of Canada Review,* an internally produced publication that deals with issues in economics, finance, and monetary policy and is intended for an external readership. Writing for the *Review* as a first-time author is widely seen within the Bank as a formidable professional challenge. Indeed, even economists who have worked in the organization for many years, and who are recognized as highly competent in producing internal documents such as "research memoranda" and "analytic notes" (of which, more later), report running up against considerable difficulty and frustration in their first brush with the *Review.*

In considering why Bank economists struggle as they do in this particular situation, I will examine the contrast between the writers' habitual, skilled participation in the Bank's mainstream discourse practices and their contrary experience with an unfamiliar, rhetorically dissimilar genre. At the same time, I will reflect on what learning to work successfully in this genre involves.

THE GENRE AND THE ANGST

The *Bank of Canada Review* has been published since 1971, monthly until 1993, and quarterly since. Issues of the *Review* contain a range of material, including speeches by the governor of the Bank, a regu-

---

[1]The Bank of Canada is the country's central bank, a counterpart to the U.S. Federal Reserve Board.

lar commentary on economic and financial developments in Canada, press releases, statistical tables, and articles by Bank staff economists. *Review* articles deal with topics such as the implementation of monetary policy, factors influencing exchange rates, theoretical issues in the economics literature, the evolution over time of important economic variables, and the role of different types of financial institutions. The circulation is approximately 4,000 copies, distributed across Canada and in some 70 other countries.

An editorial board made up of senior Bank personnel oversees the preparation of articles for the *Review*. The board currently includes twelve members: four deputy governors, three advisors to the governor, four department chiefs, a deputy chief, and the senior editor.[2]

Throughout the history of the *Review*, first-time authors appear to have experienced a high degree of angst with the genre of the *Review* article. In 1981, for example, a decade after the publication was introduced, the senior editor of the day commented that "writing for the *Review* has acquired the unenviable reputation of being an onerous and unrewarding task."[3] As we shall see, little seems to have changed in the years since this observation. For the most part, the Bank's staff economists continue to view enrollment into *Review* authorship as an obligation, not an opportunity. (In the normal course of events, an economist will be asked by his or her department chief to write on an assigned topic.) Indeed, over time a body of folklore has developed within the institution about the potential hazards of the experience.

What is striking about the way writers struggle with the *Review* is the degree to which such difficulty is an anomaly within the Bank: writing is a regular, everyday part of the job for staff economists, the institutional culture offers a number of local supports for this writing, and newly hired economists generally appear to adapt fairly readily to the regime. (See MacKinnon, 1993, on the enculturation of Bank economists as writers.)

---

[2]The Bank's executive group includes the governor, a senior deputy governor, four deputy governors, four advisors, and an associate advisor. Below this group in the institutional hierarchy are the staff economists, who are situated in one of four departments, according to the focus of their work: Research; Monetary and Financial Analysis; International; and Financial Markets. Each department is headed by a department chief.

[3]Quoted from a note written by the senior editor to the editorial board.

THEORETICAL PERSPECTIVE AND METHODOLOGY

In considering the question of why Bank economists struggle with the *Review* article, I turned first to genre theory. As recounted in detail elsewhere (e.g., Devitt, 1992; Freedman & Medway, 1994; Vipond, 1993), contemporary theorizing has reinterpreted genre as a form of social action arising in response to perceived regularities in situations and exigencies. Working within this frame, researchers examining discourse in professional sites have revealed how writers collaborate in enacting sets of knowledge-producing genres to accomplish their work (Bazerman, 1988; Devitt, 1991; Myers, 1990; Schryer, 1993; Smart, 1992a, 1993; Yates, 1989). Paré and Smart (1994) offer a view of genre that underscores this knowledge-building function:

> [W]hen an organization has a stable mandate and a well-defined structure, recurrent problems or exigencies arise, each of which calls for a different type of discourse and knowledge. [A] written genre can be seen as a broad rhetorical strategy enacted within an [organization] in order to regularize writer/reader transactions in ways that allow for the creation of particular knowledge. (p. 146)

More specifically, Paré and Smart argue for a conception of genre that includes regularities in texts, composing processes, and reading practices, as well as repeated patterns in "an organization's drama of interaction, the interpersonal dynamics that surround and support certain texts" (1994, p. 148).

Recent inquiry has begun to explore a resonance between the social-epistemic conception of genre and theory in social psychology (Bazerman, 1994; Berkenkotter & Huckin, 1993). From a perspective informed by a strand of social psychology known as "distributed cognition" (Salomon, 1993), a workplace genre set (Bazerman, 1994; Devitt, 1991) can be seen as an element in an occupational "activity system" (Cole & Engeström, 1993)—a local sphere of goal-directed collaborative endeavor, where thinking, knowing, and intellectual accomplishment are mediated by a matrix of physical settings, symbol systems, analytic methods, technologies, and structured social interaction (see Paré, this volume). In hierarchical organizations, such activity usually involves the "division of cognitive labor" (Hutchins, 1991), where technical specialists carry out analytical work, or "surrogate thinking" (Smart, 1992b), on behalf of more senior decision makers. (See Freedman & Smart, 1997, for an extended account of the discourse practices of economists at the Bank of Canada, as viewed through the lens of distributed cognition theory.)

For writers in such occupational sites, the use of the local genres is often part of a larger involvement in a complex network of knowledge-making activity. Expertise in the genres develops within a growing mastery of context-specific strategies, procedures, and tools—what Donald Schon (1983) refers to as "knowing-in-practice." As it develops, this expertise becomes an important aspect of a writer's "knowledgeably skilled identit[y]" (Lave, 1991) as a professional. (Whereas this perspective on expertise emphasizes the contextual, as discussed later in the chapter it is compatible with a "pluralistic" [Carter, 1990] or "interactionalist" [Kaufer & Young, 1993, cited in Peeples & Hart-Davidson, 1997] model of expertise that includes both context-specific and general abilities.)

To turn to the methodology used in the study reported in this chapter, interpretive ethnography—with its focus on "reading" a social group's repertoire of symbolic forms, or discourse, to learn something of how its members view their particular (self-constructed) corner of the world—offered an effective way of exploring the professional activity of the Bank's economists.

Interpretive ethnography takes seminal inspiration from Clifford Geertz, with much of its spirit reflected in the following words:

> Believing . . . that man is an animal suspended in webs of significance he himself has spun, I take culture to be those webs, and the analysis of it to be therefore not an experimental science in search of law but an interpretive one in search of meaning. . . . The whole point of a semiotic approach to culture is . . . to aid us in gaining access to the conceptual world in which our subjects live. (1973, pp. 5, 24)

(For further discussion of the assumptions and methods of interpretive ethnography, see Agar, 1980, 1986; Geertz, 1973, 1978; Hammersley, 1992; Hammersley & Atkinson, 1983; and Van Maanen, 1979, 1988).

In its epistemology, interpretive ethnography accords well with the claim in genre theory that it is a community's mutually constituted understandings of recurrent situations and exigencies that give rise to its genres, as well as with a similar concern in social psychology for "participants' construal of . . . situation[s]" (Resnick, 1991, p. 4). Consequently (or so it seems in retrospect), in the present study I have used an interpretive approach to explore how economists at the Bank of Canada perceive their experience as writers, with a view to stepping, however tentatively, into "the conceptual world in which [they] live." (See Smart, 1998, for an extended argument for using interpretive ethnography to study the discourse of a professional community.)

In constructing my account of the economists' world, I have drawn both on extensive qualitative data collected in the Bank's head office during more than a dozen years as an in-house writing consultant and on a more focused set of data gathered in the same site over a recent eighteen-month period. The recent data include the following:

- historical material on the *Review:* an extensive file that includes written commentary from the eight individuals who have occupied the position of senior editor since the inception of the journal in 1971;
- a large collection of internal Bank documents and *Review* articles, including six "research memoranda" and six matching articles (in each case, the article grew out of the memorandum);
- three interviews with each of two staff economists as they went through the process of writing a *Review* article for the first time, and interviews with three other economists who had just finished preparing their first article (as well as, in three cases, all the writer's major drafts, with annotated feedback from various reviewers);
- interviews with eight other economists who have written a number of *Review* articles and are acknowledged to be very competent in the genre (five of the eight had written three or more articles);
- interviews with six of the twelve members of the *Review's* Editorial Board; and
- observations noted while attending two meetings of the Board.

In analyzing the data, I looked for salient differences between *Review* articles and internal "research memoranda." As even experienced economists accomplished at writing for audiences within the Bank frequently have considerable trouble when they first attempt to write for the *Review,* it made sense to compare the experience of preparing *Review* articles with that of producing regular internal documents. And although Bank economists write various types of internal documents, I focused on the genre of the research memorandum because Review articles often originate as memoranda. As I compared the *Review* article with the research memorandum, three interrelated dimensions of discourse emerged from my data: the rhetorical situation, taken to include the institutional exigence for the genre, the writer's professional stance, and the readership; textual features; and the editorial process. In each area, I tried to identify contrasts between the two genres that might account for the difference, from the writers' perspective, between participation in the Bank's regular discourse practices and the experience of producing articles for the *Review*. I also attempted to identify factors associated with learning to write successfully for the *Review*.

In the next part of the chapter, as background for discussing the difficulties encountered by first-time *Review* authors, I describe the mainstream discourse practices of the Bank's economists, using a social constructionist frame. Further on, I describe the difficulties encountered by *Review* authors and then look at what experienced writers say they have learned about the genre.

THE MONETARY POLICY PROCESS

A foundational premise (so to speak) in social-epistemic rhetoric is that language is central to the construction of knowledge. According to James Berlin (1987), "all reality, all knowledge, is a linguistic construct" (p. 165), and indeed, "there is no knowledge without language" (p. 167). As Debra Journet (1990) points out, however, although language plays a major role in knowledge making, it is often used in combination with other symbolic forms such as mathematics. A case in point here is the discipline of economics, where knowledge is constituted through a discourse encompassing language, mathematical models, and statistics (Henderson, Dudley-Evans, & Backhouse, 1993; *Journal of Post-Keynesian Economics,* Summer 1991; Klamer, McCloskey, & Solow, 1988; Samuels, 1990).

In discussions of knowledge construction in economics, it has been argued that the very notion of an "economy" is an intersubjective reality created and maintained through the discursive practices of professional economists. Vivienne Brown (1993) articulates this view:

> [T]he "real economy" is not knowable as a direct or brute fact of existence independently of its discursive construction. The "economy" is represented as an object of analysis by a set of discourses which constitute it as such; it is these discourses that provide the economic concepts, modes of analysis, statistical estimates, econometric methods and policy debates that constitute the different analytical understandings of the economy. (p. 70)

But as social constructs, economies are not all cut from the same discursive cloth; their specific character is a product of social location. Professional economists are always situated *somewhere,* either in university departments or in public- or private-sector organizations. And in the case of nonuniversity economists, the occupational site—a government department, labor union, business lobby group, economic forecasting firm, or central bank—shapes the particular version of the economy that is constructed, reflecting the organization's mandate, institutional history, bureaucratic and technological systems, theoretical commitments, and so on.

For economists in such sites, the discursive realization of a stylized conceptual economy is a means to an end: they use the analytic structure of this economy, with its categories or "sectors"[4] and their interrelationships, as a heuristic for interpreting empirical data and producing "stories" that identify and explain current developments and probable future trends. (See McCloskey, 1885, 1990 on the narratives produced by economists.) Metaphorically speaking, an economy acts as an "interpretive engine" for analyzing data and transforming them into institutionally sanctioned knowledge about the state of the world, or more specifically, about the state of that particular territory that is of interest to economists in a given professional site.

Here I want to turn once more to the Bank of Canada. As a central bank, the institution's primary role is to conduct the country's monetary policy, that is, to manage the growth of the money supply by influencing interest rates and the exchange rate, with the larger intention of improving economic performance. And, according to the governor of the Bank,

> To do our job of conducting monetary policy, we have to know what's happening in the Canadian economy. So the Bank follows economic developments more closely than anyone else in the country. We monitor daily what's going on in the economy, what's going on in financial markets.

But how does the Bank go about the business of continuously transforming reams of incoming statistical data into knowledge about the Canadian economy needed by the institution's executives for making monetary-policy decisions? Adapting Charles Bazerman's (1988, p. 62) question about knowledge making in the natural sciences, how does the empirical world of economic events get transposed into the virtual world of words?

---

[4]Such sectors may include, for instance, aggregate demand, aggregate supply, consumption, government expenditure, the labor market, business investment, imports and exports, and commodity prices.

To return to the notion of site-specific "economies" constituted through organizations' discursive practices, one of the Bank's
department chiefs gives local expression to this notion: "The Bank of
Canada's policy actions are based on a theoretical and empirical view
of how the economy functions." He goes on to describe the central role
that institutionally constructed conceptual "frameworks" play in
interpreting incoming statistical data, a continuous operation known
in the Bank as "current analysis": "Daily current analysis of incoming data employs frameworks. Data or events are not merely reported—they are analyzed in accordance with the various frameworks
that have been built up over time at the Bank."[5]

Another department chief elaborates on this theme, referring
to the "various frameworks . . . built up over time" as the Bank's "paradigm" of the economy, and distinguishing between current analysis
and the "research" performed by the institution's economists:

> Current analysis involves using our paradigm of the economy—
> our view of how the economy works, that is, how it's structured
> and what the linkages are—to interpret the events of the day.
> Current analysis, in other words, is about developing stories, in
> the context of our state of knowledge. You start with the data and
> ask, "What does our paradigm say about this?" Research, on the
> other hand, challenges the current paradigm; it questions our
> thinking on how the economy works. This involves taking new
> ideas out there in the profession and adapting them to Bank use,
> so that we're continually expanding our understanding.

Within the Bank, the broad activity of constructing a conceptual
economy, using its analytic structure to interpret statistical data,
and applying the resulting knowledge in decision making is known as
the "monetary policy process" (Duguay & Poloz, 1994).[6]

To take up an idea discussed earlier, the monetary policy
process can be viewed as an activity system, one intended to produce
specialized, applied knowledge about the Canadian economy. As participants in this activity system, the Bank's staff economists play a
clearly defined role, using various disciplinary tools, such as computer-run mathematical models and statistical time-series, in tandem

---

[5]This quotation is taken in edited form from a text the department chief distributed at a presentation he gave at an orientation session for newly hired
economists.

[6]Pierre Duguay is an advisor to the governor; Stephen Poloz, at the time
their article was published, was the chief of the research department.

with a set of written genres to carry out research projects (usually documented in "research memoranda") and perform current analysis (often reported in "analytic notes").[7] The economists' expertise in the genres linked to the monetary policy process develops through intensive involvement in a complex of discursive practices—practices that encompass the joint, intermeshed use of language, statistics, and mathematics, as well as a well-defined distribution of intellectual labor and familiar patterns of writer-reviewer interaction. Contributing to the Bank's work through proficiency in these genres is fundamental to an economist's professional identity as well as to his or her career advancement within the institution.

DIFFICULTIES EXPERIENCED BY *REVIEW* AUTHORS

Theorists in social psychology have argued that human thinking, knowing, and learning are to a great extent remarkably context-specific (e.g., Lave & Wenger, 1991; Resnick, 1991; Rogoff, 1984). Bazerman (1994) strikes a similar chord in a discussion of "expertise in writing":

> [P]eople who are identifiably experts in writing frequently are only remarkably competent within one limited domain of writing or the other. They are novelists or journalists or technical writers. Competence in one domain does not particularly indicate competence in another. (p. 132)

We can easily extend Bazerman's observation to the question of why Bank economists initially experience such difficulty with the *Review*. As an unfamiliar genre, situated apart from the staff economists' everyday participation in the knowledge-making activity of the monetary policy process, the *Review* article occupies a different rhetorical "domain" than genres that are intrinsic to the process, even though all share the same larger institutional environment. And whereas economists typically develop great expertise in the genres associated with the activity of the monetary policy process, writing for the *Review* is a task of a significantly different order.

---

[7]The Bank's paradigm of the Canadian economy is instantiated in a computer-run mathematical structure known as the Quarterly Projection Model. In the model, the major sectors of the economy and their interrelationships are represented in a complex network of equations.

In the discussion mentioned above, Bazerman goes on to consider how we might account for "the specificity of writing competence." He concludes that

> we must look to the different kinds of problems posed by different kinds of writing, the different dimensions on which the different kinds of writing work, the different skills necessary to accomplish the various kinds of writing. (1994, p. 133)

In analyzing the data from this study, I followed Bazerman's lead: I attempted to discover what distinguished the staff economists' experience of the Bank's mainstream discourse practices from their experience as first-time *Review* authors. In the end, I identified a range of differences in the rhetorical situation, textual features, and editorial process that appeared to be the most significant factors setting the *Review* article apart from the genres associated with the monetary policy process. In the section below I contrast one of these genres, the research memorandum, with the genre of the *Review* article.

The Rhetorical Situation

In research memoranda, staff economists report the results of research projects carried out in their departments. The institutional exigence for the genre is the Bank's ongoing need to further develop and enhance its paradigm of the Canadian economy—"our view of how the economy works, that is, how it's structured and what the linkages are," to recall a previous quotation. This paradigm is central to the Bank's work in that it provides an analytic structure used for interpreting incoming statistical data and producing "stories" that identify, explain, and predict significant economic events and trends in Canada, knowledge needed by the institution's executives for making decisions about monetary policy. For staff economists, the ability to contribute to the development of the institution's paradigm of the economy by performing and documenting useful research is essential to establishing a credible professional identity within the Bank. As for the readership, the primary audience for a research memorandum will include a subset of senior staff economists, the writer's department chief and, exceptionally, one or more of the executives.

The institutional exigence for the *Review* article, on the other hand, is the Bank's need to communicate its views on the Canadian economy to the public (both domestic and foreign), particularly regarding matters related to monetary policy. The aim is to cast light on the Bank's policy objectives and actions and to inform public debate. According to one department chief,

> With *Review* articles on the Bank's policy role, we want people to
> comprehend why we do what we do. With articles on theoretical
> issues or on different aspects of the economy, we want people to
> know how the Bank sees the world, as background for under-
> standing our policy actions.[8]

The audience for the *Review* article, according to the board members
interviewed (and there was a high degree of agreement here),
includes four types of readers: Canadian economists and financial
analysts in business, labor, and government; business journalists;
university students given articles to read in their courses; and foreign readers interested in Canadian economic affairs. From my
research I think it more reasonable to see this portrait as an institutional construction—a case of Walter Ong's (1975) "audience
invoked"—than as a demographically informed audience profile.

I see three areas of difficulty here for economists writing for
the *Review* for the first time in their careers. First, whereas economists typically grow into a keen awareness of the exigence, the
appropriate professional stance (that of a researcher contributing to
the Bank's understanding of the Canadian economy), and the audience for research memoranda through their everyday participation in
the knowledge-making activity of the monetary policy process, they
appear to have a relatively limited understanding of the rhetorical
situation associated with *Review* articles.

For example, when I asked several economists who had
recently begun to write for the *Review* about its readership, the most
specific response was, "people with a knowledge of economics equivalent to what you'd get in a first-year economics course," a vague char-
acterization compared to the more detailed representation offered by
members of the editorial board. One author acknowledged, "To be
honest, I'm really not at all sure who they [the board members] see
as the audience for my piece." As a consequence of this limited sense
of audience, writers appear to find it hard to gauge how much background knowledge *Review* readers are already likely to have, and so
may be uncertain where to start with a topic. The author cited above
commented, "You feel you need to add some basic conceptual stuff in
plain English. But how do I know if I'm talking down to the reader?"

---

[8]This and subsequent quotations are taken from interviews with *Review*
authors and members of the editorial board. I tape-recorded most of the
interviews; in such cases quotations are taken from transcripts and edited to
remove hesitation phenomena and redundancies. On other occasions, I took
detailed notes during interviews; quotations from these interviews are reconstructed from the notes.

Second, unlike the executives, who are used to representing the Bank in the public-policy arena, staff economists are generally not in a position to comfortably take on an institutional persona and communicate the Bank view of the world to the public. One consequence of this is that economists writing for the *Review* sometimes run up against policy sensitivities (related to the publication's external distribution), and a brusque reaction from members of the editorial board, in areas where greater caution is considered necessary. According to one department chief, "This issue of sensitivity can come as a major shock for people."

Finally, there is the question of professional standing within the Bank. As suggested earlier, staff economists receive recognition (and gain promotion) for research that contributes to the institution's understanding of how the economy functions, and they tend to view writing for the *Review* as a time-consuming distraction from this "real" work. A common perception is that pieces published in the *Review,* because they do not involve original economic research, are not given much weight when an economist's performance is evaluated each year. As one author put it, "There are very few kudos attached to writing articles for the *Review.*" Another commented, "You feel you're spending your time on a marketing effort, producing a nicely packaged product for the public. And the payback in internal recognition is fairly low." Nor do economists appear to feel they learn much that will be useful to them in future research work from writing articles. Said one author, *"Review* pieces tend to be so vacuous, analytically, that you really don't get much out of doing one."

Textual Features

The research memorandum typically presents a fine-grained treatment of some issue related to the Bank's paradigm of the economy. It takes a position on the implications of the research and supports it with a carefully developed line of argument, drawing on discipline-specific concepts and rhetorical conventions. (For discussion of modes of reasoning associated with economics, see Dudley-Evans & Henderson, 1990; McCloskey, 1985, 1990; and Smart, 1993). Usually the development of the argument depends on intertextual links to previous research carried out in the Bank or reported in the literature. In general, research memoranda are extremely technical, assuming shared knowledge of economic theory, mathematical modeling, methods of statistical analysis, and specialized terminology.

Whereas the research memorandum typically presents a detailed theory-laden and empirically supported argument, the

Review article is essentially descriptive and explanatory, presenting "three or four broad themes and elaborating on them," according to an executive on the board. "It's more like a classroom lecture," said one author. When, exceptionally, an article does take the form of an extended argument, it relies "more on intuitive reasoning than on rigorous economics," according to another author. As well, the *Review* article is more self-contained than the research memorandum, in that it does not depend on references to other research work for coherence and completeness. Although on occasion an article may contain a few references to work in the economics literature, there are no references at all to internal, unpublished Bank research.[9] The *Review* article is also much less technical, neither assuming advanced knowledge of economic theory nor containing mathematical equations, complex statistical analyses, or undefined disciplinary jargon.

Economists writing for the *Review* for the first time often appear to have difficulty producing a descriptive and/or explanatory, self-contained piece built around several simply presented ideas. As one department chief commented,

> Writers have trouble bringing out broad themes. They don't think themes; they think details. Normally, that's their job—understanding the details in their particular sector [of the economy], and developing arguments. So they tend to see writing for the *Review* as another opportunity to tell someone what all the details mean; they want to include a hundred details, because the writer thinks they're all part of the argument.

Writers also appear to find it difficult to explain complex technical concepts in language accessible to the nonspecialist reader. The same department chief: "You can always give an idea in a complicated, technical way and that's the way we're used to talking among ourselves—people in the Bank know the concepts and the jargon. But that's not appropriate for the *Review*." A particular area of difficulty here is the task of translating ideas and proofs originally represented in the form of mathematical equations into prose.

Another problem for *Review* authors is knowing when to simply state a claim without going on to provide supporting evidence as one would in a research memorandum, when such technical detail would burden the nonspecialist reader. The author of an article on restructur-

---

[9]One could speculate that this is related to federal access-to-information legislation: if outsiders are made aware of specific research documents, they can submit requests to see them.

ing in the Canadian economy during the 1990s commented, "Sometimes you feel uncomfortable just asserting a point, without backing it up like you normally would. It can make you feel a little vulnerable." Paradoxically, the contrary also holds in cases where concepts tacitly understood by economists need to be illustrated with concrete examples for *Review* readers—as in a recent article on neo-classical growth theory, in which the author felt the need to provide a textbook-like explanation of the concept of "diminishing returns for capital investment."

The Editorial Process

For a research memorandum, the editorial process typically involves several cycles of drafting, reviewing, and revising involving the writer and his or her supervisor as well as, in some cases, one or two more senior people in the department. This "document cycling" (Paradis, Dobrin, & Miller, 1985; Smart, 1993) is embedded in the familiar, everyday activities of the writer's department, within the larger context of the monetary policy process. For the writer, the roles of the reviewers are well defined and the personalities are known. As well, there are various supports for the writing, including, for example, abundant informal feedback from peers and the opportunity to present draft memoranda at weekly departmental seminars for discussion.

In contrast, the editorial process for a *Review* article is situated on the margins of the everyday work of the writer's department. It is also significantly more complex and rigorous than is the case for research memoranda. Typically, an article goes through numerous (some would say innumerable) iterations, with many more reviewers involved. Further, over the course of the editorial process the writing—and the writer—are directly exposed to the judgements of Bank executives as reviewers.

To convey a sense of the complexity of the editorial process for the *Review*, I will describe the experience of one of the authors I observed. After discussing the assigned topic with his department chief, the writer wrote a two-page outline that was reviewed by the chief and three other senior economists within the department. The writer revised the outline and sent it to the deputy governor responsible for the department and to the chairman of the editorial board for comments. The writer subsequently produced a draft that was reviewed by the supervisor, the three senior economists, the chief, and the deputy governor. The writer revised the draft and sent the new version to the chairman and the senior editor. The writer then went back and forth with the chairman and the senior editor through eight further rounds of document cycling.

At this point a draft was sent to the editorial board. Less than a week before the final deadline for the article, the writer met with the twelve-member board for an hour and a half to discuss the draft. The writer then worked intensively with the chairman and the senior editor to incorporate the board's suggestions, both those made orally during the meeting and those annotated by each member on a draft copy, and produced a final version of the article. In all, the process lasted three months, involved fifteen reviewers, and resulted in a dozen drafts.

From the point of view of first-time *Review* authors, the editorial process is problematic in a number of ways. First, the overall protocol is something of a mystery, with regard to the sequence of events and the identity of the various players. "I felt in the dark about things—what the steps were going to be, and who was going to be in on it," said one author. As well, the rigor of the document cycling involved is often unexpected. Another author: "I'd heard the stories about it, but I was amazed at how many rewrites I had to do, and how long it all took." Further, the roles of the different reviewers are not defined nearly as clearly as they are for internal documents produced within the departments. As one department chief commented, "Authors find it hard to satisfy everyone involved in the process, when they don't have any real sense of who's got ultimate responsibility and authority." This can leave a writer uncertain about what to do when feedback from different reviewers is contradictory, as is frequently (if not invariably) the case. An author describes his experience:

> There are a lot more masters to please. I had all kinds of feedback from people—on the substance, on [policy] sensitivities, on style—and much of it was contradictory. Different people at different levels [in the hierarchy] had different ideas about what the piece should do and what should be emphasized. And it was hard to know whether the changes proposed were just suggestions, or changes they definitely wanted made. So I ended up endlessly reworking the piece.

Second, authors express frustration over the perception that the editorial process frequently results in a movement away from the sophisticated analysis contained in early drafts towards more descriptive writing that is "bland and vacuous—a quaint little story," as one economist put it. Consequently, authors can experience a diminished sense of voice and ownership, feeling that "at the end of it all, the piece no longer represents what you wanted to say." One economist quipped, "The disclaimer at the beginning of a piece should say 'The views in this article do not necessarily reflect those of the Bank *nor those of the author.*'"

Third, the meeting with the editorial board presents potential hazards for authors. A department chief describes how the meeting typically proceeds:

> First we go round the table, for general comments. Is the piece interesting enough for the *Review?* Does the main theme stand out well? Is the piece substantively correct? Are there any major drafting problems in particular parts of the text? Then on the second round, we go through the piece page by page, with people making comments. At the end, the chairman sums things up: "We're going ahead with the piece or we're not. And if we are, here are the things that have to be done."

For first-time *Review* authors, this is almost always the first experience with facing so many reviewers at once, and certainly the first time having a piece of writing critiqued in a forum that includes a number of Bank executives. As one author described it, "You can expect to get comments coming at you from all sides during the meeting, from people right up to the level of deputy governor." And according to another, this can threaten one's sense of professionalism: "It's hard to know how to respond to the criticism. You don't know what the appropriate role to play is, what the rules of the game are. It can be pretty unnerving."

In a moment of candor, a board member acknowledged an implicit, undeclared function of the meeting, revealing another reason authors may find the encounter disorienting:

> We're aware that writers have had problems with the editorial meeting over the years. But one reason we've resisted change is that we've always found the meetings to be a useful think-tank, a chance for Board members to get together and brainstorm among ourselves on different issues. Now admittedly, from an author's point of view, this may have meant that the meetings haven't always seemed very focused.

The encounter with the editorial board can also place an author in an unfamiliar adversarial relationship with the chief of his or her department. In principle, the chief is there to defend the article. On occasion, however, a chief can end up being quite critical when the draft ultimately sent to the board is significantly different from the last draft he or she saw prior to the author's intensive rounds of document cycling with the chairman and the senior editor. This scenario, when it has occurred, has reportedly been quite upsetting for the writers involved. One economist commented, "You hear a lot about people who've been battle-scarred by their experience at the board."

Finally, the timing of the meeting can be a problem. It occurs very late in the editorial process, sometimes only a few days before the deadline. At times, the board will end up asking for major changes to the article, leaving the writer relatively little time to revise. Consequently, according to one author, "You can really feel that you're under a lot of pressure." Another outcome may be that the board will decide to cut the article from the Review, either temporarily or permanently. For a writer, having a piece turned down after the long editorial process adds insult to injury, and can be extremely discouraging.

LEARNING TO WRITE FOR THE *REVIEW*

Despite the angst that staff economists all too frequently experience in their first encounter with the *Review,* articles continue to be produced issue after issue, year after year, and with time authors appear to become reasonably comfortable with the genre. Clearly, significant learning is taking place. But what kind of learning?

In his discussion of the local, context-specific elements of expertise in writing, Bazerman suggests that "[p]eople who manage expert performances in more than one domain must learn or reinvent the second domain after learning the first" (1994, p. 133). In this section I want to consider what such reinvention of expertise might mean for the Bank economists who eventually become accomplished at writing for the *Review.*

In part, this growth in domain-specific writing ability appears to come from the writers' increased awareness of the rhetorical situation and textual conventions associated with the genre. An important dimension of this awareness involves gaining a sense, over time, of the readership for the *Review.* As one might expect, however, given the economists' experience as writers in university (most have Ph.D.s) and in the Bank, where they regularly produce a variety of internal documents for a range of readers with different information needs, the adjustments required in this area do not appear to be a major problem. As this quotation from one economist suggests, part of this development may come from efforts to characterize an actual audience for the publication:

> I was writing a piece for the *Review* about interest rates on the real-return bonds that we issue. It was my first time, and I was thinking about the audience. I knew I'd be talking about nominal interest rates and real interest rates, and I wondered if people would know the difference. So I went to a neighbor in my apart-

ment building and said, "OK, say I told you that we're investing in some financial asset and you were going to get a nominal rate of return and a real rate of return—what's the difference between the two?" And his answer was, "Well, 'nominal' probably means small and 'real' must mean physical." I thought, "Wow, I better make sure that I explain exactly what I mean by these terms in the text."

More importantly, though, writers appear to gain gradually a sense of the institutionally constructed view of the *Review's* readership—the "audience invoked" described earlier. It is this representation of the readership that authors learn to accommodate.

Another aspect of learning to work effectively within the rhetorical situation associated with the *Review* article involves the Bank's concern for dealing very cautiously with policy sensitivities in external publications. Several authors stressed the importance of being able to anticipate what kind of reaction a piece is likely to evoke from reviewers in this regard. According to one individual, a writer needs to distinguish between two types of topic:

There are two possible tracks for a *Review* piece. If it doesn't touch on monetary policy, you can assume that you're going to move through the editorial process more easily. The closer to home a piece is, though, in terms of issues related to policy, the more knowledge and views people [on the editorial board] are going to have, and the tougher things are probably going to be. It's good to be aware of this so you know what you're up against when you begin, and can prepare yourself to deal with it.

Another author claimed to have learned a great deal in this regard by looking at previous articles on policy-sensitive topics, as models embodying the trace of reviewers' concerns and expectations:

At the start, I go to back issues of the *Review* to try and find articles on topics similar to my piece. I know these articles will have gone through the editorial process with most of the same people who are on the board now, and will have been rewritten until everyone was satisfied. So they hold a lot of "sweat equity" from other authors and can tell you a fair amount about reviewers' apprehensions on sensitive issues.

As important as gaining a sense of the rhetorical situation and textual conventions of the *Review* appears to be, an even greater challenge, from the writers' perspective, is that of learning to navigate the social currents of the editorial process. Theory in social psychology offers a lens for considering what experienced, accomplished *Review* authors appear to have learned in this respect. According to James Gee (1992), a social group's discursive practices "are never just literacy practices" (p. 32), but rather "integrate values, belief, and ways of acting and interacting with ways of using oral and often written language" (p. 40). Jean Lave (1993) suggests that taking part in such "[s]ituated activity always involves changes in knowledge and action . . . and 'changes in knowledge and action' are central to what we mean by 'learning'" (p. 5). For both theorists, learning results from individuals' gradually improving readings of their social experience and is "subsumed in processes of changing identity" (Lave, p. 64).

My interviews with experienced *Review* authors suggest that a key aspect of their rhetorical development—"changes in [their] knowledge and action"—can be defined socially, in terms similar to those advanced by Gee and Lave. A major part of the writers' growth appears to involve learning how to manage the various textual and face-to-face interactions with reviewers that occur during the editorial process. An important correlative of this learning is the reaffirmation of professional identity in dealing with comments and suggestions from people often considerably more senior in the Bank's hierarchy—an example of what Lave refers to as "the construction of new identities of mastery in practice" (p. 64).

For our purposes in this chapter, I will report three lessons that experienced *Review* authors say they have learned about the social dimensions of the editorial process. To a large extent, I will let the individuals speak for themselves.

First, authors talked about recognizing the difference between the interactions of early reviewing rounds within one's own department and those of subsequent rounds involving reviewers at more senior levels in the Bank hierarchy. One economist commented on the political angle of this:

> You need to try to get as many comments on a piece as you can inside the department. The idea is to try to enroll people into your story and hope this support gets communicated to the [editorial] board by the chief and deputy governor [responsible for the department].

Making a similar distinction, another author spoke of the need to control one's ego:

> You've got to try and keep your ego from getting too involved in things. You have to look at the reviewing process within your own

department as a chance for a creative exchange of ideas. But then once the piece leaves the department and goes up the line to more senior people, you need to disassociate from the text and try to view it as an object. The goal is just to get it published.

Second, and this was a recurrent theme in the interviews, authors spoke of upholding their sense of professionalism in the face of critiques of their texts from more senior reviewers. Below, three authors discuss how they now approach the issue of using reviewers' comments and suggestions when revising articles.

When you're dealing with feedback, you've got to strike a balance between defending your own vision of what you're trying to do in the article and addressing other people's concerns. You have to accept constructive criticism, without letting people tear out important points if you think you can defend them. After all, you'll have done more work on the topic than anyone else.

I tend to give in on suggestions for minor changes and try to hold firm on the big issues. At the same time, though, it's important to look for the larger concerns underlying people's comments, and find ways to accommodate them without compromising the key ideas. And as much as possible I try to make some use of all the feedback I get, so people can see you've used their input, even if sometimes it's only in a small way.

You can't cut yourself off from reasonable suggestions, but when you've worked out what it is you really want to say in an article, you've got to stay firm and stick by your guns. The way I see it, it's better to give a piece *your* best shot and have it cut from the *Review* than have it published as *someone else's* best shot.

These perspectives and those voiced below reflect a degree of social understanding and a capacity for informed action that appear central to the "knowledgeably skilled identit[y]" (Lave, 1991) associated with experienced and successful *Review* authors.

A number of authors pointed to the importance for one's professional self-image of holding your own in the socially and intellectually demanding face-to-face interaction of the editorial board meeting. For example, one individual stressed the need to be extremely well prepared, in anticipation of the personal "ideologies" that can come into play:

You've got to be really ready when you go to meet the board, and know your topic broadly and deeply. You have to have thought about questions they might ask, both on what's actually in the article and what's not—because people are going to come at it from all directions. So it's important to keep in mind what you know about different people's ideologies, where they're coming from as economists.

Another author pointed to the importance of playing an active role at the meeting.

You have to engage people in dialogue, rather than just sitting there silently and writing down everything they say. I try to take the initiative and talk things out. And if different people have contradictory comments, I want to get the issues reconciled right there at the meeting if I can.

Finally, several authors mentioned that, despite their original feelings of frustration, they had eventually come to see the editorial process for the *Review* as an opportunity for professional growth. As one person put it,

Despite what you often hear, writing for the *Review* can be important to your career, even though it's not about showing off your technical wizardry. Going through the process is a way of learning to represent the Bank to the public. It involves going beyond the purely technocratic part of the job.

This indeed would appear to be the apotheosis of the *Review* writer's education in "the drama of interaction, the interpersonal dynamics" associated with the genre.

What are we to make of this testimony? On the one hand, we need to recognize that writers are highly individual in how they engage in, and learn from, social interactions such as those constituting the *Review's* editorial process. As Bazerman (1994) points out, "higher psychological functions, such as those employed in writing, [are] the result of each individual's unique pathway of interactions with other individuals" (p. 139). On the other hand, however, significant commonalities appear in authors' accounts of learning to participate confidently in the genre of the *Review* article. Perhaps foremost here, if one can judge from the fervor of the authors, is the importance of standing one's ground in textual and face-to-face interactions with reviewers more senior in the Bank, while at the same time finding strategies for accommodating these reviewers.

CONCLUSION

In this chapter, I have reported a study that employed an interpretive approach to explore the experience of Bank of Canada staff economists in two different domains of writing. I compared the economists' participation in the Bank's mainstream discourse practices with their experience preparing articles for the *Bank of Canada Review*. I found that for first-time authors, writing for the *Review* meant stepping outside the familiar realm of knowledge-making activity associated with the monetary policy process and could result in much difficulty and frustration. I also found that making a successful transition to the genre, as most writers eventually do, involves adjusting to a complex array of new rhetorical constraints, textual forms, and social relations. Perhaps the most challenging part of adapting to the *Review* involves learning to participate in interactions with more senior reviewers in a way that allows for the reaffirmation of professional identity.

The overall conclusion I draw from the study is that writing expertise is *not* easily transferable from one domain of discourse to another, even by highly skilled professionals working within a single occupational setting. When achieved, the reinvention of expertise required to succeed in a new domain means learning to play a role in an unfamiliar sociorhetorical "game" (to use Wittgenstein's term) and involves development on various different levels, development that can only come from experience.

I will close the chapter with a qualification to this conclusion and then a question. First the qualification: In my view, it would be unwise to let ourselves be seduced by the intuitively satisfying insights and claims of social psychology (more specifically, those of distributed cognition) to the point that we assume writing expertise to be an *entirely* local matter. Rather, I agree with Michael Carter (1990) when he argues for a "pluralistic theory of expertise" that distinguishes between domain-specific knowledge and skills and general, transferable rhetorical ability and holds that effective writers possess both. (Elaborations on this distinction have been made by Geisler, 1994; Kaufer & Young, 1993; and Peeples & Hart-Davidson, 1997.)

My experience as an in-house writing consultant in the Bank of Canada (as well as freelance work with other organizations) suggests that on a textual level, general, transportable ability may include knowledge of how reader-centered pieces of writing tend to be structured (assuming there to be certain parallels across genres), while on a social level it may involve skill at "reading" a newly encountered domain of discourse in order to recognize goals, values, and social relations that are significantly intermeshed with writing. With respect to the writing process (and here I would deny that we can ever become a "post-process" discipline, given our role as teachers of writing), general rhetorical ability appears to include, for example, the command of particular computer technologies, the skills required to collaborate effectively with other people, as well as practices such as profiling intended readers, whenever possible taking the initiative to talk to them about their concerns and information needs; using multiple drafts to generate and shape ideas, understanding that a draft is just a draft is . . . ; sharing work-in-progress with colleagues, taking care to describe the intended audience and purpose and to specify the kind of feedback wanted; and leaving intensive editing efforts to the end of the process.

After all, and here is the question: Let us imagine that you are the head of a newly formed community environmental group and are responsible for assigning the job of producing a lengthy, complex piece of writing—say a brief contesting a local airport's plans to expand into an old-growth forest. Let us also imagine that no one in the group has prior experience in the genre and that you have to choose among Bazerman's novelist, journalist, and technical writer, and a fourth person who, in his or her walk of life, has for years done little more writing than jotting down weekly grocery lists, filling out forms, or composing a short note to a friend. Who would you strike off the list immediately, and why? I guess that we would all likely eliminate the fourth individual, making certain assumptions about the general writing abilities that the remaining three could bring to the task from their experience in other domains of discourse.

The issue of local versus general ability matters a great deal for our teaching, of course. As Carter observes, "what we do in our writing classrooms [and, I would add, in workplace training venues] is determined, explicitly or implicitly, by our concepts of what it means to be an expert writer and how writers obtain expertise" (1990, p. 280). Indeed, the conundrum of where the local ends and the general begins is a vital concern for all who teach in academic and professional settings, and needs to be taken up in further qualitative research. This inquiry would explore the experience of individuals moving from one domain of writing to another, in an effort to identify those aspects of expertise that are transportable across boundaries and those that can only be developed locally within a specific site. Of particular value would be longitudinal studies in which researchers had ample access to both domains in question. (Whereas there would no doubt be a considerable degree of variation among individuals, nevertheless certain generalizations could reasonably be inferred from the results of the research.) Such inquiry might, for example, focus on one of the following: university students moving from an introductory composition course into the realm of discipline-specific writing; students moving from undergraduate studies into graduate work in a discipline; students moving into the workplace, either temporarily as interns in a co-op program or permanently as employees; members of a business organization moving from one division or department to another; people changing careers; and individuals returning to university after a number of years in the workplace. (The other studies reported in this volume begin to explore certain of these boundary crossings; see, also, Dias, Freedman, Medway, & Paré, 1999.)

For classroom instruction or workplace training intended to prepare writers for experience in known future domains, this research could help us identify and teach those general, transportable aspects of expertise that appear most relevant to our students and trainees. On the other hand, for instruction and training designed for writers who are newcomers to a particular domain, the research could lead to pedagogies that support, and possibly accelerate, the development of the local, context-specific aspects of expertise that come with experience and enculturation, focusing on those that are both essential and/or difficult to learn and amenable to teaching.

EPILOGUE

Genres inevitably evolve over time. As Gunther Kress (1987), cited in Devitt (1992), suggests

> If genre is entirely imbricated in other social process, it follows that unless we view society itself as static, then neither social structures, social processes, nor therefore genres are static. Genres are dynamic, responding to the dynamics of other parts of social systems. (p. 42)

Recent changes to the *Review* illustrate this point. While I was writing this chapter, the chairman of the editorial board and the senior editor were successfully lobbying for a reform of the editorial process. (Whether or not my research on the genre of the *Review*, which included interviewing these two individuals and sharing many of my findings with them, played a role here is difficult to say.) One part of the reform, according to an internal memo, will be to encourage "more sharply pointed and focussed articles, left in the voice of their authors," in the hope of making economists more enthusiastic about writing for the *Review*. This will require a measure of self-restraint on the part of the editorial board—and here only time will tell.

The second part of the reform involves the board meeting, the traditional forum for author-reviewer discussion. The board has agreed, on a trial basis, to forego its meetings with *Review* authors altogether. Instead, each of the board members will comment on the preliminary outline of an article and then later provide written feedback on a draft, at a point early enough to leave the writer ample time for revising. A "final" draft will be circulated to board members, any one of whom could call a meeting of the board to discuss the article with the author and negotiate further revisions. (Interestingly, in two departments local editorial groups have been already formed to consult with authors.) There is also to be a clearer delineation of authority, with the author collaborating with his or her chief and the deputy governor responsible for the department to decide on how best to interpret and incorporate suggestions from reviewers.

Clearly, these modifications to the editorial process will bring with them a host of role-related changes for writers and reviewers alike. For writers, the new arrangement could even mean a reinvention of attitude toward the *Review*. In a world of evolving genres, almost anything is possible.

ACKNOWLEDGEMENTS

I am grateful to Jim Reither and Joyce Simutis for the opportunity to discuss many of the ideas presented in the chapter. As well, I thank the editors of this volume and an anonymous reviewer for comments on earlier drafts. My thinking about conceptual economies was prompted by conversations with Peter Medway regarding his notion of the "virtual building"—a discursive construct created by architects, builders, municipal authorities, and site workers to guide the planning and construction of a material building (see, for example, Medway, 1994, 1996). I also wish to acknowledge the insightful feedback offered by members of a graduate reading group at Purdue University: Michelle Comstock, Bill Hart-Davidson, Tom Moriarty, Tim Peeples, and Mike Zerbe.

REFERENCES

Agar, M. (1980). *The professional stranger: An informal introduction to ethnography.* New York: Academic Press.

Agar, M. (1986). *Speaking of ethnography.* Beverly Hills, CA: Sage.

Anson, C., & Forsberg, L. (1990). Moving beyond the academic community: Transitional stages in professional writing. *Written Communication, 7,* 200-231.

Bazerman, C. (1994). *Constructing experience.* Carbondale and Edwardsville: Southern Illinois University Press.

Bazerman, C. (1988). *Shaping written knowledge: The genre and activity of the experimental article in science.* Madison: University of Wisconsin Press.

Berkenkotter, C., & Huckin, T. (1993). Rethinking genre from a sociocognitive perspective. *Written Communication, 10,* 475-509.

Berkenkotter, C., Huckin, T., & Ackerman, J. (1988). Conversations, conventions, and the writer. *Research in the Teaching of English, 22,* 9-44.

Berlin, J. (1987). *Rhetoric and reality: Writing instruction in American colleges, 1900-1985.* Carbondale: Southern Illinois University Press.

Brown, V. (1993). Decanonizing discourses: Textual analysis and the history of economic thought. In W. Henderson, T. Dudley-Evans, & R. Backhouse (Eds.), *Economics and language* (pp. 64-84). London: Routledge.

Carter, M. (1990). The idea of expertise: An exploration of cognitive and social dimensions of writing. *College Composition and Communication, 41,* 265-286.

Cole, M., & Engeström, Y. (1993). In G. Salomon (Ed.), *Distributed cognitions: Psychological and educational considerations* (pp. 1-46). London: Cambridge University Press.

Devitt, A. (1991). Intertextuality in tax accounting: Generic, referential, and functional. In C. Bazerman & J. Paradis (Eds.), *Textual dynamics of the professions* (pp. 336-357). Madison: University of Wisconsin Press.

Devitt, A. (1992). Generalizing about genre: New conceptions of an old concept. *College Composition and Communication, 44,* 573-586.

Dias, P., Freedman, A., Medway, P., & Paré, A. (1999). *Worlds apart: Acting and writing in academic and workplace contexts.* Mahwah, NJ: Erlbaum.

Dudley-Evans, A., & Henderson, W. (Eds.). (1990). *The language of economics: The analysis of economic discourse.* ELT Documents No. 134. London: Modern English Publications in association with the British Council.

Duguay, P., & Poloz, S. (1994). The role of economic projections in Canadian monetary policy formation. *Canadian Public Policy, 20*, 189-99.

Freedman, A. (1987). Learning to write again: Discipline-specific writing at university. *Carleton Papers in Applied Language Studies, 4*, 95-114.

Freedman, A., & Medway, P. (1994). *Genre and the new rhetoric.* London: Taylor & Francis.

Freedman, A., & Smart, G. (1997). Navigating the currents of economic policy: Written genres and the distribution of cognitive work at a financial institution. *Mind, Culture, and Activity, 4*, 238-255.

Gee, J. (1992). Social-cultural approaches to literacy (literacies). *Annual Review of Applied Linguistics, 12*, 31-48.

Geertz, C. (1973). *The interpretation of cultures.* New York: Basic Books.

Geertz, C. (1978). *Local knowledge.* New York: Basic Books.

Geisler, C. (1994). *Academic literacy and the nature of expertise: Reading, writing, and knowing in academic philosophy.* Hillsdale, NJ: Erlbaum.

Hammersley, M. (1992). *What's wrong with ethnography?* London: Routledge.

Hammersley, M., & Atkinson, P. (1983). *Ethnography: Principles in practice.* London: Routledge.

Henderson, W., Dudley-Evans, T., & Backhouse, R. (1993). *Economics and language.* London: Routledge.

Hutchins, E. (1991). The social organization of distributed cognition. In L. Resnick, J. Levine, & S. Teasley (Eds.), *Perspectives on socially shared cognition* (pp. 283-307). Washington, DC: American Psychological Association.

Journal of Post-Keynesian Economics, Summer 1991.

Journet, D. (1990). Writing, rhetoric, and the social construction of scientific knowledge. *IEEE Transactions on Professional Communication, 33*, 162-167.

Kaufer, D., & Young, R. (1993). Writing in the content areas: Some theoretical complexities. In L. Odell (Ed.), *Theory and practice in the teaching of writing: Rethinking the discipline* (pp. 71-104). Carbondale: Southern Illinois University Press.

Klamer, A., McCloskey, D., & Solow, R. (1988). *The consequences of economic rhetoric.* London: Cambridge University Press.

Kress, G. (1987). Genre in a social theory of language. In I. Reid (Ed.), *The place of genre in learning* (pp. 35-55). Geelong, Victoria, Australia: Deakin University.

Lave, J. (1991). Situated learning in communities of practice. In L. Resnick, J. Levine, & S. Teasley (Eds.), *Perspectives on socially shared cognition* (pp. 63-82). Washington, DC: American Psychological Association.

Lave, J. (1993). The practice of learning. In S. Chaiklin & J. Lave (Eds.), *Understanding practice: Perspectives on activity and context* (pp. 3-32). London: Cambridge University Press.

Lave, J., & Wenger, E. (1991). *Situated learning: Legitimate peripheral participation.* New York/Cambridge: Cambridge University Press.

MacKinnon, J. (1993). Becoming a rhetor: Developing writing ability in a mature, writing-intensive organization. In R. Spilka (Ed.), *Writing in the workplace: New research perspectives* (pp. 41-55). Carbondale: Southern Illinois University Press.

McCarthy, L.P. (1987). A stranger in strange lands: A college student writing across the curriculum. *Research in the Teaching of English, 21*, 233-265.

McCloskey, D. (1985). *The rhetoric of economics.* Madison: University of Wisconsin Press.

McCloskey, D. (1990). *If you're so smart: The narrative of economic expertise.* Chicago: University of Chicago Press.

Medway, P. (1994). The language component in technological capability: Lessons form architecture. *International Journal of Technology and Design Education, 4*, 85-107.

Medway, P. (1996). Virtual and material buildings: Construction and constructivism in architecture and writing. *Written Communication, 13*, 473-514.

Myers, G. (1990). *Writing biology: Texts in the social construction of knowledge.* Madison: University of Wisconsin Press.

Ong, W. (1975). The writer's audience is always a fiction. *PMLA 90*, 9-22.

Paradis, J., Dobrin D., & Miller, R. (1985). Writing at Exxon ITD: Notes on the writing environment of an R & D organization. In L. Odell & D. Goswami (Eds.), *Writing in nonacademic settings* (pp. 281-307). New York: Guilford.

Paré, A., & Smart, G. (1994). Observing genres in action: Towards a research methodology. In A. Freedman & P. Medway (Eds.), *Genre and the new rhetoric* (pp. 146-154). London: Taylor & Francis.

Paré, A., & Szewello, H. (1995). Social work writing: Learning by doing. In G. Rogers (Ed.), *Social work field education: Views and visions* (pp. 164-173). Dubuque, IA: Kendell/Hunt Publishing.

Peeples, T., & Hart-Davidson, B. (1997). Grading the "subject": Questions of expertise and evaluation. In L. Allison, L. Bryant, & M. Hourigan (Eds.), *Grading in the post-process classroom* (pp. 94-113). Portsmouth, NH: Boynton/Cook.

Resnick, L. (1991). Shared cognition: Thinking as social practice. In L. Resnick, J. Levine, & S. Teasley (Eds.), *Perspectives on socially shared cognition* (pp. 1-22). Washington, DC: American Psychological Association.

Rogoff, B. (1984). Thinking and learning in social context. In B. Rogoff & J. Lave (Eds.), *Everyday cognition: Its development in social context* (pp. 1-8). Cambridge: Harvard University Press.

Salomon, G. (Ed.). (1993). *Distributed cognitions: Psychological and educational considerations*. London: Cambridge University Press.

Samuels, W. (Ed.). (1990). *Economics as discourse: An analysis of the language of economics*. Boston: Kluwer Academic Publishers.

Schryer, C. (1993). Records as genre. *Written Communication, 10,* 200-234.

Schon, D. (1983). *The reflective practitioner: How professionals think in action*. New York: Basic Books.

Smart, G. (1992a). The social dimension of a workplace genre, and the implications for teaching. *Carleton Papers in Applied Language Studies, 9,* 33-46.

Smart, G. (1992b). The ecology of genre. *Inkshed, 11,* 2-22.

Smart, G. (1993). Genre as community invention: A central bank's response to its executives' expectations as readers. In R. Spilka (Ed.), *Writing in the workplace: New research perspectives* (pp. 124-140). Carbondale: Southern Illinois University Press.

Smart, G. (1998). Mapping conceptual worlds: Using interpretive ethnography to explore knowledge-making in a professional community. *The Journal of Business Communication, 35,* 111-127.

Van Maanen, J. (1979). The fact of fiction in organizational ethnography. *Administrative Science Quarterly, 24,* 539-550.

Van Maanen, J. (1988). *Tales of the field: On writing ethnography*. Chicago: University of Chicago Press.

Vipond, D. (1993). *Writing and psychology: Understanding writing and its teaching from the perspective of composition studies*. Westport, CT: Praeger.

Winsor, D. (1996). *Writing like an engineer: A rhetorical education*. Mahwah, NJ: Erlbaum.

Yates, J. (1989). *Control through communication*. Baltimore, MD: Johns Hopkins University Press.

Author Index

A

Ackerman, J., 223, *249*
Adam, C., 2, *9,* 31, 36, 41, 46, 48, 53, 55, *59,* 129, 130, 133, 142, *144,* 168, 171, 175, 181, *182,* 184, 195, *196*
Agar, M., 227, *249*
Aldrich, P. G., 167, *181*
Alvarez, A., 152, *165*
Alvesson, M., 220, *221*
Anderson, P. V., 1, *8,* 200, *221*
Andrews, J. D., 167, *181*
Anson, C. M., 53, *58,* 129, *144,* 167, *181,* 223, *249*
Applebee, A., 96, *128*
Atkinson, P., 227, *250*

B

Bachelard, G., 102, *128*
Backhouse, R., 229, *250*
Bakhtin, M. M., 4, *8,* 33, 44, *58,* 131, *144,* 184, 194, 195, *196*
Barabas, C. P., 183, *196,* 219, *221*
Bataille, R. R., 1, *8,* 167, *181,* 200, *221*
Bateson, G., 152, *163*

Bazerman, C., 3, *9,* 15, *27,* 85, *87,* 149, 154, 155, *163,* 183, *196,* 219, *221,* 226, 230, 232, 233, 240, 244, *249*
Bednar, A. S., 167, *181*
Beer, A., 22, *28*
Bereiter, C., 49, *58*
Berkenkotter, C., 3, *9,* 183, 188, 193, *196,* 223, 226, *249*
Berlin, J., 12, *27,* 229, *249*
Bitzer, L.F., 129, *144*
Bizzell, P., 12, *27*
Blakeslee, A. M., 183, 195, *196,* 220, *221*
Bourdieu, P., 4, *9,* 145, 160, 162, *163*
Bracewell, R. J., 4n, *9*
Brandt, D., 169, *182*
Britton, J., 13, *27*
Brown, J. L., 200, *221*
Brown, K., 151, *164*
Brown, V., 229, *249*
Bruner, J. S., 40, *60*
Burgess, T., 13, *27*

C

Carter, M., 227, 245, *249*
Chao, G. T., 200, *221*
Chinneck, J., 132, *144*
Clews, R., 147, *163*
Cole, M., 3, *9,* 16, *28,* 152, 154, *163, 164,* 226, *249*

D

de Montigny, G. A. J., 145, 151, *164*
Del Río, P., 152, *165*
Department of Education and Science, 96, *128*
Devitt, A., 3, *9,* 155, *164,* 226, 247, *249*
Dias, P., 1, 3, *9,* 15, 22, *28,* 31, 31*n,* 48, *58,* 92, 122, *128,* 129*n,* 130, *144,* 155, *164,* 169, *182,* 183, *196,* 202, *221,* 247, *249*
Dobrin, D., 51, *59,* 150, *165,* 237, *251*
Douglas, M., 4, *9,* 21, *28,* 151, 152*n,* 154, 162, *164*
Dudley-Evans, A., 235, *249*
Dudley-Evans, T., 229, *250*
Duguay, P., 231, *250*
Duxbury, L., 132, *144*

E

Ede, L., 190, *196*
Edwards, D., 151, 152*n,* *165*
Elbow, P., 57, *58*
Emig, J., 13, *28,* 96, *128*
Engeström, R., 151, *164*
Engeström, Y., 16, 20, *28,* 146, 151, 152, 153*n,* *164,* 226, *249*

F

Faigley, L., 12, *28,* 167, *182,* 200, *221*
Fairclough, N., 122, *128*
Flanagan, J. C., 202, *221*
Flower, L., 13, *28*
Flynn, E., 160*n,* *164*

F

Forsberg, L. L., 53, *58,* 129, *144,* 167, *181,* 223, *249*
Foucault, M., 122, *128*
Freedman, A., 1, 2, 3, *9,* 15, *28,* 31, 31*n,* 36, 41, 46, 48, 53, 55, 58, *58, 59,* 63, 84, 86, *87,* 92*n,* 122, *128,* 129, 129*n,* 130, 133, 142, *144,* 155, *164,* 168, 169, 171, 175, 177, 181, *182,* 183, 184, 195, *196,* 223, 226, 247, *249, 250*

G

Gardner, P. D., 200, *221*
Garvey, W. D., 185, 187, 189, 190, *197*
Gee, J., 242, *250*
Geertz, C., 5, *9,* 227, *250*
Geisler, C., 245, *250*
Gilbert, G. N., 188, *197*
Gilsdorf, J. W., 167, *182*
Giltrow, J., 3, *10,* 135, *144,* 155, *164*
Goetz, J., 37, *58,* 201, *221*
Goswami, D., 1, *10,* 15, *29*
Greene, S., 12, *29*
Gutierrez, K., 57, *59*

H

Hagstrom, F., 152, *166*
Hammersley, M., 227, *250*
Hanks, W. F., 34, 50, 55, *59*
Hart-Davidson, B., 227, 245, *252*
Hayes, J. R., 13, *28*
Heath, S. B., 38, 58, *59*
Henderson, W., 229, 235, *249, 250*
Herndl, C., 3, 4, *10*
Herrington, A., 53, *59*
Hubboch, S., 57, *59*
Huberman, A. M., 201, *222*
Huckin, T. N., 3, *9,* 183, 188, 193, *196,* 223, 226, *249*
Hutchins, E., 152, 158, *164*

J

Jolliffe, D. A., 11, *28*
Journet, D., 229, *250*

K

Kanter, R. M., 204, *221*
Kaufer, D., 227, 245, *250*
Klamer, A., 229, *250*
Klein, H. J., 200, *221*
Kleinmann, S., 201, 219, *222*
Knoblauch, C. H., 12, *28*
Koistinen, K., 151, *164*
Kress, G., 247, *250*

L

Langer, J. A., 183, *197*, 215, *222*
Latour, B., 183, *197*
Lave, J., 3, *10*, 32, 33, 34, *59*,
   147, 148, 154, 158, *164*, *165*,
   168, *182*, 184, 195, *197*, 227,
   232, 242, 243, *251*
Lawson, B., 110, *128*
LeCompte, M., 37, *58*, 201, *221*
Ledwell-Brown, J., 1, *10*, 22, *28*,
   200, *222*
Leont'ev, A. N., 16, 17, *28*
Leontyev, A. A., 65, 85, *88*
Lunsford, A., 190, *196*

M

MacKinnon, J., 46, 53, *59*, 129,
   144, 150, *165*, 223, 225, *251*
Magneson, H., 147, *163*
Martin, J., 200, *222*
Martin, N., 13, *27*
McCarthy, L. P., 53, *59*, *60*, 223,
   251
McCloskey, D., 229, 230, 235, *250*
McLeod, A., 13, *27*
Medway, P., 1, 3, *9*, 15, *28*, 31,
   31n, 48, 58, *58*, *59*, 86, 87, 92n,
   95, 103, 122, *128*, 129n, 130,
   144, 155, *164*, 169, *182*, 183,
   195, *196*, 226, 247, 248, *249*,
   250

Middleton, D., 151, 152n, *165*
Miles, M. B., 201, *222*
Miller, C. R., 3, *10*, 18, *29*, 63, 86,
   88, 129, 131, 135, *144*, 151,
   165, 168, *182*, 184, *197*
Miller, R., 51, *59*, 150, *165*, 237,
   251
Miller, T. P., 167, *182*
Mintzberg, H., 218, *222*
Morgan, G., 200, 201, *222*
Murray, D., 13, *29*
Myers, G., 183, 186, 195, *197*,
   226, *251*

N

North, S., 12, *29*
Nystrand, M., 12, *29*

O

O'Leary-Kelly, A. M., 200, *221*
Odell, L., 1, *10*, 15, *29*
Olney, R. J., 167, *181*
Ong, W., 234, *251*

P

Paradis, J., 15, *27*, 51, *59*, 150,
   165, 237, *251*
Paré, A., 1, 3, *9*, *10*, 15, 22, *28*,
   31, 31n, 48, *58*, 86, *88*, 92n,
   122, *128*, 129n, 130, *144*, 155,
   160n, *164*, *165*, 169, *182*, 183,
   195, *196*, 223, 226, 247, *249*,
   251
Pea, R., 153, *165*
Peeples, T., 227, 245, *252*
Petraglia, J., 57, *60*, 169, *182*
Pittenger, C., 22, *28*
Poloz, S., 231, *250*
Popken, R., 53, *60*

R

Radar, M. H., 167, *182*
Resnick, L., 227, 232, *252*
Robbins, D., 4, *10*
Rogoff, B., 33, 37, 38, 40, 42, 57,
   58, *60*, 232, *252*

Rosen, H., 13, *27*
Rosenblatt, L. M., 215, *222*
Ross, S. G., 40, *60*
Russell, D. R., 3, *10,* 16, 18, *29*

S

Sackmann, S. A., 200, *222*
Salomon, G., 152, 154, *165*
Samuels, W., 229, *252*
Sathe, V., 200, 218, *222*
Scardamalia, M., 49, *58*
Schön, D., 117, *128,* 227, *252*
Schryer, C. F., 3, *10,* 15, *29,* 86, *88,* 131, *144,* 226, *252*
Scollon, R., 64, 65, 66, *88*
Scollon, S. W., 64, 65, 66, *88*
Schein, E. H., 201, 220, *222*
Sigband, N. B., 167, *181*
Smagorinsky, P., 96, *128*
Smart, G., 2, 3, *9, 10,* 31, 36, 41, 46, 48, 51, 53, 55, *59, 60,* 86, *88,* 129, 130, 142, *144,* 150, *165,* 168, 171, 175, 177, *182,* 195, *196,* 201, 219, *222,* 226, 235, 237, *251, 252*
Smircich, L., 220, *222*
Smith, D., 145, *165*
Solow, R., 229, *250*
Sommers, N., 13, *29*
Spilka, R., 15, *29*
Swales, J., 63, *88,* 169, *182,* 183, *197,* 200, *222*
Szewello, H., 223, *251*

T

Tebeaux, E., 200, *222*
Tulviste, P., 152, *166*
Valiquette, M., 3, *10,* 135, *144,* 155, *164*

V

Van Maanen, J., 227, *252*
Vipond, D., 226, *252*
Vygotsky, L. S., 13, *29,* 32, 34, *60*

W

Walvoord, B., 53, *60*
Wenger, E., 33, 34, *59,* 146, 147, 154, 158, *165,* 168, *182,* 184, 195, *197,* 232, *251*
Wertsch, J. V., 16, 25, *29,* 33, 40, *60,* 152, *165, 166*
Wiemelt, J., 12, *29*
Willard, C. A., 135, *144*
Winsor, D., 95, *128,* 149, 150, *166,* 195, *197,* 223, *252*
Witte, S. P., 4n, *9,* 95, 96, *128*
Wolf, S., 200, *221*
Wood, D., 40, *60*
Woolgar, S., 183, *197*
Wunsch, A. P., 167, *182*
Yates, J., 226, *252*

Y

Young, R., 227, 245, *250*

Subject Index

A

Academy and workplace, 64, 74-82
Action (AT), 17
Activities (AT), 17
Activity systems, 3, 162, 226
  Bank of Canada, 231-232
Activity Theory (AT), 3, 11, 16-19, 152
  genres, 64, 65
  three tiers, 16-19
  writing classroom, 16-19
  writing course, 19-21, 25-27
Apprenticeship, 148
Architectural work
  writing, 125-126
Architectural writing, 6, 89-128
  design notebook, 95, 105-117
  design studio, 91, 92
    characteristics of writing, 93-96
  design thesis, 96-98
    case study, 98-117
    précis, 97, 104-5, 126-28
  design tool, 117
  four elements of design, 99-103
  history (architectural and cultural), 90
  intention and artifact, 99, 103
  invention (creation), 93-94
  language, 95-96
  research thesis, 96, 97
  vocational value of writing for design, 122-24
  work, 125-26
  writing for architecture, 91-92
Artifact, 153
AT. *See* Activity Theory
Attenuated authentic participation, 35, 43-53, 55-56, 207
  attenuation, 47-49
  evaluation, 50-51
  goal of writing, 45-46
  guide-learner role, 49-50
  improvisatory quality of learning opportunities, 48
  learning sites, 51-53
  messiness of workplace context, 48-49
  role of authenticity, 46-47
  social work, 147

257

B

Bank of Canada, 224, 230
Bank of Canada Review, 222-225, 233-235, 236-237, 237-240
Business school writing, 131-133

C

Case study (Innes Yates), 98-117
Classroom and workplace writing
    differences between, 48-53
Cognitive consensus, 162
Cognitive labor, 226
Collaborative process of writing, 183-196
Community
    definition, 3
Composition studies. *See* Writing classrooms
Culture, 227
    See also Organizational cultures

D

Design (architecture)
    four elements, 99-103
Design notebook (architecture), 95, 105-117
Design studio (architecture), 91, 92
    characteristics of writing, 93-96
Design thesis (architecture), 96-98
    case study, 98-117
    précis, 97, 104-105, 126-128
Desired outcomes, 212, 213-214
Discourse community, 169, 200, 201
Discourse practices, 3, 63
Distributed cognition, 6, 226, 245
    social work writing, 152-155, 158-163

Document cycling, 171, 207, 237, 238, 239
Domain-specific writing ability, 240

E

Economy
    definition, 229-230, 231
Enculturation, 3, 4
Engineering students, 61-87
English as a Second Language (ESL), 68-70
English as a working language, 66
Everyday cognition. *See* Situated learning
Experienced writers and new genres, 223-248
    Bank of Canada, 224, 230
    Bank of Canada Review, 224-25, 233-235, 236-237, 237-240, 240-244
    daily current analysis, 231
    differences, 233-240
    difficulties, 232
    genre theory, 226, 227
    interpretive ethnography, 227
    research memorandum, 228-229, 233, 235, 237

F

Facilitated performance, 35, 37-42, 55-56
    collaborative performance, 39-40
    discursive content, 40-42
    evaluation, 50-51
    goal of writing, 45-46
    guide-learner, 49
    learning sites, 51-53
    messiness of workplace context, 48-49

G

Genre, 4-5, 62-63, 155
    Activity Theory, 18-19, 64, 65

classroom, 38, 40, 42, 53
community-specific, 200
cultural differences, 72-73
definition, 130-131, 155, 168-
  169, 226
design studio (architecture),
  92
differences, 74
distributed cognition, 152-155
experienced writers, 8, 233-
  248
reconceptualization, 168-169
respond-aloud protocol, 170
sets (social work), 153-155
social action, 3, 184
social motive, 135
social work, 151
systems (social work), 155-158
transitions, 86-87, 223-224
workplace, 43
writing, 85
Genre studies, 15
Guided participation, 33-34, 37,
  42
Guides. See Oldtimers

H

Habitus, 4, 162

I

Identity, 3
Iliad (Homer), 97, 106, 107
Individual consciousness
  social construction, 4
Induction of learners, 8, 219
Intercultural communication, 6,
  61-87
  academy and workplace, 64,
    74-82
  engineering classes, 64, 82-85
  engineering students, 63-64
  former country and new coun-
    try, 64, 68-73
  involvement and indepen-
    dence, 64, 65-67

writing courses, 64, 82-85
Internships. See Social work
  writing
Interpretive ethnography, 227

L

Language, 33, 153, 229
Learners. See Newcomers
Learning, 174
Legitimate peripheral participa-
  tion, 34-35, 148, 150
Linguistic market, 145, 160

M

Medical chart (social work), 155-
  156
Metaphor of possession, 25
Myth of the autonomous individual, 16, 27, 54
Myth of transcendence, 11, 12,
  13

N

Newcomers, 46, 49, 145, 157,
  160, 169, 177, 178, 181, 200,
  201, 206, 207, 209, 219, 220
New genres and experienced
  writers. See Experienced writers and new genres

O

Oldtimers, 49, 147, 148, 149,
  150, 168, 169, 170, 181
  respond-aloud protocol, 169-170
Operations (AT), 18
Organizational cultures, 199-221
  definition, 201
  desired outcomes, 212, 213
  expectations for writing, 203-
    208
  mottoes, 203-208
  prescriptions, 212-213
  respond-aloud protocols, 215-
    218
  setting, 202
  subcultures, 209-218

P

Plagiarism, 174
Practical cognition. *See* Situated
    learning
Practicum writing, 137-141, 142-
    144
Prescriptions, 212-14

R

Reading texts, 169-176, 177-180
Research articles, 183-196
    collaboration, 190-193
    editor, 193-195
    referees' criticism, 186-190
    setting the stage, 184-186
Respond-aloud protocol, 169-170,
    172-173, 176, 215-218
Rhetorical competence, 168
Rhetorical theory, 3

S

School-based simulations, 3, 26,
    36, 84
    workplace writing, 133-136
Scientific discourse, 86
Scientific research articles. *See*
    Research articles
Situated activity, 242
Situated cognition, 169
Situated experience. *See*
    Situated learning
Situated learning, 5, 6, 31-58,
    163, 169, 184
    attenuated authentic partici-
        pation, 35, 43-53, 55-56
    cognition-plus-view, 32
    facilitated performance, 35,
        37-42, 55-56
    guided participation, 33-34
    interpretive view, 32
    language, 33
    learning again, 53-55
    legitimate peripheral partici-
        pation, 33, 34-35

situated social practice, 33
    students, 35-55
    zone of proximal development,
        34
Situated social practice, 33
Social work writing, 145-163
    attenuated authentic partici-
        pation, 147
    community of practice, 154
    distributed cognition, 152-155,
        158-163
    genre, 151, 155
    genre sets, 155-158
    genre systems, 155-158
    internships, 147-151
    learning to write, 150-151,
        153-154, 156-157
    legitimate peripheral partici-
        pation, 148, 150
    observing, 147
    reports, 149, 150
        medical chart, 155-156
Socially shared cognition. *See*
    Situated learning, Distributed
    cognition
Students
    attenuated authentic partici-
        pation, 35, 43-53
    classroom to workplace, 53-55
    facilitated performance, 35,
        37-42
    situated learning, 35-55
    writing courses, 25, 26-27
Surrogate thinking, 226
Symbolic action. *See* Discourse
    practices

T

Teaching, 21-22
    facilitated performance, 35,
        37-42
    writing courses, 23-27
Transitions, 3, 4, 5, 8
    genre to genre, 223-224

university writing to work place writing, 43, 51, 53-55, 122, 129-144, 167-181

U

University writing, 39-42, 45-46, 48-53, 169-176

University writing and workplace writing

bridging the gap between, 129-144

business school writing, 131-133

case-study simulation, 133-136, 142

contextualization of the text, 179

differences between (in reading texts), 169, 170-176, 177-180

genre, 130-131

iterative process, 177-178

practicum writing, 137-141, 142-144

respond-aloud protocol, 169-170, 172-173, 176

response to the text, 179-180

successful transition between, 167-181

V

Vygotskian school of Russian psychology, 5, 16

W

Workplace and classroom writing differences between, 48-53

Workplace tasks, 48

Workplace writing, 43-53, 129-144, 167-181

Workplace writing and university writing. *See* University writing and workplace writing

Writing

Bank of Canada Review, 222-225, 233-235, 236-237, 237-240

business school writing, 131-133, 170-176

cognitivist view, 13-14

collaborative process, 183-196

design studio (architecture), 93-96

engineering students, 61-87

experienced writers, 223-248

organizational culture, 199-221

practicum writing, 1371-41

research articles, 183-196

school writing, 39-42

situated activity, 14-15

situated learning, 35-55, 163, 169

social action, 15

social perspective, 13-16

social practice, 15-16, 22, 25-27

social work, 145-163

students, 35-55

university writing and workplace writing, 129-144

workplace, 43-45, 133-136

workplace writing and university writing, 129-144

Writing classrooms (university), 5, 7-27

Activity Theory (AT), 16-19

service course, 12

skills, 12

teaching, 21-22

Writing Courses, 19-27

Activity Theory (AT), 25-27

engineering classes, 82-85

students

teaching, 23-27

Y

Yates, Innes, 98n
  See also Case study

Z

Zone of proximal development,
  34